W9-BOM-440

My

Brother

the

Killer

My Brother the Killer

A Family Story

Alix Sharkey

HARPER

An Imprint of HarperCollins*Publishers*

MY BROTHER THE KILLER. Copyright © 2021 by Alix Sharkey. All rights reserved. Printed in the United States of America. No part of this book may be used or reproduced in any manner whatsoever without written permission except in the case of brief quotations embodied in critical articles and reviews. For information, address HarperCollins Publishers, 195 Broadway, New York, NY 10007.

HarperCollins books may be purchased for educational, business, or sales promotional use. For information, please email the Special Markets Department at SPsales@harpercollins.com.

Originally published in the United Kingdom in 2021 by Mudlark, an imprint of HarperCollins Publishers.

FIRST U.S. EDITION

Library of Congress Cataloging-in-Publication Data has been applied for.

ISBN 978-0-06-305134-8

21 22 23 24 25   LSC   10 9 8 7 6 5 4 3 2 1

For my mother,
my daughter and my wife.

Tilbury Docks … are very modern, but their remoteness and isolation upon the Essex marsh, the days of failure attending their creation, invested them with a romantic air. Nothing in those days could have been more striking than the vast, empty basins, surrounded by miles of bare quays and the ranges of cargo-sheds, where two or three ships seemed lost like bewitched children in a forest of gaunt, hydraulic cranes. One received a wonderful impression of utter abandonment, of wasted efficiency.

Joseph Conrad, *The Mirror of the Sea* (1906)

My

Brother

the

Killer

Prologue:
My Last Prison Letter, Part One

Dear Stuart,

Almost 20 years have passed since we last met, on a muggy afternoon in August 2001. Shortly afterwards you were arrested for Danielle's abduction and murder, and remanded in custody to await trial. Ever since your conviction in December 2002, you have been serving a life sentence behind the watchtowers, razor wire, steel doors and three-foot brick walls of a Victorian prison in West Yorkshire. I assume that's where you are now, as you read these words.

Despite never having visited, I've read that HMP Wakefield is Western Europe's largest maximum-security prison, housing over 700 of the UK's most dangerous offenders: serial killers and rapists, child murderers, psychopaths and paedophiles. Apparently, even the guards call it *Monster Mansion*.

I guess by now it must feel like home.

In your absence the world has changed drastically. Smartphones and tablets, video streaming, Google Maps, YouTube, Skype, WhatsApp, surveillance drones – none of these things existed when you were last a free man.

What else has changed? My attitude.

In my previous letters – sent during your first few years in prison – you must have noticed my soothing tone, the way I avoided any hint of accusation, any suggestion that you might be guilty. I was trying to start a conversation in the hope you might one day tell me what you'd done with Danielle's body.

This time, I won't mince my words.

You know how I know you're guilty, Stuart?

I mean, leaving aside all the overwhelming evidence? Circumstantial, perhaps, but strong enough for a jury to convict you in under eight hours. But all that aside?

Your silence.

Imagine if we swapped places. If I were innocent and unjustly convicted – as you once claimed to be – while you were walking around free as the breeze? My screams for help would have deafened you. My letters of outrage would have swamped you. I would have begged, hounded, shamed and harassed you until you secured my release.

Likewise, if you were innocent, I would never have heard the end of it.

For the first few months after your conviction I waited, giving you the benefit of the doubt. I thought, Maybe he's still angry with me because I suspected him. But if he's truly innocent, as he claims, and this is all some terrible mistake, then sooner or later he'll explain his side of things. Eventually he'll ask for my help.

You never reached out. Not a peep.

That's how I know you're guilty.

So why kick this hornet's nest? In many ways it would be easier to let you continue your charade and eke out your days, slunk in your corner, cut off from the world. And certainly, for a long time, my best course of action seemed to be denial, pretending not to know or care about you. I felt ashamed to be your brother, a nauseating fear of being associated with your crimes, of being judged along with you. That fear turned in on itself, until I began to wonder if we shared the same genetic predisposition, the same pathological tendencies. Even after I managed to quell those doubts, there was still the lingering fear that maybe I couldn't access the darkest parts of my psyche. Perhaps my deepest nature was inaccessible, hidden even from myself?

I tried to run away. And for a while at least I managed to escape. After I moved to America, I sometimes forgot that I had a brother serving life for killing his teenage niece. And you made that easy, because you never reached out to me. Perhaps you wanted to be forgotten, in the hope that your crime would be forgotten, too.

Trouble is, I can't go on pretending that I don't remember, or that this is out of my hands, or all in the past, or nothing to do with me. Maybe you've found a way to compartmentalise or trivialise your crime, but I won't be able to look myself in the mirror unless I try one more time to put this right.

The impetus for this book was anger. I was enraged when I realised you might be released without ever telling Danielle's parents what you did with her body. Then I got angry with myself. I'd left it far too long to speak out. And many times during the writing of this book, I became furious whenever I thought about you. But though I despise you for what you did, I'm no longer angry with you. And even though the law has now changed, making it far less likely that you will walk free without giving up Danielle's body, I still feel a responsibility to challenge you.

And so I'm hoping that if I tell the truth, maybe you can, too. Not only would that be the right thing to do, but I suspect deep down you want to make amends and ask forgiveness. To give closure to Danielle's parents, Tony and

Linda, who welcomed you into their home as part of their family.

Equally, I have come to rescue our mother from an ugly legacy. I'm not going to let her life story be defined by your imprisonment for the murder of a little girl who trusted you. I want people to know that she tried her best, even if her naive attempts to protect you sometimes enabled your depravity. Despite those failings, she was and still is the best thing about our family, and if there is anything honest or kind or brave or noble in any of us, we learned it from her.

Naturally, she still loves you, and has never abandoned you.

My feelings towards you are a little more complex.

But Stuart, I do not hate you. I have no hatred for anyone. True, I cannot love you as I once did. Your cruelty makes that all but impossible. Yet I still feel something, some kind of brotherly affection – or at least, attachment. Some desire to save you from yourself, to prevent you from wasting the few years that remain to you.

Over the last three decades I have moved often, from London to Paris, Miami, New York and Los Angeles. Along the way I have discarded piles of ephemera, including photographs, artworks and numbered editions, sketchbooks, notepads and scads of personal documents. Yet when I set out to write this book and went searching through the small trove of personal papers I had always clung to, I found your prison letters, many dating back to the late 70s. Across tens of thousands of miles, over continents and oceans, for almost five decades those letters came with me.

And I'm still trying to understand: *why?*

Anyway, here we are again.

This is my last prison letter to you, an attempt to

reconcile your brutal crime with the memory of a beautiful young boy, my little brother Stuart.

I want to believe that kid still exists.

I want to believe I can still find him and rescue him.

Maybe after I lay out the story of how we got here, we'll have a better idea of what comes next. So let's pick this up at the end of the book.

See you on the other side.

Alix

1

Thursday 2 August 2001
45 days since Danielle's disappearance

It's a mild Thursday afternoon and the sky is the colour of gunmetal, a typical British summer day. Having left Paris on the 10.15 Eurostar, I arrive at London Waterloo around lunchtime. Running early, I buy six newspapers at WHSmith and settle into a corner of Costa Coffee with my sandwich and Americano. I really don't need the caffeine because my pulse is already racing as I leaf through the British press, dreading the moment when I turn the page to find a photo of myself, and learn they've finally linked me to the missing girl.

But today there's no news about the case.

Which is good news, and not just for me: there is still hope.

I take the tube to Tower Hill and walk to Fenchurch Street. Around 2 p.m. the Southend train lumbers out of the station on an elevated track through the City of London towards Essex, a journey back to my roots. The first few miles overlook a warren of bustling East End streets, but gradually the train descends to ground level and dense terraced housing gives way to suburban sprawl. By the time we pull out of Rainham I'm scanning a flat green landscape, dotted with cows and straddled by electricity pylons. Beyond this, the tugs and barges on the river. This strip of Thames Estuary, a mix of reclaimed marshland and light industrial hangars, always stirs an uneasy nostalgia. Even under normal circumstances I would rather not make this trip.

Today is anything but normal.

The journey to Grays takes around 25 minutes but carries a lifetime of memories, starting with family trips to London tourist attractions: the Tower, the Zoo, the British Museum. At 15, I would change at Barking and jump the fence at South Tottenham to join the thousands swaggering up the High Road to White Hart Lane. Soon I was riding into the West End and lying about my age to nightclub doormen. Escape velocity was attained in 1976. After bluffing my way into East Ham College, I teamed up with fellow art student Rob Brown and broke into a condemned council flat in Whitechapel. We changed the locks, jerry-rigged the electricity and became punk rock squatters.

I was finally a Londoner.

Since then, any return to Essex would alter my mood. I never again felt fully at home, not even visiting my family, who – at least on my mother's side – are warm, loving and generous people, quick to see the funny side of things. Despite my best efforts, friends and relatives could sense this reluctance to visit more often, stay longer than necessary. Whatever they suspected, the problem had nothing to do with any sense of superiority. I respected the community I'd left behind but couldn't be part of it. Lurking at the back of my mind was always the fear that I was only ever a couple of poor decisions from being sucked back into the bleak, violent haze of childhood.

Perhaps that is why, almost a quarter of a century later, I look out across these haunted fields at the barges on the Thames with the feeling that I never truly left.

And maybe never will.

I try to picture the man I'm about to meet – my little brother Stuart. Little as in younger, but no longer smaller. Physically, much bigger. That's always my first thought, how much bigger he became. And then? Not much else, really. Despite having shared an intensely violent childhood and adolescence in Tilbury, separated by only 14 months, we have long since grown apart. These days he is almost a stranger.

Of course, I can list a handful of facts. He's a 44-year-old self-employed builder, a one-man firm called Right Price Builders, doing odd jobs around the local area, erecting walls and fences, replacing doors and windows, fixing broken paving. I think he told me a couple of years ago that he'd built an extension on someone's house. But his personality? Hard to say. Quiet, I suppose. Private. Doesn't drink alcohol. Years ago, he would spend hours in the gym, weightlifting and bodybuilding, but he no longer pumps iron. At one point he rode a powerful motorcycle – a Kawasaki. But again, not for years. Same with Shotokan karate. In his thirties he was a keen practitioner and trained regularly, but he dropped martial arts long ago. I heard recently that he likes taking photographs. Otherwise, not much to talk about. He lives a tranquil, respectable life with his wife Debbie, who is expecting their first child in about a month. They've worked hard and bought a semi-detached, three-bedroom house in a pleasant residential street.

Apart from that I know little about him. I tell myself this is only natural. After all, I moved away from the area decades ago, while he has always lived here – at least during those years when he was not in prison. We grew even more distant after I first moved to Paris in 1996, and since then we've rarely seen each other, let alone socialised.

Still, we've never lost touch. Always a call on birthdays and at Christmas, a bland chat for 10 minutes – never more, just a check-in – but enough to maintain brotherly bonds. In February 2000 I even called from Nepal to wish him happy birthday, which seems quite conscientious.

Or maybe I was just showing off.

The last time I saw him – and Essex – was in 1996. It was the last Friday in August when I took this same train, the day before the wedding. Stuart and Debbie were waiting in the car park outside Grays station, waiting to drive me to the hotel where their guests would be staying. I remember thinking how precisely everything was planned. How they liked to have everything under control and leave nothing to chance.

And here I am, five years later, riding the same train, back into my past.

Our past.

I get off at Grays and walk out to the car park, where a grey Vauxhall is parked facing the perimeter wall. As I climb into the back seat, both occupants turn to face me. Two plain-clothes officers from the Major Investigation Team of Essex Police.

You made it, says DS Keith Davies with a tight smile.

He's glad I kept my word. He wasn't sure I would.

He introduces his colleague, a female detective called Jo Antcliffe, and then runs me through the drill once more, repeating almost word for word what he'd said on the phone a few days earlier.

This isn't about accusing anyone, he says. In fact, it's best if you keep an open mind, a cool head. Don't judge him. Forget what you've learned from us about the case. Yes, we have strong suspicions, but we could still be wrong. So it's important that you remain detached, unemotional. Accusations or aggressive questions, any kind of confrontation would almost certainly be counterproductive, and perhaps even fatal.

Does that mean – ?

He shrugs.

If Stuart has abducted Danielle, he says, there's still a chance – even now – that she might be alive, locked away somewhere with food and water. That's the only reason he's out on bail. If he decides to go check on her, we'll be following, right behind him, so let's not alert him to the fact that he's being watched.

My task is simple: get Stuart to talk about his life, his thoughts and feelings. Listen carefully to his answers and observe his behaviour, develop my own impressions. Be sure not to mention any facts about his past that could only have been learned from the police. Afterwards, we'll regroup and go over everything, and they'll ask for my *gut feeling*.

You know him as well as anyone, maybe better, says Keith Davies. You're his brother. If anyone can tell whether or not he's lying, it's probably you.

We all look at each other and nod. Nobody in the car wants to speak the words that hang in the air: it is now over six weeks since Danielle vanished and at this point her odds are virtually nil. But we cannot give voice to the unthinkable, not yet. Until she is found, one way or another, there is still hope.

I ask where we should meet up when I'm finished.

Head back here, says DS Davies, indicating the train station.

Okay, I'll call you when I'm on my way.

Don't bother, he says. You won't see us, but we'll be watching.

*   *   *

We drive to Long Lane, not far from Stuart and Debbie's house, and I get out to walk the last hundred yards or so. As I approach, a few minutes early, I notice the curtains drawn at every window, an oddly mournful look for late summer. I'm about 20 yards away when the front door opens. Stuart emerges, swiftly locks and deadlocks the front door, and strides out to meet me before I can reach the front gate. It feels like a magic trick. He must have been watching, peering through a tiny gap in the curtains

11

as I walked up to his house. He nods and grunts at the neighbour in the next garden but doesn't introduce me.

We shake hands and greet each other in our curt, masculine way. The way we've grown accustomed to down the years.

Good to see you, I say.

Yeah, he says. How'd you get down here, take the train?

Of course.

You didn't walk from the station? You should have called me to come and get you.

No, got a cab, but had him drop me off at the corner. You know, more discreet.

Oh, right, he says, eyeing me suspiciously.

Ten seconds in and I'm already lying. I suspect he knows, and wonder if I've already failed in my mission.

Let's walk, he says.

We're not going inside?

No, he says. Got to buy a pump filter from the hardware store around the corner. It'll only take five minutes, then we can get something to eat.

At three o'clock in the afternoon?

Maybe just a coffee then.

On our way to the hardware store I sneak sideways glances, trying to size him up, while we stumble through his generic questions – about my health, work, life in Paris – and my equally generic answers. I ask how he has been doing himself.

The street is empty but he glances around before replying.

We'll talk about that later, he says. I don't like to discuss anything in public.

This strikes me as paranoid, but then again I'm not the one suspected of abducting and maybe killing a 15-year-old girl. I'm not sure how I would react under those circumstances.

What about Debbie? How is she?

She's gone to stay with her mum and dad while all this is going on. Too much stress with the baby on the way.

He is unshaven and out of shape, his muscular torso running to flab. His face looks puffy, like someone who slept on the couch. His deep brown eyes, once gleaming and full of mischief, are smaller than I remember, as if shrunken into his head. He wears a black T-shirt and battered dark blue jogging pants with a small hole in one thigh, a pair of scuffed trainers. Work clothes. Or maybe that's what happens when your wife goes home to her parents, you end up looking dishevelled and exhausted. I wouldn't know – at this point, I have never been married.

So I suppose the police have been to see you, he ventures in an airy, no-big-deal tone, not so much a question as a statement.

Yes.

And what did they have to say then?

Well, they said they had followed several leads but none of them had amounted to anything so far. And they said that so far, you are their main suspect.

Their *only* suspect, he mouths, with a look of exasperation, as we enter the hardware store.

When we get back to the house I'm expecting to be invited in, but instead he suggests we go for a drive and get *a bit of grub*. We climb into the blue Transit van parked in his driveway.

Blue van, I mutter.

Of course, like everyone else who has been following the case, I know that one of the last witnesses to see Danielle alive, a fellow pupil at her school, had seen her climb into a blue van the morning she went missing. That sighting has been widely reported in the national news, so Stuart must understand why I mentioned it. He doesn't respond.

Once we get on the main road, I'm expecting him to open up – there are no prying neighbours now. But he volunteers nothing about Danielle, her disappearance, the investigation, his arrest and brief incarceration, his feelings on the matter. I find this odd. I know that he was close to Danielle and often spent time at her home. Still, recalling Keith Davies's words and avoiding any rush to judgement, I ask how he has been coping. You know, with constantly being in the news, with being accused of this terrible crime. He sighs and shrugs.

I just want to get back to my life, he says. To make sure Debbie is alright.

He repeats a phrase he'd used when we spoke on the phone back in June, after he'd been arrested on suspicion of Danielle's abduction, questioned and released on bail.

This should be our time, he says. We should be together getting ready for the baby's birth and what d'you call it, going to antenatal classes.

But he says nothing about injustice or media persecution, expresses none of the outrage I'd expect from someone wrongly accused. Instead, he stares straight ahead and talks almost nonstop about the flat Essex countryside, and how some company is developing that piece of land over there, and how that factory over there belongs to another company, and how that land on the right is where the new Eurostar train line will run, and how the traffic is usually much busier along this road at this time of day, and how you have to be on the lookout for hidden turns and cars that can pull out in front of you without warning.

I sit and say nothing. I want him to fill the silence.

Somehow our conversation turns to my childhood friend Andy Hollington, who at this point is living in Southend-on-Sea, the eastern terminus of the Fenchurch Street line.

So how is Andy?

Good, I say. He's a student now. He enrolled at Southend Tech.

Oh yeah? says Stuart, with the hint of a smirk. When we were kids, *student* was a synonym for *dosser* among local lads, who generally left school at 16 to work on building sites, or in the local asbestos factory, or maybe Ford Works in Dagenham if they were lucky.

Yeah, I say, studying photography.

I wait. No response.

Yeah, I add. He's got a Nikon, really nice camera.

He glances over at me, tight-lipped, but says nothing.

Stuart is a keen amateur photographer. Normally I'd expect him to engage in conversation about cameras and photography. Instead, he turns his face to the side window as we take the roundabout. I tell him that Andy says he has his eye on an even better camera, one with a fancy zoom lens. Still nothing. Odd, because the police told me all about the cameras and photographic prints they found when they searched Stuart's house. The images on his computer. The white business cards he'd had printed, advertising himself as a photographer.

CINDERELLA'S

Photography: Beauty, Glamour, Fashion, Portrait.
Portfolios for new & established models.

Beneath that, just *STUART* and his mobile phone number. No office or home number.

No email or home address.

No last name.

The silence between us hums like an electromagnetic field. His mind is churning, trying to calculate how much I know.

And then he begins to list our fast food options.

By now his attempts to normalise this situation are verging on the surreal. Here is a man accused of abducting a teenage girl – his niece, a girl he has known for years and who may still be locked in a basement somewhere – and he's asking what kind of grub I like. As we pull into the car park behind a Harvester restaurant, I can barely conceal my contempt. What does he think we're doing?

He jumps out and lifts the van's hood to fiddle with the engine, then heads inside. I find myself following him, almost in a daze. He picks up a menu from a table, offers it to me.

What d'you fancy? You could have a burger and chips, or they do a decent ploughman's if you're just peckish.

He's pointing at tables, asking where I want to sit, maybe by the window? I turn in search of the strange whirring and tinkling noises. Perched on wooden stools in front of an electronic bingo machine are two sallow middle-aged men in T-shirts, cigarettes clamped in brown fingers. They don't even look our way.

I feel like saying, What the fuck is wrong with you? Do I look like I want to sit in a Harvester and eat chips while you talk about the fucking wallpaper?

Instead I say, I'm not really that hungry. Why don't we go to Lakeside instead, maybe get a sandwich?

Later, I'll wonder. Is this how we get ourselves gaslighted, too polite to confront rank absurdity? Too timid to look madness in the eye and shout it down?

Out in the car park he lifts the hood again, flips the engine kill switch back on, and we climb into the van and drive off.

Sensing my mood, he says, Sorry, I thought the Harvester would be a nice place to go.

Really?

Well, me and Deb had a really nice evening there not so long back, just about the last good evening we had together. You know, before all this … this whole saga blew up.

Saga.

As in a long, tedious and often pointless series of events.

I remember my instructions from DS Keith Davies: *No accusations. No provocations. Just listen, watch and pay attention.*

We head west towards Lakeside, a cavernous shopping centre just a mile or so up the road. As we sit in silence I recall DS Davies saying that Stuart would sometimes run Danielle to school or pick her up in this van. A dark thought occurs: am I the first person to sit in this passenger seat since Danielle last occupied it?

I look at Stuart and wonder: is he thinking the same thing?

I doubt it. Right now, his mind is scuttling like a rat in a barrel, desperate to find a way out. I know, because once again he starts pointing to factories and roadworks, this piece of land up here, that church over there, the turn-off back that way. Always toward the horizon, always away from himself. It's the same with his time references. Later, tomorrow, next week, next year. Any place and any time, except right here and now. There's no way he will inhabit this moment, acknowledge what's actually happening in this van.

I turn to him and ask what he thinks about everything.

Eh?

Y'know, I say, with Danielle's disappearance. What's your take on it? What do you think happened to her? What's your *theory?*

Oh mate, he says wearily, I wish I knew. I've gone over it a million times, but it could be anything. The place where she disappeared, it was a really busy street and it was rush hour, so you would have thought that someone would have seen something. But so far there's nothing. We've just got to wait for something to come up.

How do you *feel* about it?

Well I could do with a few days away from it all.

All what?

All this pressure. I'm the main suspect, so the police are just playing mind games, hoping I'll crack.

What do you mean?

You know, coming round the house again and again, putting pressure on Mum, trying to frighten Debbie, telling tales to my neighbours and Debbie's family ...

But how do you mean, *playing mind games*?

Well, they're just trying to wear me down, get me to crack ...

Yeah, but why would you *crack*? What's to wear down?

Eh?

He seems genuinely confused.

If you haven't done anything, I say, then you don't have to worry about mind games – cos you've got nothing to hide, right?

There's a glimmer of something like recognition in his eyes and then it's gone. Does he understand my argument? If so, he's pretending otherwise. Again, I stop myself from stating the obvious: only someone with a false narrative to maintain would perceive this situation as a battle of wits, between two parties *playing mind games*. Again the silence swells, the air charged with unspoken meaning. He can't even look at me.

At Lakeside we get out smack in the middle of a vast car park.

This is the safest spot, he says, because it's properly covered by CCTV.

He points up at the cameras and explains that some areas are blind spots. I ask myself how he worked this out and why. He lifts the hood and incapacitates the van again. He seems obsessed with surveillance and security systems, and terrified someone will steal his vehicle. Or maybe impound it.

We enter the mall under the Warner Bros sign and walk through the Disney Store, its floor littered with candy-coloured T-shirts that have slipped from their hangers and now lie waiting for the teenage staff to gather them up. I tell him I need to piss. He walks me over to the men's room, but doesn't stop there. Instead, he actually ushers me inside and pushes open a cubicle door, points to the bowl and says, There you are.

I want to ask if I look incapable of finding a toilet bowl in a public lavatory. Instead, I glare at him for a long beat and say, Yeah, I know how this works.

Once again he seems puzzled by my reaction, as if *I'm* the one acting strangely. But now it's all starting to make sense to me.

Thinking back to the way I have seen him behave with his wife, I realise that Stuart has been doing this for so long that he doesn't even realise how odd it is. For two decades, ever since he started dating her as a teenager, he has pointed Debbie in the direction he wanted her to look, preventing her from stumbling across awkward truths, ushering her through certain doors and away from others, telling her what to do and where and when. And eventually this weird dance came to seem normal to them. No wonder she performed her role so well. Twenty years of meaningless babble about curtains and wallpaper, tiles and taps, gardens and fences, jeans and trainers, *a nice bit of grub* and God knows what else. Twenty years of his constantly pointing to the horizon, deflecting her attention away from the present – and most of all, his past.

Since this is my first visit to Lakeside I tell him I want to take a look around. After all, just a couple of years earlier the BBC had put this place on the map with a docusoap TV series called *Lakesiders*. For a while we wander through this echoing mall –

19

two million square feet of white shopping space rich with the smell of cleaning products and cooking oil – while he provides a running commentary on the obvious, as if I'm Prince Charles or something.

Ratners, jewellery, not bad for watches … JD Sports, good for tops and trainers … that Chinese place, decent rice and spring rolls there … or the Italian, they do pizzas and pasta, that kind of thing, not bad … or you can get a baguette, like a long French bread roll … Of course, you know about those …

We sit and eat sandwiches together, which he insists on paying for. He eats in a dainty manner, little finger pointed out as he nibbles his sandwich. I notice his fingernails are still chewed down to the quick, a habit he has had since the age of four or five.

I remind him that I'm taking my 13-year-old daughter Fiona on holiday in a couple of weeks, so I should buy myself some trainers, maybe some shorts, perhaps some insect repellent.

Right, he says. Where you going?

I pause before answering, because he already knows. He stops chewing and looks up.

Malaysia, I say. We want to see the rainforest.

Oh, very nice. Can't sneak me into one of your suitcases, can you?

This is so weird that for a second I suspect he's toying with me, but no.

He notices that I'm staring at him, head tilted.

What?

Nothing, I say.

Three weeks ago I'd told him on the phone that we were going to Malaysia and he'd said exactly the same words about sneaking him into a suitcase. Yet while I recall that exchange, he clearly doesn't. Maybe the stress is affecting his memory. Or maybe there's some part of his mind actively *trying* to forget. Or maybe it's not a joke at all. Maybe he's genuinely asking for my help, but framing it as a jokey throwaway line to test the waters. After all, it wouldn't be the first time I'd conspired with Stuart to help him evade justice.

As we continue strolling through the mall I tell him how shocked I'd been on learning he was a suspect in Danielle's disappearance.

It seemed unreal, I say. I really couldn't believe it.

He doesn't query my use of the past tense, but instead points to a boarded-up shop.

Yeah, he says, the rents here are pretty high. And of course, you can't tell them you're having problems paying the rent, because all the tills are centrally linked so the landlords can see exactly how much everybody is taking.

This latest mention of surveillance reminds me that we are being watched and recorded, and I look up at the CCTV cameras. An image comes to mind: seen from above on a grainy monitor screen, two middle-aged men amble through a mall, pausing to look in shop windows. One of them keeps looking around to see if they're being followed, while also guiding the other, pointing the way. When we were kids, a few miles down the road in Tilbury, two men loitering in a shopping district with no discernible purpose would have been stopped and questioned by the police. These days it's just normal consumer activity.

Then I notice something and say, Oh, look.

Barely 10 yards ahead, taped to a pillar, is an Essex Police poster with the word MISSING and the now-familiar colour photo of a pale teenage girl in school blazer, white shirt and striped tie. Blonde ringlets tucked behind one ear, her face tilted up and gazing doe-eyed into the camera, she smiles in a bashful way, revealing a gap between her front teeth.

Stuart acts as if he hasn't heard me, and then as if he doesn't understand me.

There, I say.

By now we are almost in front of it, but he's still turning his head side to side, supposedly unable to see what I mean.

Danielle, I say, pointing.

Oh yeah, he says, with another weary sigh. Yeah, they're all over the place. Not a very good photo of her, actually.

He mumbles something about a much better picture they could have used. I glare at him, astonished. I know he can see the sardonic edge in my gaze, defying him to tell me that he's innocent, that this is all some terrible mistake, that the police have the wrong man.

We walk back out to the car park and he lifts the hood and flicks the switch then we get in the van and he says he'll drop me off at Grays station. He can't wait to get rid of me, it seems. We barely speak during the 10-minute drive.

We get out and shake hands. I lean in, embrace him and kiss his cheek. I want him to feel something, because maybe that will allow him to open up, let the tears fall and tell the truth. He smells sweeter than I imagined and the scent of his skin brings back memories of the beautiful little boy I once knew, of his childhood laughter. And that, of course, makes me think about the beautiful little girl who is now missing, presumed dead.

Take care, I say, and stay in touch. Don't forget you can always talk to me.

He smiles, but there's a dark glint in his eye, as if some unspeakable secret has just passed between us. Almost daring me to recognise and accept it.

Don't worry, he says. I'm not dead and buried yet.

2

Tilbury, 1961

I am five or six, lying on the living-room floor with my head resting on one arm, drawing a picture. I hear the familiar sound of the Old Man slamming the front door and grunting at my mother in the hallway, so I don't look up as he enters, don't turn to greet him. I go on drawing my picture. I don't want to talk to him or pretend I love him, which is what he wants, and why he always asks: *Y'happy to see me?*

I can smell his stockinged feet before they appear on the carpet beside my face, and I'm vaguely aware of his arm above me when something strikes the back of my head and something else knocks the pencil out of my hand. There's a black splash on my drawing. He has dropped his dirty wet shoes on me. Confused, holding my head, I turn to look up at him, squeezing out a thin smile.

Oh Al, says my mother. Why'd you do that ...?

Her meek protest confirms what I'd suspected – that it was wrong, nasty and spiteful to drop dirty shoes on your child's head – and tears spill down my cheeks. He scowls at me, then turns to her with that rattling in his throat, the sound that means he's about to strike.

Aaach, look what you done now, made him bawl like a fucking baby. He was fine until you opened your fucking trap.

He cocks a backhander. She flinches, but doesn't back down. He snarls again, Get tae fuck out of my sight.

But she doesn't. Instead, she kneels and dabs at my eyes with a crumpled tissue and wipes the dirt off my hair and tells me it's alright.

Daddy didn't mean to hurt you, he was only playing.

We both know better. He needs to inflict pain and humiliation on his wife and children every time he enters the room. Nothing less can put him at ease.

My little brother glares up at him with undisguised malice, but the Old Man ignores him. Sometime I wonder if he's frightened of Stuart, sensing that one day his younger son's white-hot rage will explode. If anyone is ever going to avenge our mother, we know it will be Stuart. He says as much whenever the Old Man's not around.

When I grow up, I'm going to kill him.

No, she says. You mustn't say that, Stuart. That's wrong.

I *am*, I'm going to kill him.

Then you won't go to heaven, will you?

Don't care.

Don't say that, Stuart.

As small children, Stuart and I live the tensions of sameness and difference. We share the usual things: surname, address, school, favourite television programmes. But we don't look alike at all, and perhaps for this reason our mother dresses us near-identically, in matching shirts and trousers and shoes. Only our hand-knitted cardigans and elasticated bow ties are in different colours: scarlet for me, baby blue for him.

Our temperaments differ, too. He is headstrong and daring, I am more cautious. I tend to think before I react, while he doesn't give a damn, displaying a self-assurance I can only envy. But we cannot remember a time when we didn't both exist, and for now we are deeply bonded. We play out violent fantasies with our toy guns, as secret agents or spacemen or Tommies fighting Germans. Soon we'll discover Marvel and DC Comics and become violent superheroes.

Even the discipline at St Mary's Roman Catholic Primary school is enforced with violence. The nuns are free to smack or cane us, and Father Byrne is even more ferocious. On overhearing some blasphemy he once slapped a boy's face so hard it left a red welt. But playtime is free and energetic, the girls lining up to take turns skipping Double Dutch while the boys chase a tennis ball across the tarmac, goals marked by the concrete posts supporting a green PVC chain-link fence. Sometimes weird men stop on Dock Road and peer through this fence at us, before being shooed off by one of the male teachers.

* * *

Though the Old Man beat her savagely and frequently, my mother refused to be cowed. Even as a small child I knew that she would never give him the satisfaction of breaking her spirit. One time in the kitchen we three kids were clinging to her skirt and bawling while the Old Man brandished a frying pan of sizzling fat, threatening to throw it at her.

You want this in your fucking face? I'll scar you for life!

Go on then! Do it, you bastard! I'm not scared!

Perhaps because it would have burned his children too, he hurled the pan into the corner of the room.

As we got older, we became valid targets. Early one Sunday morning when I was nine or 10 he came downstairs and caught me in the living room lighting strips of newspaper on the electric fire and tossing them into the fireplace. He threw me against the wall and started smashing his fists into my ribs so hard I couldn't breathe, couldn't even squeal for mercy. I was thinking, *I am going to die now*, when my mother burst in and pulled him off, taking an elbow to the face for her trouble.

And yet when I think back to those days, it's not the violence that stands out. It's my mother's singing voice, suddenly fluttering through the house as rare and beautiful as a bluebird, a sound so wonderful because, just for a fleeting moment, she felt some kind of joy.

Or it's the many little ways she found to show us love and tenderness. Somehow, despite the constant threat of mindless rage, we knew hours of happiness and laughter. Weekend nights, when the Old Man was invariably out on the piss, the four of us would dance in the living room, doing The Twist to The Beatles or Stones or whatever band was appearing on *Sunday Night at the London Palladium*. Because she insisted we had to pair off older-younger, I would reluctantly dance with our younger sister Sinéad, while Stuart got to dance with our mother. Although a little jealous, I didn't really mind.

When she was happy, we were all happy.

* * *

My mother's father Jack Sharkey was born in 1907 in the port town of Dún Laoghaire, 10 miles south-east of Dublin. He grew up working the fields with his farmworker brothers before becoming a merchant seaman. Sometime around 1930 he disembarked in Tilbury, already one of England's busiest docks. There he met Elizabeth, my grandmother. She had been born in 1913 to an unwed teenage mother and adopted as a baby from a Southend orphanage by a childless couple who worked in service in a grand house in Westminster. Lizzie's earliest memories, she once told me, were of cleaning silverware and sweeping out fire grates, using the back doors and back stairs, eating in the basement and sleeping in the attic, working for people whose eyes she was forbidden to meet, speaking only when spoken to. Little wonder she developed a lifelong scorn for unearned privilege and inherited wealth, and revulsion for the trappings of nobility. (Asked if she would accept the customary telegram from the Queen on her 100th birthday, she told the royal footmen, *Why's she sending me a bloody card? I don't know her. Tell her I won't be sending one back.*)

Jack and Lizzie had three girls in short succession: Julie, my mother Molly, and the baby, Ruby. In an era marked by the Great Depression, poverty oozed like a noxious gas from Tilbury's marshy ground. In December 1931 the Tilbury Distress Committee found 900 local families on the verge of starvation and established an emergency soup kitchen. My mother was born into this world just two years later. Yet despite the hardship all around them, the Sharkeys had enough to eat, clean clothes, a comfortable home and a decent education. The family was humble, but with aspirations to improve their lot.

When I ask about her own childhood, my mother recalls love and happiness.

We grew up in a nice home, she says, with a mum and dad who loved us. Of course, my dad could be strict if we messed about. My mum would say, Wait till your father gets home. And he was strict, but never severe. If he said, You better do this, then you'd do it, no questions asked. But the worst you'd ever get was a clip round the ear, nothing worse than that.

Jack Sharkey never drank at home. Indeed, the only time he drank was on Sunday afternoons. Since there was little else to do, the family would wander country lanes for hours – like the nine-mile hike to the village of Laindon – stopping on the way back at a country pub, where Lizzie and the girls would sit in the garden with a soft drink while Jack had a brown ale. The parents never spent on themselves, saving every spare penny to buy clothes or Christmas presents for the girls.

And as children our mother does the same for us, saving up for birthday presents, or summer holiday train outings to seaside towns like Pitsea or Leigh-on-Sea. There, we unpack our sandwiches and drinks and potato crisps and lie on the sand, greased up and smiling in the sunshine, while people shoo angry wasps off melting ice-cream cones. Then we'll swim a few yards into the cold, salty, dark green water, or run along the beach squinting into a billion diamonds of light glittering on the Thames Estuary.

Every Friday we have a fish feast for tea, which is what we call our evening meal. Like everyone else we know, we eat breakfast, dinner and tea. Lunch is some meal we've only heard about, something posh people eat, perhaps involving caviar. But on Fridays we know Mum will return from the fishmonger with a couple of pounds of sprats, double-wrapped in white butcher's paper. She unwraps the package in the kitchen and the silvery mass slithers across the yellow Formica table. She takes each sprat between finger and thumb, dabs it in white flour and drops it into sizzling fat. We eat fish on Fridays because that's what Catholics do, but she also likes sprats because she's doesn't have to gut them, so they're easy to prepare. So full of goodness, she says, and tasty, too.

Of course, we all know we eat them because they're cheap.

By now her teeth have already begun to rot and fall out. Much later, I would realise this was due to calcium deficiency. Four kids in just over five years? Raising them with no money, having to breastfeed them well after they could walk?

We literally sucked her bones dry.

Tilbury, 1962

Fraser was the youngest of the four children. I had just started school when he was born. I barely saw his face – I was allowed to peer into the cot, but only for a few seconds. My mother was worried I might give him a cold or some other germs from school.

Those late autumn days were stranger than normal. First, because a jolly black lady came to the house. She spoke with a sing-song accent that Mum said was Caribbean, and she made me promise to be a good boy and look after my brother and sister, because my mum would be very tired when the baby was born. Auntie Ruby, an NHS nurse, also came to help with the delivery. The Old Man celebrated by going out and getting even more drunk, as if he needed an excuse.

In those days we still lived at 10 Seymour Road on the dockyard side of town. Our two-up, two-down Victorian terraced house had an outdoor toilet and no bathroom. With a loan from Jack Sharkey my parents had bought it at a knockdown price because it came with a sitting tenant, an elderly lady called Mrs Whitlock, who rented one of the upper rooms.

One evening shortly after we move in, my mother is upstairs when her shriek of terror rips through the house. My father bounds up the stairs, barefoot in singlet and khaki trousers. After a lot of whispering and sobbing, he comes back down with the small, rigid body of Mrs Whitlock in his arms. I hide behind my mother's skirt as my father carries the dead lady into the living room and places her on the sofa. Then my mother goes next door to ask the neighbor to fetch the priest, who will call the doctor, who will call the police. In this Catholic home we respect the natural hierarchy.

My father is out at the pub one afternoon when I carefully lift the mysterious bottle of amber liquid on the mantelpiece, known to us all as *Daddy's medicine*. Imitating the Old Man's gestures I unscrew the cap and take a quick slug. Halfway down the liquid explodes from my face in a mist, as the bottle falls and shatters on the pink-tiled hearth. I cough and gasp and flutter my hands, the fiery blast scorching my throat and sinuses, forcing hot tears from my eyes. Wheezing, I suck air into my lungs. My mother strides into the room, takes one glance and slaps me so hard my head rings like a bell. She's not angry at me, but at the hiding she now has coming: he will beat her for negligence, for allowing me to waste good booze.

And now it's a Sunday afternoon in summer 1962 and we're out in the back garden, my mother, brother, sister and myself. Happy in the sunshine, radio tuned to the weekly chart show, an unvarnished plank fence towering over us on three sides. Mum likes to bring a chair out and sit prepping food, peeling potatoes or stringing green beans while we attack the soil with buckets and spades, or kick a yellow plastic ball. Sometimes she will spend a couple of precious pennies on caps for our toy guns and my brother and I will chase each other, firing imaginary bullets – *bang bang bang*. After we shoot all our caps, we hold the zinc alloy guns to our noses and savour the sulphurous tang, amazed at the wonder of explosive chemicals.

I'm waiting to hear this summer's hit, *I Remember You*. This song is always playing somewhere, drifting out of a window or burbling from a shop radio, Frank Ifield's glossy yodel at odds with the earthy smells and the mud-spattered vegetables scooped up by our horny-handed grocer, with his check shirt and tie, brown apron and cloth cap.

But instead of Frank Ifield, a new song plays. I like the melody but the words confuse me. They talk of a foreign place, and while I know foreign places because my father is always sailing to or from them, I don't know this one. When the song ends, I ask, Mum, what's Spanish Harlem?

She tells me it's a place in America where Puerto Ricans live. Beautiful people with olive skin, she says, who love to dance. I can tell from her voice that she'd like to live there, to dance with them. And in a moment of awakening, I become aware of distant lands full of shimmering promise and exotic people. I realise that songs contain emotions I don't yet understand, a yearning for other worlds, for imagined lives. And finally I realise that my mother, if she could, would wish herself into another existence. She is 28 and has already given birth to four children.

This garden is a place of fear and wonder. Another time, we are out here together when my mother leaves her food prep and goes indoors to fetch something. I pick up her paring knife and Stuart, knowing this is forbidden, tells me to put it back. I refuse, so he grabs the blade and tries to take it from me. I snatch the knife away, slicing his palm to the bone. My mother has to rush her screaming, hysterical three-year-old to the doctor for stitches and a tetanus shot to prevent infection.

This is the first time I wound Stuart. One day he will wound me, balancing the books.

In next door's garden a fierce, stupid mongrel called Bonzer barks incessantly. The fence is too high for us to see him, but sometimes we take our fish paste sandwiches and when Mum's not looking, toss scraps over for him. This makes Bonzer bark even more, which amuses us. Until his owner, an Australian called Pat, complains to Mum, who slaps me around the head because I'm the oldest and should know better.

The world beyond the back gate is a bomb-cratered waste-land strewn with trash and pockmarked with enormous black puddles. The docks had made Tilbury a prime target during the

Blitz, but Tilbury is not unique. Industrial towns and cities all over the UK still have huge chunks blasted away, places where you can turn off a busy street and find yourself staring up at buildings with entire sides missing, like giant dolls' houses, their living rooms broken open to expose wallpaper and picture frames, bathroom porcelain dangling three storeys up like Surrealist artwork. And below, shattered roads overgrown with weeds, stagnant water, rusty iron rods protruding from broken concrete. Such are the urban playgrounds of the early sixties in a nation still gaunt and wizened by collective sacrifice.

But with the Baby Boom under way and industry quickly recovering, a new generation is fast becoming self-aware. And while this is happening, my mother is coming to terms with the fact that she is trapped in a loveless marriage to a violent alcoholic, her already narrow options reduced even further by her young children.

After Fraser's birth our mother stayed in bed a whole week. We'd never known her spend so much time in bed, even when sick. With three small children and no help to raise them, she didn't have time, so we sensed something was wrong. Although the baby was a blessing from God, she seemed sad and weary. She struggled to dress me for school. One morning she screamed at me when I refused to wear a hand-me-down seersucker shirt we'd been given. I started crying, whining that I didn't want to wear a girl's blouse. She insisted it wasn't, but I could tell because it buttoned up the wrong side.

Other mornings she would cry for no reason, or none we could understand. Of course, she would sometimes cry when our father hit her. And then he would hit her again for crying. That was normal. Everyone cries if you hit them hard enough. And everyone gets hit if they won't stop crying. These were the facts of life by the time we could talk. But now she would weep silently while he was out, dabbing her eyes with a balled-up tissue. And then she'd try to smile and tell us she was just being silly. That it was going to be alright. That she loved us all very much.

Then one day, the cot was empty. The house was silent. Fraser was gone.

What happened to our baby brother?

Nobody spoke, nobody knew what to say.

For a moment I wondered if it was my fault. Despite my mother's warnings I'd been sneaking up to the cot, peering in at the baby when she wasn't looking. Was it my germs? Had I killed him?

That evening she sat us all down on the sofa, and then sat on the pouffe before us, her swollen calves laced with spidery veins.

Fraser has gone to heaven, she said. God wants him to be with the angels. He's happy now.

We never talked about the baby again.

*   *   *

At night, when my father was out drinking and acting the tough guy, boasting he could kill any man in the room, I would hear my mother crying in the dark, in their bedroom, alone.

Cot death was the official cause, but he didn't care what the doctor said. He screamed at her, beat her, damned her to hell.

He needn't have bothered. She blamed herself.

Many years later, when I asked her about it, she mumbled some words I didn't really hear, but somehow understood.

Fraser had known.

She had tried to pretend, tried to hide it from him. But a mother cannot hide how she feels from a baby suckling at her breast. Fraser could sense her broken heart, taste her sorrow and pain. She couldn't hide how battered and frightened and lonely she was, how close to giving up herself.

And Fraser had simply let go.

Tilbury, 1961–63

Where is Daddy?

He's away at sea, you know that.

But where?

Maybe New York. We'll find out tomorrow.

The city's name is familiar from TV shows yet still impossibly alien. The fact that Daddy could be in such a place makes him godlike, a traveller to distant galaxies.

Once or twice a week my mother takes us to the public library in Civic Square, but we never check out any books. While we sit hushed on the wooden bench, she walks over to the newspaper rack and lifts out a wooden rod, the broadsheet hanging from it like a tattered flag, then lays it on a desk and spreads it out. *Lloyd's List*, which provides daily news on mercantile shipping, is not readily available in local newsagents, a special order, so this trip saves her a few pennies she can use on food. She stands bent over it in her thick, slubby overcoat, a plume of dark curls peeking over her forehead from the printed rayon headscarf she wears tied under her chin, as she runs her finger down the long dense columns of print, checking vessels and ports and time zones to see where he has set sail or dropped anchor, tracking his progress across the globe, counting the days until the beatings begin again.

From an early age we know the library as a place where you can learn about the real world. Like when Daddy will get back from his work and become a real person again. Other kids, their dads eat breakfast with them before going to work every morning. Other dads, their work is physical or mental toil requiring sweat and grunt and strain. Work that may take place behind walls, but in docks and factories we can see, on roads we know.

Our dad's work is not like that. In the library my mother will tell us he has just arrived in Cape Town or departed from Buenos Aires, at a time when those places seem as distant as Mars or Venus. Our dad's work is not a daily task, but one that requires many months. It's a vanishing act, a sacramental mystery that takes place out on the high seas. In those rare moments when he returns and deigns to answer our childish questions about where he has been, the answers leap out like technicolor movie credits: South Pacific, Indian Ocean, Zanzibar, Shanghai. And so we grow up thinking of work as something unworldly and enigmatic, executed in some unknowable dimension.

Other dads come home every day in dirty clothes and wash up before eating.

Our dad comes home after four or five months wearing a new Burton suit and gleaming new shoes. And now he doesn't need to work for weeks on end. Now he has paper money in his pockets, lots of it, and all the time in the world.

Other dads celebrate New Year's Eve with the family, rolling back the carpet to do the Hokey Cokey in the front room. Our dad is always at sea. We mark his absence in the kitchen, listening to the foghorns of ships in the dock, long mournful blasts booming through the frigid night, Tilbury's ghostly stand-in for midnight fireworks.

Other dads save for predictable annual events, for birthday presents and Christmas gifts. Our dad is never around for those events. Instead, like some Slot Machine Santa he appears in the middle of the night, tie askew and reeking of drink, to pay out phenomenal jackpots.

Like the time he returns from a two-month journey with stops in Africa and America. We kneel on the living-room floor, vibrating with excitement as he places a green and yellow batik knapsack before us and whips it open to reveal a pile of glittering plastic trinkets: toy soldiers with detachable weapons, dolls with nylon hair, revolvers and handcuffs, rockets and racing cars, magnifying glasses and sheriff's badges, eyepatches and moustaches, beads and bangles and hair grips, red transparent dice and miniature playing cards. There are also American sweets – what he calls *candy* – and packs of chewing gum, too. He had probably stopped the cab on his way to the ship, run into a Chinatown general store and told the cashier to wrap up 20 dollars' worth of cheap junk in this strip of African fabric. But to us, this is a fabulous treasure, exquisitely gaudy, unlike anything our friends' parents will ever find locally. And scattered in among these wonderful baubles are dozens of little cowrie shells, with delicate mottled backs and glossy white bellies, looking eerily like living creatures.

My sister turns one over in her palm, peering into its tiny crenelated mouth.

Are these toys, Daddy?

That's money, sweetheart.

No, don't be silly.

Aye, really. That's African money. And so is that, and that.

And now, as he points, we see the strange coins, some square, others with holes punched in them. And then the dainty leaves of paper money in impossible colours like pink and orange and purple. In our eagerness to rifle through the toys, we hadn't even noticed the fistfuls of foreign currency mingled in our plastic bounty.

At weekends he appears in the kitchen mid-morning, still in his singlet and pyjama trousers. He drinks tea and eats toast while reading the paper, circling a few horses, and then gets washed and shaved and groomed, putting on his clean shirt and nice suit to go out and drink all day with his mates.

Sometimes he'll be back for tea at six, but most evenings he's still missing when we go to bed. And then we'll jolt awake as the front door slams, Stuart and I in our bunk beds, listening wide-eyed in the darkness. Downstairs, he starts shouting about the state of his dinner, which is never right.

Too hot. Too cold. Too salty. Too dry.

Fucking slop, you stupid fucking bitch, what the fuck is that meant tae be?

The shattering of the plate against the wall. A shriek as he slaps her, an explosive groan as a punch lands in her ribs.

Sometimes she pleads, her voice echoing up the stairs, *Please, Al, I'm sorry.*

Sometimes she roars her defiance, *Go on then, do it! You're such a big man, go on … you big, tough man, you, hitting a woman! Do it!*

Eventually his shouting fades to a low grumble and then dies out. Even as infants we know this is the booze slowing him down, lulling him into oblivion – his inevitable destination.

In the morning, we say nothing about last night.

He eats breakfast, picks out his nags, gets shaved.

He smells good again.

He smells of Old Spice, a blend of citrus and musk in a milk-coloured flask with a blue sailing ship on it. Sometimes I'll creep into the bathroom to take it off the shelf and run my fingertips across the creamy glass, tracing the rough edge of the painted ship like braille, sensing its coded message. One day, I too will smell like a man, dress like a star, drink my way around the tropical ports of the world.

He gets dressed and smells even better: worsted wool and the fresh cotton shirts hand-washed and ironed by my mother, laced with the medicinal zest of Vitalis hair tonic.

In the evening, he smells bad again.

He reeks of stale bitter and Senior Service butts, the phosphorus snap of Swan Vestas and that cool mix of pine disinfectant and evacuated bowels that lingers in tiled public toilets marked GENTS. He smells of damp Victorian terminus buildings and sweaty palms clutching smooth copper coins. He smells of the hiss and gush of steam and babies wailing and guard's whistles and clickety-clack heels and porters with sack trolleys crying, *Mind your backs*, the weary must of old newsprint as it swirls up into the vaulted wrought ironwork and frosted glass overhead.

He smells of a dying era, of failure, surrender, defeat.

But even staggering drunk he is never dishevelled, never seen in public unless suited and booted, topped off with his trademark trilby. And never ever seen in jeans.

Jeans, he tells me one day, are for kids and imbeciles who get paid from the neck down.

As a chef, he is paid from the neck up. Sometimes I think the only reason captains and shipmates and friends gave him so many second and even third chances – knowing full well he'd always let them down again – is the impeccable way he presented himself.

And then one morning, he's gone again.

No goodbyes, no explanations. Just vanished.

The house seems oddly calm. Now we sleep through the night without being woken by the sound of breaking glass or crockery, without my mother's cries of pain.

A couple of weeks later and she starts taking us to the library again, to trace his passage across vast oceans to far-flung continents, bracing herself for his return.

And then one day in the middle of the night we are roused from deep childish slumber to find the carpet once again scattered with strange coins and plastic toys and comics. For a few days everyone seems happy and we all eat meat, and then the beatings resume and he stops going to the pub, buying bottles of cheap plonk and hanging out in bus shelters or on park benches to stretch out his drinking money.

Until it's time to go earn some more, and the cycle repeats.

Perhaps the strangest thing is that I never see him cook. Despite his brutal dismissal of the food my mother dutifully prepares – which is only dry because she keeps it warm, expecting him at midnight, although he rarely returns until hours later – despite all this, not once do I recall him in the kitchen, preparing a meal. Not for his children, not even for himself. Of course, after months at sea preparing three meals a day for 30 or 40 men, home cooking must seem like the ultimate busman's holiday.

But he doesn't even enjoy eating, let alone cooking. To look at him, to talk to him, you'd never guess his job involved preparing food. Despite his fancy French credentials I never once hear him talk about food as a sensuous experience, never once remark on flavour or texture or odour, never once speak of restaurants, recipes, ingredients or techniques.

Oh, he likes the idea of being a chef, of being in charge, of telling people what to do. He loves to explain how important he is, doling out sustenance. But his focus is always on the power structures and logistics of feeding large numbers of men while thousands of miles from dry land – rather than any aesthetic consideration, any gastronomic pleasure.

I have only a single memory of learning something from him in the kitchen. One morning I ask him about the strange breakfast he sometimes prepares, breaking a raw egg into a pint glass, adding salt and pepper and a couple of slugs of Worcestershire sauce. He stirs the mix gently to avoid breaking the yolk and then swallows it in one shot.

Why do you drink that raw egg stuff, Daddy?

That's a Prairie Oyster, he says. It's good for you.

After he has left for the pub, I ask my mother if she ever drinks it.

No, she says. I don't need it.

Why does Daddy need it?

Because it's a hangover cure. And it lines his stomach so he can drink all day.

*   *   *

Every weekday morning our neighbour's nine-year-old daughter Anne collects me and walks me to St Mary's Roman Catholic Primary School. This school is the centre of our universe. It shares a tree-shaded garden with Our Lady Star of the Sea, the church where our parents were married in March 1956. Next to that is the Convent of Mercy, which houses our teachers, nuns of the Sisters of Mercy. On the other side stands the priest's house, occupied by Father Byrne. As the school's spiritual adviser, his opinion outweighs even that of the headmaster, Mr Fitzgerald.

A year later, Stuart and I are old enough to walk to school together without Anne. But while we dress alike, physically we are dissimilar. Stuart has the thick curly hair, heart-shaped face and softer features of my mother, while I have inherited my father's straight dark hair, oval face, hooded eyes and high cheekbones. I also have the Old Man's thick lower lip and beneath it a scar that makes it even thicker, thanks to having fallen face-first onto a paving slab at the age of three. The impact smashed my lower teeth straight through the skin under the lip, requiring two stitches at the hospital.

The overall effect is of vaguely Asian features, which mark me out as an alien, an object of scorn and abuse. I'm taunted and mocked as a Chink or Jap or Ching-Chong Chinaman. Older boys sometimes spit at me, or sneer that my mum must have fucked a Chinese milkman. The girls chant a rhyme at me in the playground:

Chinese, Japanese
Dirty knees,
What are these?

They pull the corners of their eyes, slap their *dirty knees* and tug imaginary nipples for *What are these?*

I am not so much hurt as confused. First, I know they are wrong. I'm not Chinese or Japanese. But I don't understand why it would matter – especially in a dock town full of sailors from all over the world. I know they're wrong because my father explains this one night, lolling drunkenly in his armchair, while I sit on his lap and ask about the blurry, dark blue tattoo on his left forearm. Above a sailing ship on the ocean waves, two muscular hands lock in a handshake. Below the ship is the bannered slogan, *Hands Across the Sea.*

At sea, he tells me solemnly, every man is your brother. When you reach for a hand at sea, you don't look at its colour.

Fortunately, I have a brother of my own to lend a hand in the school playground when Tony Carter or some other bully starts smacking me around, kicking me and calling me Chink. Because no matter how often or how viciously we fight at home, Stuart and I always defend each other. And while I'm rarely called on to save him – his pretty-boy looks seem to function as a protective force field – he frequently comes to my rescue. If an older boy hits me, no matter how big or tough, Stuart piles in, fists swinging wildly. This much at least we've absorbed from both parents: nobody hits one brother without catching hell from the other.

As for our future, it seems straightforward. Even in primary school we know enough about the grown-ups in our orbit to be dimly aware of our options. Neither of us wants to follow in our father's drunken footsteps and join the Merchant Navy, so it's a clerical job in the City if we're lucky, or shift work on a factory floor, maybe Ford Works in Dagenham. Otherwise, a life on the dole, with early marriage and fatherhood, council houses and working men's clubs, community halls and magistrates' courts. And though my mother talks to us about becoming doctors or lawyers, we can tell this is just her way of encouraging us, giving us hope.

Similarly, she always tucks us into bed with a kiss and the back of her fingers brushing our foreheads, before pausing at the door to sing-song a little chant, one we repeat back to her, a kind of homespun nursery rhyme:

Night night, God bless, sleep tight, see you in a minute, see you 'morrowdays, I love you.

We need this reassurance because our dreams are troubled. Sometimes Stuart talks in his sleep, muttering angry sounds of refusal and defiance. I have a recurrent dream where I'm standing in a place both strange and shockingly familiar, looking up at a massive castle beyond a wide moat, its towering walls covered with bitter green ivy, gleaming in the sunlight. In my dream I live here, it's my home. Only I cannot enter because the drawbridge is up. Even at six or seven, long before I learn about reincarnation, I know I'm dreaming of a previous life.

A life I can never return to.

3

Paris, February 2000–2001

While the nascent internet economy was helping fuel a finance and property boom, I was working in London as a freelance journalist, but covering catwalk shows and interviewing designers in Paris. Having lived there for two years in the mid-nineties, I knew the city and spoke French, and since my work was secured by phone, written at home and delivered by email, why not move back and work from Paris? After comparing property prices and exchange rates, I realised I could trade up.

My daughter Fiona was almost 13, old enough to take the Eurostar on her own, provided her mother Jane saw her off at Waterloo and I was waiting on the platform when she arrived in Paris, or vice-versa. Though we'd separated when Fiona was still a baby, Jane and I remained on friendly terms and took our parental duties seriously, consulting closely about her upbringing.

That February I placed my tiny one-bedroom flat on the market and flew to Nepal for a month. After celebrating Tibetan New Year in Kathmandu, I went trekking in the Himalayas and visited several Buddhist shrines before returning to London to find my property had sold in a bidding war. The move to Paris was on.

The next steps unfolded with almost dreamlike ease. By mid-September I had moved into a two-bedroom apartment in

La Chapelle, a funky working-class district in the 10th *arron-dissement*, 10 minutes' walk from the Gare du Nord Eurostar terminal. My first night as a property-owning Parisian, too excited to sleep, I stood in the darkness against a louvred window, looking down at black cobblestones gleaming in the moonlight, and then up at clouds streaming through the night sky like God's own screensaver.

I wasted no time getting plugged into the social scene of hotel bars and bistros, or fabulous events like the Miu Miu party at the Communist Party HQ building, Niemeyer's modernist labyrinth of undulating lines and voluptuous forms. Maybe for the first time in my life, I felt successful. I'd hit the hyperspace button at the perfect moment and landed safely in another part of the universe with spending money in my pocket, far from the constrictions and violence of my early life. I was living in Europe's chicest city – yet just a two-hour train journey from friends and family in London and my mother's flat on the Hertfordshire border. And only an hour more from my dockland hometown and the suburbs where my brother Stuart and his wife Debbie still lived, along with my aunts and uncles and cousins. Far enough to be out of mind, near enough to be close to heart.

Truly, the best of all possible worlds.

As well as drinking too much while acting the big shot at parties and fancy dinners, I was trying to manage an on-again, off-again relationship in London. Celia was barely half my age, an artist and part-time receptionist living in a studio flat on a Southwark council estate. Ours was not a well-balanced relationship and now seems inappropriate, but I was impressed by the way she shifted gears from Sade to The Stooges, Vivienne Westwood to Valerie Solanas, Wesley Snipe's *Blade* to Kierkegaard's *Either/Or*. She was smart and sassy, with a line of banter that more than matched my own. But her Zambian passport meant she couldn't visit France without spending weeks obtaining a visa, so we mostly stayed at her place. It was there in late February 2001 that I used her computer to log into my French webmail account, and found a momentous announcement from my sister-in-law:

> Hi Alix,
>
> How are you? Not sure if you are travelling still or back home in Paris. Anyway, just thought I would pass on some good news, I'M PREGNANT !!!!!!!!!

At the foot of the email, after some jokey aside about a scan that showed a clear resemblance to my side of the family, was a stock colour photo of a smiling baby, its features contorted using crude software to make it look gormless. I couldn't help but think this might be tempting fate, but decided to keep my reply upbeat.

> Hi Debbie,
>
> Just got your email. I'm in London at the moment and hadn't been able to access my French email account until yesterday. So, anyway … CONGRATULATIONS!!! That's really fantastic news, I'm sure you and Stuart must be delighted. Do you know whether it's a boy or girl yet? I told my mum last night and she was very happy. Anyway, I wish you both all the best of luck as parents, and look forward to meeting my first niece/nephew. Keep me informed of developments! And please give Stuart a hefty slap on the back on my behalf.
>
> love, Alix.

Looking back, it seems weird that I asked her to congratulate my brother for me. Maybe I was too self-important to call him myself. Maybe I wasn't entirely convinced of his joy – or my own goodwill. The baby certainly would not be *my first niece/ nephew*. There was the small matter of Stuart's previous child, Jennie-Lee, long since abandoned. Despite our mother's efforts to maintain contact while she was still a toddler, somewhere along the line Jennie-Lee, by my calculations now a young woman of 24, had been consigned to our familial storehouse of secrets, mysteries and half-truths too embarrassing, contentious or unpleasant to mention in company – all of them locked away behind a door marked *None of Your Business*.

I knew better than to rattle that door. And so I followed the old familial pattern, suppressing feelings of doubt and mistrust to go with the flow. Besides, Stuart had matured and outgrown his youthful recklessness. He was now a happily married man with his own small business and a loving and supportive extended family. Debbie's pregnancy only confirmed this. Why upset everyone by dredging up his failed first marriage and long-lost daughter?

No, I would play my ordained role as the uppity elder brother, the one who'd symbolically broken with his past by adopting our mother's maiden name, who'd got shot of his Tilbury accent and now spoke like a Fancy Dan. I knew that Stuart – who still used our father's surname and retained his Estuary diphthongs – would sometimes mimic my vocal mannerisms, making me sound like a pompous, dim-witted James Bond wannabe.

Yeah, I was the one who fancied himself a bit too much, who thought himself better than the rest, even though he'd never admit as much. I knew how they saw me. And I was okay with it. They weren't completely wrong.

And so I continued drinking and philandering, while filing stories from Lille, Bordeaux and Marseille. By now I had been studying Buddhism and trying to practise meditation for some years, and every few months I would travel overseas to attend teachings or spend a week or more in retreat, thankful to find myself isolated in a single room or same-sex dorm, with no booze or weed or coke or pills.

On 30 May I flew to Vancouver and travelled to a cluster of wood cabins deep in the Canadian Rockies. To underwrite my 10-day retreat, I flew back via San Francisco to interview beat poet Lawrence Ferlinghetti, founder of City Lights bookstore. Life seemed good by the time I got back to Paris, and the following day a telecom engineer hooked up my long-awaited ADSL line. Now I could browse the internet at high speed all day long. No more glitchy dial-up modem and pay-by-the-minute access. I had no idea how important this new technology was about to prove. On Saturday 16 June, I wrote and filed a piece on Dutch footballer Marco van Basten for *GQ*, then went out to meet friends at yet another fashion party. The evening would take an unexpected turn, as I wrote in my diary the next day:

Early morning of 17 June 2001, walking home along Boulevard de Clichy near Blanche station you notice people lining up outside a sketchy joint called Le Magnum. Everyone in line is black and male, except for one rough-looking blonde girl. You join the line. Because you're dressed in a suit, you get waved inside, €11 admission comes with a free drink, so you grab a whisky coke and start moving to the dancehall reggae, which gets better, sleazier, funkier as you go along. The place is packed. The whisky coke tastes even better. Next thing you're dancing to all kinds of great tunes you've heard on porno websites and thinking how your moves are really quite camp compared to these boys around you. The DJ drops a remix of Independent Women *by Destiny's Child and the place goes bonkers. Then you're dancing to some kind of fucked-up Raï music crossed with techno and thinking,* Levi's ad! I could make a million if I ripped this off and sold it to them. *Then some awesome gal comes up and starts dancing, then talking. You can't hear a word, so she gestures to the bar: she wants a whisky coke. Her name is Aida, like the opera. You dance together to* Get Ur Freak On *by Missy Elliott and you know the lyrics better than she does, and then she wants a pack of Marlboro and you realise where this is heading. So you slip out the door, sliding the coat-check gal your number just in case, and head home to find Norton Utilities has worked its magic and fixed all the bad blocks on your hard disk. And then at 3:00 a.m. you get a call from a Cambodian girl in New York who says she wants to marry you, only she thinks you are in a bad mood, when in fact everything is just about as good as it ever gets.*

About as good as it ever gets.

These words mark the end of my blissfully glib Playboy Life.

Although I don't know it yet, tomorrow the world will change forever.

Tomorrow is Monday 18 June 2001.

4

Tilbury, 1964–65

The police cannot protect my mother. They have no right to enter a man's house unless he asks them, or a third party reports a crime. His wife and children? As long as he stops short of murder, how he treats them is his business. Essentially, they're his property.

One time, the Old Man summons us and lines us up in front of his armchair. My mother had dared suggest otherwise, so now he demands the truth.

He asks each of us in turn, Do you love me?

Yes, I lie, looking at the floor.

But Stuart scowls, sticks out his chin and barks, *No, I hate you!*

The Old Man squints at him, jaw clenched. Nobody dares talk to him this way. We're all trembling, waiting for the inevitable backhand blow that will send Stuart flying across the room. But at four, he is still a little too small for the Old Man to strike. At five, I have already taken a fist to the temple and know better than to test him.

Not long after this our mother decides to leave him. No note, no forwarding address. She opts for Scotland. Grandad accompanies us to the station – just in case we bump into the Old Man and he gets violent – and we board the overnight train to Glasgow, sleeping on the seats of our 2nd class carriage. Our mother will throw herself on the mercy of the Old Man's older sister Mary, an affluent and happily married childless woman who lives in a nice part of town. Mary has always been kind and sympathetic and my mother believes she'll put us up in her big house until we get settled. But on our arrival, Mary takes us in a taxi to see her wee brother Johnny. Although he is not happy to see us, Johnny grudgingly agrees to take us in.

It's a dismal living arrangement: Johnny Campbell and his wife and four small children live in a mould-stained, three-bedroom prefab, the nastiest kind of council housing. Worse, just like his elder brother Alec, our father, Johnny pisses his money up the wall before coming home to beat his wife and kids.

Our mother tells us we have to make this city our new home, but we cannot overcome the weirdness, the otherworldliness of it all. Stuart and I try to play football with some kids in the street, but suddenly all the energy drains from my legs and I fall down, unable to move. I know it has something to do with the way everyone speaks, this accent that makes me feel like a visitor to another planet. Stuart puts his arm around me and consoles me as we both walk home crying, too young to understand our profound homesickness. Back at Uncle Johnny's we huddle in a damp-smelling bedroom with cardboard walls, and listen to the screams as he punches his wife. We have travelled 400 miles to trade one nightmare home for another.

A few weeks pass before one afternoon when the Old Man turns up. Someone in his sprawling family has told him that he can find his missing wife and kids in the last place he'd have thought to look: his hometown. We sit around the kitchen table with our cousins and listen to the hushed voices in the living room. My mother weeps and sniffles while the Old Man coos and purrs and makes all kinds of promises. He'll quit drinking, get a job in Tilbury, no more going to sea. He'll be a good husband and a father to his kids. He'll do whatever it takes to win her back. Can't she see how much he loves her?

He calls her Wops, her childhood nickname, which he had picked up when they were courting.

Wops, as in slang for Italian, for her curly black hair, olive skin and dark eyes.

Alright, she says, sniffling. As long as you promise, Al.

I promise, Moll. I swear on my life.

*   *   *

It wasn't the first time my mother had tried to escape Tilbury. At the age of 20 she'd taken the Fenchurch Street train every morning to work as a secretary in a City law firm. Within a year she was engaged to a man called Jim, a junior lawyer from Clapham Junction. At weekends she would visit him and they had plans to rent a flat in that part of town when they got married. Maybe one day they'd move to Pimlico or Chelsea.

Then she met my father in The Ship, and everything changed. He must have pursued her doggedly, because she was a good Catholic girl and not interested in hanky-panky before marriage. God knows she must have extracted promises and assurances from him before shifting allegiance.

But Alec Campbell was not the stable, loving provider she was looking for. He was a 27-year-old merchant seaman who lived most of the year on the high seas, sailing colonial routes via African ports to Asia and Australia, or to South America via New York when Manhattan's piers were still working docks, as opposed to the tourist attractions they've since become.

Did she swap dull certainty for dashing unpredictability? What convinced her to give up Jim for Alec? She says she can't remember.

*   *   *

So we all returned to Tilbury and tried to act as if things were normal, even though we didn't really know what *normal* meant. And this man we had never met moved in with us, a complete stranger who looked exactly like the Old Man but acted like someone else entirely.

He kissed our mum, something we'd never seen before.

She smiled at him, which seemed very odd.

We watched suspiciously, uneasy witnesses to this new-found affection.

Unable to understand what was happening, we struggled to accept this new arrangement. Should we try to love him again? Or should we continue to hate him? I tried to split the difference, inching towards letting him back into my heart. But Stuart remained stony-faced, refusing to forgive him or show him the slightest affection.

On the rare occasions when we addressed him directly, Stuart and I might call him Dad, but never Daddy. That word was always too sweet, too gentle, too intimate. Dad suited him better: monosyllabic, blunt, factual. Yet even that was a stretch. Until this point we had no memories of being with him the way kids are supposed to be with their fathers, laughing or hugging, playing in the garden or going on little trips together. Yet here we were, back in the family home.

Only now he was different. For the first time he was fun to be around. He played games with us and read books and laughed aloud at the cartoons in the paper. Children forgive quickly and we learned to like him. Almost love him. After a while even Stuart no longer seemed to burn with rage. We were still getting used to this new normal when everything changed again.

She'd taken him back, but he came bearing gifts.

*　　*　　*

It's a Monday morning when Sister Annunciata announces that the whole class will be seeing the nurse today to get a special test, a kind of check-up. We file into the echoing hallway and line up with all the other pupils – 120 kids chattering and giggling, excited by the novelty of a medical examination. One by one we shuffle into the tiny secretarial office which doubles as a sick bay.

The school secretary seated at the desk ticks off my name and rolls up my left shirt sleeve. The nurse twists my wrist and swabs my forearm with alcohol, then smears the skin with a pungent fluid chemical. She applies the cool metal kiss of a spring-loaded gun to my arm. A ratcheting click, a *pop* and the biological agent is fired into my skin on the tips of six tiny needles. She dabs away tiny drops of blood with cotton wool and applies an Elastoplast. No explanation, no advice.

Next!

Two days later I peel off the plaster to find a weeping blister, a circle of angry red dots where the needles punctured the skin. I'm horrified, especially as my brother and sister have no such reaction. Clearly, something has gone wrong.

But when the nurse returns at the end of the week to inspect our arms, she tells me this itchy inflammation is a good sign. Unlike my brother and sister I won't need the full vaccination, which can cause several days of sickness.

Why not? I say.

Because you have antibodies.

What's that, Miss?

It means you've already been exposed to tuberculosis but your body fought it off, so you now have natural immunity. You don't need the vaccination.

In the playground I brag about my new status to the other kids. *Natural immunity.* You might get sick with TB, but it can't hurt me.

The root of my natural immunity, of course, is the Old Man.

He had brought his drunkard's disease with him, infecting me with tuberculosis.

Within weeks he was so sick that he had to move out of the marital bed and into Sinéad's single bed in the so-called box room over the front door, while she began sleeping with my mother. Stuart and I were happy to be farthest from him, sharing bunk beds in the bedroom overlooking the back garden.

We were told not to disturb him, which seemed odd given how his periodic appearances had always involved shouting and screaming and slamming of doors, the smashing of crockery and glasses and bottles. Now the explosive violence we'd grown to associate with his presence gave way to a church-like hush, as we tiptoed up and down the stairs, hissing at each other instead of shouting.

Meanwhile the Old Man lay in bed sweat-drenched, coughing and wheezing and groaning and hawking up phlegm into a plastic bowl, while my mother scurried back and forth with towels and hot water, bed pan and medicines and clean pyjamas. After several days of this she gathered us in the front room and warned us that Daddy was very sick and might die.

I shrugged, unable to work up any real emotion, while my brother was characteristically blunt.

I hope he dies, said Stuart. I *hate* him.

Stuart and I were shocked when two priests arrived at the door, grim-faced and speaking to our mother in breathy murmurs. Not just our family priest Father Byrne, but another priest we'd never seen before, older and clearly superior. My mother had summoned them to perform Extreme Unction, the Roman Catholic sacrament for the dying, which we all knew from our catechism lessons would involve penance, communion and prayers, followed by the anointing of the body with holy water and holy oils to prepare for death.

They were ushered upstairs into the box room.

This was it, then.

It would be horrible for a while, but then everything would be so much better.

While my mother and the older priest were upstairs, Father Byrne joined us in the living room and said we should pray for our father. So we all knelt and mumbled along with him, Our Father who art in Heaven, yadda yadda ... Hail Mary, full of grace, yadda yadda ... while Stuart and I glanced at each other sideways, rolling our eyes.

If prayers were answered, they certainly weren't ours. A few days later the Old Man made a near-miraculous appearance like some consumptive Lanarkshire Lazarus, up and walking to the bathroom, albeit at a glacial pace and with one hand on the wall for support, the other clutching the waistband of his now-oversized pyjamas. The old priest came back to check on his progress, perhaps himself amazed at what had happened. I listened at the door as he admonished the sinner.

No, he said, it's *more* than a miracle. It's a *second chance*. I hope you'll use it wisely.

A few days more and the Old Man was washed and dressed and sitting in the living room with his bare feet up on the pouffe, wearing baggy khaki trousers and a cotton singlet, laughing at the cartoons in *Reader's Digest*. I don't think I'd ever seen him so relaxed and casual. For a couple of months, he was almost a regular father, someone who ate with us, helped our Mum prepare the odd meal, stayed home and watched television in the evenings, did small DIY jobs around the house. In those fleeting moments of sobriety, I encountered someone I'd never known, a quirky man who seemed to understand how the world worked. And even if he'd never used that knowledge to his own profit, I began to glimpse why my mother had fallen for him – his cynicism was balanced by a sharp Glaswegian wit and a keen sense of the absurd.

*   *   *

One afternoon, I was going out to play with friends when he called my name.

What's that on your neck? he said.

I knew he meant the bruise I'd got playing football but I put my fingertips to my neck, as if trying to understand the question.

That? That's called *skin*.

You cheeky fucking monkey, he said, leaping out of his chair. Come here.

With a squeal of delight I bolted out the front door and across the road, to duck down the alley. I was shocked when he came sprinting around the corner after me. I'd never seen him run before, not even a brisk stride. Here was a previously unknown athleticism. I turned and started running again. He was gaining on me fast when I heard a loud *pop*.

Fuck, he said.

The waistband button had snapped off and his khaki trousers had slipped down to his knees. I laughed and pointed as he clutched the waistband in his fist, no longer able to give chase.

Fat man, you burst your trousers!

And then the strangest thing happened: he started laughing, too.

You little fucker, he said.

I saw your underpants!

You'll see something else later.

Can't catch me!

He smiled and shook his head, then turned back to the house. And that was it, the high point of our relationship.

* * *

After he stopped drinking my mother said he had to get another job. He couldn't go back to sea because he always drank at sea. But he didn't have any other skills. The only thing he could do was feed dozens of men three times a day while hundreds of miles from dry land. He was really good at this job, one he'd learned from the ground up as a galley boy, running up and down decks with buckets of water, peeling and chopping vegetables, cutting up salted fish, stirring enormous vats of rice or stew. Sometimes I tried to imagine him working in a kitchen with the ship pitching up and down on 10-foot waves. After a storm, he once told me, the crew is always famished.

But even with his Cordon Bleu, what could he do in Tilbury? There were no five-star hotels in this dockyard town. Of course, he could have moved to London and got a job in a fancy restaurant or hotel there, but that would have meant separating from his wife and children – the one thing that had convinced him to stop drinking in the first place.

Whether he looked for another job or not, he didn't get one. My mother was going out and earning what little money came into the house, waitressing at Jim's Cafe, a lorry drivers' stop on the edge of town, at the top of Feenan Highway.

So the Old Man had no money and sat at home feeling useless. Soon the atmosphere started to shift, naive optimism giving way to creeping anxiety. Now my mother circled him warily, burned too many times to have fully dropped her guard. And then she found an empty beer bottle, and the next day a couple more, tucked away in a cupboard under the stairs. She pleaded with him tearfully and he apologised and said he'd stop, swore it was just a momentary relapse – he wasn't going back to drinking.

Shortly afterwards another empty bottle appeared, and then another, until they weren't hidden anymore, and then beer bottles became whisky bottles. Soon he was openly drunk, no longer hiding it, coming home drunk at midnight, shouting and swearing and smashing the plates of food she'd kept warm for him, and soon he started hitting her again.

Around this time my mother told me how she had learned too late about my father, how he had spent his whole life letting people down, squandering every chance and opportunity. She'd spoken with Merchant Navy captains, serious and thoughtful men who understood the hard life of a merchant seaman and made allowances. These captains told her they'd had to sail without him, the ship's chef, because he had literally *missed the boat*. But then, because he was good at his job, they'd given him a second chance, only to have him repeat the trick – the ship sailing at high tide while he lay face down on some park bench, blind drunk and flat broke.

God knows how she found the strength and single-minded purpose, but she managed to force him out of the house again. It happened incrementally, with several angry doorstep scenes. More than once the police had to come and politely request that he leave the premises, as we stood behind our mother in the hallway while he told her what a fucking piece of shit she was. The policemen would restrain him as he lunged at her, and then he'd pull his arm away and turn on one of the coppers, threatening to punch his fucking lights out, while Mum would be telling us to go back into living room and watch the telly.

The evening of my eighth birthday, a young but hulking police officer appears at the front door with the Old Man, who has come to collect the last of his belongings. He is drunk, of course, snarling at my mother as she hands him his suitcases. The copper grips his elbow tight, so he can't force his way in or lunge at her. Stuart and I watch him from the hallway, standing behind Mum. He sees us but doesn't speak to us or mention my birthday. In fact, I don't believe he ever knew our birthdays – he'd never given any of us so much as a card, let alone a present.

And then one day we wake up and realise he's gone for good.

For some time we still find it hard to believe she has finally got rid of him, that he won't be back. It feels like the lull before the storm, one we'd lived through countless times – an explosion of rage in the middle of the night, as he stumbles through the house swearing and snarling, smashing plates and glasses and hurling abuse and punches. But gradually we learn to trust the silence, to relax in his absence, and no longer hide our heads under our blankets at night.

Tilbury, September 1966

On school days the four of us have coffee with our breakfast. Usually it's Nescafé, although sometimes my mother brews fresh coffee in her stainless-steel percolator. I love the way the brown liquid gurgles and rattles the percolator, then spurts up into the glass bubble on the lid. On dark mornings we sip coffee and eat cornflakes while Radio Caroline or Radio London blares from the Japanese transistor radio on the kitchen windowsill. Like working people all across the country we love these songs, and feed off their energy to start the day. For a few weeks each hit becomes a family friend, a cheap, sugary emotional high. We try to guess each song's progress up and down the charts, claiming expertise if we're right. Occasionally our Mum will sing along – just a few bars or a couplet – with a tone so pure it makes my heart flutter.

Even as children we are keenly aware that many of these songs are loaded with nostalgia and a sense of loss, lamenting something old and valuable that is passing away even as we sing along. The national mood seems inconsolable – even songs of pride and plucky defiance are tinged with sadness or profound yearning. We seem to be saying goodbye to a simpler world, with simpler emotions. Are we mourning the mythic Blitz spirit that supposedly united the nation in its moment of greatest peril? Quite possibly, since at this point the Second World War is barely 21 years behind us, still fresh in the popular memory. The military conscription of all healthy males aged 17–21, known as National Service, has only recently ended, and most of the young men in Tilbury have done their mandatory 18-month stint. Little wonder that everyday speech is rife with military jargon, and our values tinged with bluff nationalism.

This is the culture Stuart and I try to grasp with childish minds, this dissolution of a postwar colonial mentality, a mindset shaped by communal hardship, rationing and discipline. We first engage the world at this moment of tremendous upheaval, where the old and new cannot agree to co-exist, one era fading before the next is yet formed. On television the Prime Minister is talking about forging a new Britain in the white heat of scientific revolution, while rag and bone men on horse-drawn wooden carts still come clip-clopping along our street, crying out:

Ol' rags and lumber! Any old iron!

My Brother the Killer

Their plodding carthorses leave behind piles of sharp-smelling dung in the middle of the road, and local men come out to scoop it up with their coal shovels, to put on the potatoes and carrots they grow in their back gardens.

5

Friday 22 June 2001
4 days since Danielle's disappearance

Later, as the pieces begin to fall into place and I start to grasp the who and the what – although the how and the why are still too horrific to contemplate – it will dawn on me that I had literally skimmed over the story. My scalp will tighten and the flesh on my arms will crawl as I recall sitting at my desk just a few days earlier, drinking coffee and browsing websites, looking for scraps of information, data, trends, rumours ... anything that I might work up into a feature, one of the ways that I earn my living.

And how, while scrolling down through the BBC News website, I'm vaguely aware of a photo in the bottom right-hand corner of some blonde girl, a geeky little thing in her school blazer and tie. I don't bother to read the article, because I can see without looking it's just another missing schoolgirl, one of dozens reported every year. A brutal and ugly fact of life: little girls and the sick men who abduct them.

That's not the kind of story I write about. I scroll past without a second thought.

In the evenings I drift through the streets of La Chapelle like smoke, some pale remnant of a fireworks display, to meet with Paul, Phil, Randall and Anthony at our favourite local restaurant, a no-frills Sri Lankan place called Dishny, where we like to get loud over several bottles of Lion Stout. In the morning my main concern is securing my *Carte de Séjour*, the official ID document all noncitizen residents are supposed to carry. But first I must amass, complete and submit a half-dozen supplementary forms along with supporting evidence, just to establish my right to *apply* for this document. French bureaucracy has invaded my life. Perhaps this is why I'm caught off guard a day or two later, when I get a call from my mother and hear the strange tone in her voice, a kind of sobbing, pleading sound.

What's wrong, Mum?

The police knocked on my door this morning. They said they wanted to talk to me about Stuart.

What? Why would they want to talk to *you* about *him*?

They asked me when I last saw him, she says. If he'd been to visit me recently.

Why would they ask that?

They said they wanted to *trace his movements over the last few days.*

I don't understand, Mum.

About that missing girl, they said.

What girl?

You know, down in Essex.

Mum, I don't know what you're talking about.

A young girl has gone missing, she snaps, as if I'm being wilfully obtuse. *15 years old.* And they say he may have something to do with it.

No, Mum. They've got it wrong.

I'm trying to reassure her while also trying to calculate the ages of friends and acquaintances in Essex who might have a 15-year-old daughter, but nothing comes to mind.

They said it's his niece, she says. They said Stuart knows her.

Okay, I say. That's it … yeah, don't worry, Mum.

Now I realise. Just a routine check. Nothing to worry about. This missing teenager is obviously some distant relative, probably in a far-flung part of the country, and the police are literally grasping at straws, exhausting every lead. Meanwhile, my mother's voice is quivering.

I don't know … what to think, she says.

And now the sobbing tone bleeds through again and she starts to weep.

Don't be silly, Mum. That's not Stuart, I guarantee you it's not him, I'm telling you. They're bullshitting, they just need a suspect because they've got nothing to go on. He wouldn't do it.

But she continues crying and now I feel my temper rising, because she's as good as judging him guilty without the slightest evidence.

Mum, I say. What are you crying for? Are you stupid? Just because the police say he did it, doesn't make him guilty.

Will you talk to him? she asks, between sobs. Please?

Of course, I'll get in touch with him right now. Yes, I'll call you back. Don't worry, Mum. The police made a mistake, they've got it wrong. You'll see.

Fucking police, I'm thinking, picking on my brother just because he's been inside a couple of times. That's all it is. They ran his name and found his criminal record, decided he looks like an easy pinch. Lazy fuckers.

It never occurs to me, not even for a second, that he might be guilty. The idea that he might be involved in a young girl's disappearance is unthinkable.

I call Stuart and leave a message on his answering machine. Then I call back instantly and leave another message, explaining in more detail why we need to talk. I send him an email saying that I'm worried about him, that we need to speak urgently.

He doesn't get back to me.

*　　*　　*

An hour later I'm still waiting, trying to suppress my creeping unease. I start to wonder why my mother referred to her as *that* missing girl. Finally, something clicks and I start to dredge up the memory of being at my desk a couple of days earlier, idly scrolling past the blonde schoolgirl on the BBC News website.

I get online. A few seconds later, I'm reading the BBC News item. This must be her, *that* missing girl. Only by now there are several more reports about her and her distraught parents. There have been appeals for witnesses, search parties, possible sightings. It's clear that this story has taken on a national importance. Her name is Danielle Jones, it says.

Last seen leaving her home on the morning of Monday 18 June, on her way to catch the school bus in East Tilbury. And now that I look at the photo properly, her face seems vaguely familiar.

The floor lurches beneath me and my heart sucks itself into a quivering knot.

Danielle?

As in Danielle, the little blonde girl who was one of two bridesmaids – my eight-year-old daughter Fiona was the other – at Stuart and Debbie's wedding five years ago?

They wore matching pink satin gowns.

His niece, now 15.

Now missing.

That Danielle.

6

Tilbury, Summer 1967

This stone is smooth and hard and heavy. One side is cool and damp, where I plucked it from the earth. The size of a large egg and the colour of lead, it fills my hand. It is Sunday in the middle of the summer holidays and the sun is directly overhead. The air is thick with heat and a haze shimmers off the gravel.

In a moment I will throw this stone, and nothing will ever be the same.

I'm hot and angry, telling him again and again to turn back, to stop following me and my friend Stanley Hall.

Stanley and me, we're off to find trouble. When the holidays end in September we will both start secondary school, so we're big kids now. My brother is still in primary school, too young to hang around with us. But he will not do as he's told. Stuart has always been cocky and fearless – that's why he won't listen.

I have warned him several times to turn back. But every time I turn and start walking, he follows. I stop and snarl, grab for him, but he jinks and dances away, too fast for me. He does this again and again.

I throw a couple of pebbles at him. He smacks them away and mocks me.

So I kick up this fat grey stone and weigh it in my palm, giving him a sense of its ominous mass.

Don't make me throw it. Fuck off, go home. Don't follow me.
I start to walk away again, and he follows.

Why is he doing this? Doesn't he have his own friends? Why must he follow me and Stanley? Neither of us want him with us. We're going to look for birds' eggs, or maybe stuff we can steal, probably copper wire we can sell for a few bob to that barrel-shaped bloke in the greasy overalls who works at the scrapyard called Yallop's. He buys copper for cash. Silver coins – *jingle*, we call it – no questions asked. Jingle to spend on chocolate and sweets. Maybe a packet of ten No. 6 and a box of matches. Or if we can find them, fireworks.

Stuart knows I'm not allowed to cross this piece of wasteland at the back of Feenan Highway. He knows it leads only to corn-fields, ditches and boggy grassland with cows and horses, ringed with rusty barbed wire. To pig farms and gypsy camps and junk-yards. To thorny trees thick with birds' nests that we older boys plunder for our egg collections, kept in shoeboxes under our beds. And then to a building site with recently installed electrical wiring. Those thin, coppery shoots sprouting from unpainted walls, awaiting their switches and plastic sockets.

Ripe for the plucking.

That's why I don't want him with us. And anyway, doesn't he have any friends of his own? It's not like he can't make friends. Especially girls. All the girls seem to like him, even the older ones. He's so pretty, I guess. Almost like one of them.

It never occurs to me that maybe he just wants to be with his big brother. That maybe I should invite him along and look after him. That maybe *I* should be his friend.

No, I want to be distant, unknowable, menacing. Like the Old Man.

Stuart says that if he can't come with us, he's going to tell Mum where we went.

That's all the trigger I need. He can see in my eyes what's coming and he starts to run. He knows that I'm going to throw it, and my aim is good.

He's fast, already 20 yards away. Instinctively, I factor this in. Birds, cats, dogs, other kids, sometimes even passing cars, I'm practised at hitting a moving target. I lean back, whip my arm and let fly. The instant the stone leaves my hand, I know.

I freeze, seized by terror at what I have done, what I have become. I watch the stone soar through the blue sky and start to fall, closing on its target. Although he is fast, I know the stone will hit the back of the head and smash his skull, killing him instantly.

I want to scream, to warn him, but there's no time and anyway, he wouldn't stop.

This moment expands and swells. The stone falls through the sky. My brother's silky hair bouncing in the sunlight. The tension in Stanley's jaw as he watches, appalled that I have split the universe to let in something vast and horrific.

My mind is saying, *No, no, no, no, no no no,* squirming, frantic for a way to undo this, to unsee this. A way to reverse time, annihilate this sin. But it's too late. The stone slams into the back of his boyish head with an ear-splitting crack, dashing him to the ground.

I'm running towards him.

He's not moving.

My brother my brother my little brother. Oh God, what have I done.

Oh no, please no.

*   *   *

We now live in Cowper Avenue, at the other end of Tilbury from Seymour Road and the docks, in a two-and-a-half-bedroom council house at the end of a street that simply gives up at the edge of a rough field, on which local gypsy families graze fat-bellied horses, chained by 20 feet of heavy link to iron stakes in the ground.

My mother had to sell the Seymour Road house to the local council in a compulsory purchase scheme. It went for a pittance, and the Old Man drank most of it, but she held out against the order for months, insisting we be re-housed in a few years after the old Victorian terraces were finally demolished and the new council houses went up in their place. She got it in writing – after all, she was trained as a legal secretary. One day we'll move back to the other side of town, into a nice new council house.

Now she is also divorced, having initially dallied with a separation. Despite years of unremitting abuse, physical and mental, she always resisted the idea of divorce, not least because it is forbidden by the Catholic Church, which insists marriage is a covenant with God. But under the Family Law Act of 1966, England's new divorce legislation, the so-called 'cooling-off period' has now been reduced from six months to six weeks. Shortly after I turn 11, my mother goes to Southend Crown Court with an attorney and a barrister to get a decree nisi.

Despite her fears, the Old Man doesn't turn up to try and defend himself. He must have known it was all over. Maybe he was too drunk to care. Either way, she becomes one of the first divorced women in the UK to get her six-week decree nisi converted to a decree absolute. She explains these things to me because she is happy about this, finally free of this monster that Stuart and I call the Old Man. Or as she now refers to him, The Other Thing. And she has also secured the Exclusion Order that prevents him from coming within 100 yards of the house, or approaching or talking to any of us.

Right now, she's our hero.

Of course, the Old Man still lurks around town. She has told us not to talk to him, to turn and walk away quickly if he addresses us, and if he follows, to run. If we see a policeman, we should tell him our father isn't allowed to talk to us by law. But we have already learned to walk the streets scanning the horizon. We're eagle-eyed when approaching bus shelters or tree-shaded public benches, anywhere with a seat for three or four, anywhere he and his buddies can gather with a bottle of Buckfast or a quart of Olde English. My father and his mates pool their resources and buy booze from a local off-licence, rather than pay pub prices. Anyway, they are all banned from local pubs, for fighting or intimidating the clientele.

If we encounter him on the street, our reactions are very different. Stuart won't even acknowledge his existence and the Old Man doesn't bother trying. But I can't help but be fascinated. Once every couple of months, I'll walk over to say hello and spend 10 minutes observing him and his pals.

In a guttural baritone, he speaks an idiosyncratic fusion of Glaswegian brogue, American slang and naval jargon. Instead of using the toilet, he hits the head. He never says fool, but galoot or imbecile. Clothing is always schmutter or gear or mufti.

Even when he's not holding the bottle, the others look up at him in awe and wonder. While they wear cheap, ill-fitting clothes scavenged from homeless hostels and church hall jumble sales – nylon car coats, grimy shirts, scuffed shoes, trousers unravelling at the seams – he's clean-shaven and sports a dark, single-breasted suit, cut in the close-fitted Italian style, a white or cream shirt, knit tie and pocket square. Plain Oxfords polished to a high shine, Trilby at a jaunty angle. He's 5 ft 10 ins and 140 lb max, so he can carry off the narrow-brimmed hat.

Sinatra style on a Burton budget: Alec Campbell, Laird of Inebriation.

No matter how hammered he gets, his hands are impeccably clean and manicured. And though he can never quite remove the orange nicotine stains from his right-hand index and middle fingers, he keeps them well-scrubbed. Often he will take a large steel file from inside his jacket and ceremoniously scrape under his nails, filing and blowing them while holding forth on historical topics. He talks about the Suez Crisis or Kennedy's assassination, or the fabulous zoology of New York, or how Cockney sparrows, just like real sparrows, cannot sing or fight and are full of shit. He smokes Senior Service and frequently hawks up phlegm, and spits into the gutter, but mitigates this vulgarity with the pristine handkerchief he'll pluck from his pocket to wipe his lips. He reeks of cheap aftershave and cheaper booze.

* * *

For months now Stuart and I have been growing apart. Having spent so long dressed alike and expected to behave in the same way, we start to assert separate identities. And perhaps it's just his headstrong attitude, or that he absolutely must defy authority, but by the time he is 10 my brother has started to display antisocial behaviour at school. Not just fights and mischief, but threats to teachers.

It is strange to watch someone so beautiful, so full of innocent song and laughter, become so angry and embittered, especially when he still exudes charm and innocence. While I gravitate towards darker songs on the radio, The Stones and The Kinks and Jimi Hendrix, Stuart still sings along in a high tenor to pretty pop songs, The Monkees' *I'm A Believer* and Peter Sarstedt's *Frozen Orange Juice*.

But now that beauty and innocence is about to disappear.

I have destroyed it.

I have committed the second great biblical sin. I have raised a stone and struck my brother dead.

As I run towards him my legs feel like sandbags, as if they might collapse beneath me. Every fibre in my being tells me to turn and run the other way and never stop, never look back to confront the fact that he is dead and I have killed him.

He is sprawled on the ground, but by some miracle his legs are twitching. And now I hear the high-pitched whine of agony that springs directly from his body. His hands wrapped over the crown of his head, blood oozing through his fingers and down his neck, soaking his shirt collar. He groans and rocks gently in the dirt. I take his shoulders and turn him over:

Sorry sorry Stuart I'm so sorry, I'm sorry.

His face is a mess of blood and tears and dirt and sweat. Snot bubbles from his nostrils and runs across his lips to mix with the drool on his chin and he's saying something terrible:

I can't see … I can't see.

Oh my God, I've blinded him.

Stanley starts laughing, *Hahahaha*. Pointing at Stuart and laughing.

I don't know how to react. This is horrible: I have blinded my brother, yet my friend finds this hilarious.

I look again at Stuart and realise there is dirt and blood in his eyes.

He blinks and wipes his eyes with the back of his bloodied hands. I take off my shirt and hold it to the angry pink mouth puckered on the back of his head. As I dab at the wound, I tell him to stay still. He turns and lashes out, catching me flush in the face.

Fuck off, you bastard, leave me alone!

Not blind, then.

Realising we won't be making any jingle today, and that he doesn't want to be around when our mother finds out, Stanley says he'll see us later and walks off.

I help Stuart to his feet and tell him I'll take him home, make sure he arrives safely. We walk back to the house slowly, in near-silence. I follow half a pace behind him, our attitudes and positions now completely reversed. I try to engage him, asking if it still hurts, reaching out and offering to look at it. He pulls away and stares straight ahead, refusing to acknowledge me. A short distance from the house I stop and watch as he continues walking, his head and neck and shirt all dark and sticky with blood. As he opens the front gate I turn and run. I'm only postponing the inevitable, but right now I can't face my mother. When she sees how close I have come to killing him, there will be hell to pay.

Returning at dusk, I get the beating that I knew was coming. Bent over a vinyl armchair in the living room, as she grips my left wrist and twists it to lock me into place, the swish of the dowel coming down hard on my backside, again and again, I scream and bawl:

I'm sorry I'm sorry, please no Mum, I'm sorry.

Years later I will ask her why she had to beat us like this, and she will say that she was terrified, that she had nightmares about her sons turning out like their father: vicious, brooding, woman-hating brutes. She could see how fast we were growing up, and was trying desperately to stop us going off the rails. But no matter how often she tried to explain right from wrong, no matter how often she asked for our help, nor how many tearful promises we made, her logic and reason didn't work on us.

In the end, exhausted and unable to control us with love and kindness, she decided to beat some sense into us. By the time she realised this was just creating a feedback loop – the more she beat us, the more steely and unruly we became – it was too late.

Afterwards I whimper, damp-eyed and balled-up at one end of the sofa. I have been punished and tomorrow all will be forgotten and we will never speak of it again.

Because that's how we deal with horror. We choke down our feelings and we move on. Silence is how we survive. And that realisation, that sense of relief, makes me feel weightless, blissful, as if I'm about to float up to heaven.

My brother is still alive.

But Fraser?

I don't recall a funeral or a service of any kind.

To this day, I have no idea where his grave might lie.

Tilbury, 1968

Growing up in the mid-1960s Stuart and I are too young to be aware of the so-called sexual revolution, but we can sense great changes playing out, and the era's rapidly evolving social attitudes undoubtedly shape our understanding of the world. Even as kids we understand that talk of sex is no longer quite taboo. By the time we are old enough to recognise idealised images of female beauty we can already see a dramatic cultural shift. In media and music and consumer products, everything staid and familiar is peddled with images of curvaceous but prim adult women, wholesome housewives who look more or less like our mother.

Conversely, everything modern and vital is marketed with a new kind of woman – younger and leaner, flat-chested and boyish. These androgynous girl-women look like our friends' teenage sisters – long-limbed and gamine, cute and cool, button-nosed and sexually available. Just as we start to develop sexual awareness, these new models of feminine desirability are emerging, doe-eyed waifs like Twiggy and Jean Shrimpton.

Of course, none of this is new: the sexualisation of pubescent girls has been grist to pop's mill at least since Chuck Berry's 1958 hit *Sweet Little Sixteen*. But in an age of dolly birds and miniskirts, this atmosphere of sexual liberation – which simultaneously infantilises young women to usurp their powers while pressuring them to be sexually available – creates an entirely new dynamic. Under the banner of free love, older men enjoy an incredible predator moment, where they can pose as hip and groovy lovers, while being sharks in the pool. And perhaps the most skilful exploiter of this cultural naivety is murderous cult leader Charles Manson, who at this very moment is capitalising on the free love creed to create his incestuous Family of teenage runaways. This is the cultural atmosphere in which we start to grow into young men.

Stuart and I also share another major source of sexual awareness. A hidden and unspoken source that we research secretly, sometimes together and sometimes independently, whenever our mother and little sister are both out of the house. In the corner of our living room is a cupboard we have been told never to open. We know in some abstract way that it's the closest thing we have to a library in our house, this forbidden space crammed with haphazard piles of paperback books and magazines – stuff for grown-ups, as our mother calls it.

One day when everybody else is out of the house, I finally open the cupboard door. What I find is weird and disturbing and electrifying. A lot of it was left behind by the Old Man, although by now even my mother has forgotten what lies behind this door. While most of the magazines are dog-eared copies of *Reader's Digest* and *TV Times* and *National Geographic* and *Life*, I learn that my father also kept magazines with names like *Mayfair* and *Fiesta*: softcore porn, full of women wearing only stockings and garter belts and heels, pouting and posing provocatively.

I have never seen real-life female genitalia, and the erotic thrill is all the stronger because I know I shouldn't be looking at this, the stuff of adult mystery, the source of all that whispering and smirking while we children peer from face to face, trying to fathom the big secret.

But there is more.

Most of the paperbacks are bland potboilers – westerns, thrillers, spy novels – but peppered among these are several paperbacks with lurid illustrated covers that depict snarling Nazis and wide-eyed naked females. These pornographic pulp fantasies, a genre known today as Stalag Fiction, fetishise sexual violence by concentration camp guards against emaciated, defenceless young women and girls. While I can barely comprehend this combination, I can't help but be exhilarated by this material, whose illicit content simultaneously scares, thrills and disgusts me.

And so my nascent *eros* is shaped by stolen moments with these books and magazines, and since I know Stuart also spent furtive hours browsing through that cupboard, I am almost certain the same is true for my brother. Our earliest notions of sexuality involve waif-like and passive girl-women, secret pornographic lusts and sinful desires, narratives of imprisonment and sexual torture of women-objects. And because we are good little Catholic kids, the guilt involved in acquiring this forbidden knowledge only strengthens an already intoxicating mix.

Of course, children can be exposed to inappropriate imagery and still grow into well-balanced and law-abiding adults. But I wonder how many of these themes took root and still endure in my brother's psyche. It's curious and disturbing to me that several of these elements are present in the case of Danielle Jones's murder: the lingerie and white stockings found in his home with traces of her DNA on them; the waif-like girl-woman as object of desire; the abduction, possession and ultimate annihilation of that object. I cannot help but see that cupboard, a trove of hidden lust and long-forgotten dark desires, as a metaphor for a certain modus operandi.

Returning secretly over a period of months, I studied these dark treasures, piecing together an increasingly sophisticated understanding of a hidden adult world. From those stacks I would later dig out *Some of Your Blood* by Theodore Sturgeon, a 1961 gothic novella that tells the story of George Smith, a taciturn GI in an unnamed war, whose letter home to his young wife is flagged by a censor. Challenged over its contents, Smith strikes his commanding officer and is sent to a military psychiatric clinic. Asked to write his autobiography in the third person, he produces a detailed portrait of a young boy badly abused by his violent and drunken father – a theme that struck home. Crippled by repeated beatings by her husband, his mother dies and George falls into a life of petty crime, a deeply disturbed young man whose only confidante is his teenage wife. The climactic revelation is that at times of stress George needs to drink blood that, while not stated explicitly, must surely be his wife's. This work electrified me, making me aware that books could reflect contemporary lives and families that resembled my own, and yet still serve up chilling flights of fantasy.

Yet the book that first shapes my understanding of art, the first novel I will ever read, is placed in my hands by a fellow pupil at school. One day in 1968, a kid called Simon Brown approaches me in the corridor of the Science block and presses a hardback book against my solar plexus.

Your name's Alex, right? Maybe you can make sense of this, he says.

What's it about?

No idea, load of gobbledygook.

So why are you giving it to me?

Read the first paragraph, you'll see. Just make sure you return it to the school library when you're finished.

At this point, I haven't even been inside the school library. But I open the book and glance at the first couple of lines:

'What's it going to be then, eh?

There was me, that is Alex, and my three droogs ...'

I flip it over and look at the cover:

A Clockwork Orange.

*   *   *

Our mother is always on her pushbike, cycling all around Tilbury. She tells us she likes cycling. It's faster than walking, she says, and it keeps her fit and slim, and she likes that. She cycles to work at Jim's Cafe, a lorry drivers' stop on the northern edge of town, where she cooks and serves hefty servings of fried food, scraping together a meagre wage to supplement the Family Allowance she receives from the Department of Health and Social Security. And then she cycles home to make dinner, get us washed and into our pyjamas, and watch telly with us.

At weekends or during school holidays, if we're not home in time for dinner, she cycles around town hunting for us. She stops our friends and asks them, Have you seen Alexander and Stuart?

These kids will tell us, Your mum's looking for you two. She's gonna kill you when you get home.

Even though she works hard and tries her best to bring us little treats – plastic toys or board games, the occasional ice cream – we know our place. We're chemically poor, in a way we instinctively assume will always be the case. But our mother instils us with pride. Though she will sometimes beat us, she always consoles us afterwards. Some of our friends' mothers judge her for her failed marriage. We can tell by the way they look at us when we knock on their doors to ask if their kids can come out to play.

She knows how these people gossip. How they assume any single woman with three children must resort to the obvious way to bring extra money into the house. She despises these people with their hypocrisy and supposed piety. Though still a good Catholic girl, she won't stoop to their backbiting and snobbery. She teaches us to be the same way.

These people, she tells us, who think they're good enough to judge you? Don't waste your breath on them. You're better than them and they're jealous. Sneer at them and move on. You have better things to do.

It's the same psychological self-defence instilled in a million other working-class kids. This insistence on our exceptionalism, and by extension her own, is her way of trying to protect us. She helps create a hard shell around us to prevent us from being crushed. It's understandable. This pride and fierce defiance is all that has kept her own spirit alive.

Around this time my mother tells me she has seen a ghost. Well, not exactly *seen*. More like *felt*. She says the ghost comes and visits, watching from the stairs as she does the washing-up in the kitchen.

Don't turn around and look at me, the ghost tells her, or I'll have to go.

But she knows it is there: she can feel it, sometimes even hear it. The ghost doesn't mean any harm, the ghost is her friend. The ghost believes in her.

I wonder if the ghost is Fraser, but I don't dare say so.

I'm not sure what to do with this information. Perhaps there really is a ghost. After all, ghosts must be real. They're on the telly. Grown-ups talk about them.

On the other hand, how can I be sure they exist if I've never seen one? Maybe they're like Father Christmas and the Tooth Fairy, silly stories for little kids.

I tell my mother that I want to see the ghost, too.

Well, she says, you have to listen very carefully and wait. It doesn't come when you're looking for it. You just have to wait.

Now I'm really spooked. Either there really *is* a ghost, and my mother has some kind of psychic power, maybe even the power to attract the spirits of the dead. But even more frightening is the alternative: she has started losing her mind. Although I don't yet fully understand words like psychosis or hallucination, I'm aware that maybe she's seeing and hearing and imagining things. At 11 years old, I'm seriously concerned that she might be losing her grip on reality.

And then she ups the ante.

One time, she says, the vicious beatings, abuse and humiliation finally became unbearable. She made up her mind to run away, just leave and never return. But then she realised she would be abandoning her children. And she couldn't do that, couldn't leave her babies alone with that monster.

Instead she came up with a plan. This was years ago, she says, when we were all very little and the domestic gas supply was still toxic. Late one night she roused us from our beds and led us downstairs, telling us we were going to play a game where we slept together on a blanket she had spread out on the kitchen floor.

She told us to lie down and close our eyes. And then she waited for us to fall asleep. Once we did, she would turn on the gas, lie down with us, and together we would drift into death.

I was really going to do it, she says, wiping away tears. I'd made my peace with God. I'd prayed to Him and I knew He would forgive me because my heart was pure. I was doing it because I couldn't leave you with that Other Thing, because that would be worse than death. I was ready to kill myself, absolutely. But then I looked at you, my babies, sleeping. And you were so beautiful, I just couldn't do it.

I say something like, I'm sorry, Mum.

She wipes the tears away with her fingertips and says, I realised I would just have to shut up and get on with it. That's what you do when you've got no choice. Just get on with it.

Years later, when I come to write this book and ask her how she survived, she will tell me that every morning, she would wake up and will herself to forget the horrors of the previous day. It was the only way to keep going.

That's why my memory is so bad now, she says, because every day for years, I had to train myself to forget what had happened to me the day before.

What a bitter irony that the Campbell clan's motto is *Ne Obliviscaris*: Do Not Forget.

My mother literally inverted it: Do Not Remember.

7

Grays, Saturday 23 June 2001
5 days since Danielle's disappearance

At 8 a.m. there's a knock at the door of Stuart Campbell's semi-detached suburban house. When he answers, dressed in his work garb of faded T-shirt, sweatpants and trainers, he finds two detectives and two uniformed officers from Essex Police. They arrest him on suspicion of Danielle Jones's abduction, read him his rights, handcuff him, palm the crown of his head into the back of an unmarked car and drive him to Brentwood station. He'll spend the next 60 hours in custody, his time split between a basement cell and the interrogation room, where detectives question him repeatedly.

Even if Stuart doesn't confess, they reason, there's a chance he'll get mixed up in his lies, or let slip some otherwise innocuous detail that could be a clue to Danielle's whereabouts. At this point they're not yet ready to accept the worst, hoping against hope that he has Danielle locked up somewhere – in some basement, garage or deserted building – awaiting his return.

Terrified and traumatised, but still alive.

Throughout their long hours of questioning Stuart stubbornly maintains his innocence, insisting he has no idea where Danielle might be. The detectives know his story has holes you could drive a bus through, but can find no obvious giveaways, no clues or pointers to the truth.

One more time, they say. Where were you on Monday when Danielle disappeared?

I already told you, he says. I've told you half a dozen times.

Tell us again.

Sighing with exasperation, he tells them how he left home just before 8 a.m. and drove straight to Wickes, a warehouse-sized hardware store in Rayleigh, about 10 miles east of his own house and seven miles north-east of Danielle's, to buy some special bolts he needed for a job. And no, he didn't go anywhere near Danielle's home or see her at any point.

After calling Debbie at 8.25 – and telling her specifically where he was, a point she confirms – he spent some time looking in various bins for the bolts, he says, before finding them. The journey, he agrees, is normally a 25-minute drive each way. But on his way back he got held up in traffic – which explains the extra 45 minutes or so that he otherwise cannot account for.

So, the detectives point out, if we factor in the time you spent in the store, the whole trip was more like 100 minutes. Or a solid two hours if, as we suspect, you never made the trip at all.

He shakes his head.

So, they ask, why was the traffic so bad on your way back? Was there an accident?

I don't know, he says. I decided to get off the main road and take a back route.

And then?

I went straight to my neighbour's house, arriving around 11.30 a.m., to resume the decking job I'd been working on for the last few days.

The detectives know that the neighbour has confirmed that she saw him working on the deck – but about 30 minutes after he claims to have arrived. And there are other problems with his story. The CCTV footage from Wickes' car park shows no sign of Stuart's blue transit van entering or leaving. Same with the CCTV footage in the store: no sign of Stuart during the time he says he was there, or any other time that day.

Stuart doesn't have a receipt for the bolts he says he bought. He says this is because he paid cash, rather than using his debit card. Although he *had* used his debit card in the same store only a week earlier.

The detectives tell him they asked the manager to check the till receipts against inventory. Those special bolts Stuart needed? Nobody bought any of those bolts on the day in question. Nobody has bought any of those bolts in the last six weeks.

And while Debbie has provided a statement that supports Stuart's alibi, the detectives don't believe it. In fact, they suspect she will eventually retract it on advice from legal counsel.

When the detectives circle around to repeat their questions for the fifth or sixth time, Stuart flatly refuses to answer.

Instead, he decides the interview is over.

He responds to every question with two words, delivered in a flat and robotic tone.

No comment.

* * *

Of course, I don't have this information at this point. All I know right now is that my brother has been arrested on suspicion of Danielle's abduction. Is he guilty? I have no idea. But I know what I'd want from my family if I were accused of a heinous crime – at least until certain facts had been established, witnesses questioned and hypotheses put to the test. I'd expect my family to presume me innocent, rather than condemn me based on gossip and tabloid reports.

My limited understanding is also tainted by the mixed signals I'm getting during phone calls with my mother who, in fairness, is herself getting mixed signals about members of the Jones family. Some of them seem to believe Stuart is innocent, although Danielle's parents – who are now certain that Stuart is the culprit – have been urging police to arrest him and hold him until he confesses.

Meanwhile, Stuart is still not returning my calls and I can't get in touch with Debbie because I don't have her latest mobile number. I consider calling the City firm where she works, but decide against it. Who knows what problems that might unleash? There's a good chance this scandal has already undermined her career: having her journalist brother-in-law call the firm, trying to track her down? That certainly won't help. I'm not even sure she's still going into the office: my mother says she's due to start her maternity leave any day.

Most importantly, she is now almost seven months pregnant. And her husband, the father of her soon-to-be-born child, has already spent more than two days in custody being questioned about the abduction and possible murder of their 15-year-old niece. I cannot imagine her stress, but it must be close to intolerable. I certainly don't want to add to her anxiety, and possibly trigger another tragedy.

But I'm baffled and frustrated by their silence, by the fact that neither of them has reached out, not even for advice. They know I'm trying to get in touch: my mother assures me she is passing on my messages whenever Debbie calls her. Surely if Stuart is innocent, he would ask for my help? And even if – God forbid – he is somehow involved, who else could he possibly turn to?

I find myself twice-removed from the inside track. Self-exiled in Paris, far from this rapidly evolving and increasingly ugly situation, and cut off from my brother and his wife, who refuse to take or return my calls. I try calling aunts and cousins, but keep hitting a dead end. I can't even call one of my London editors to pin down some basic facts, because that might alert them to my personal involvement. And I have precious few other resources.

This is life in 2001: a time before smartphones, internet radio and streaming TV. Facebook is still three years away, and Twitter won't launch for another five. News websites are still almost entirely text-based and updated only sporadically. Despite my state-of-the-art ADSL line and tangerine iMac, there's no way for me to follow live UK TV news from Paris. In an era before social media, before a billion citizen paparazzi started uploading phone footage of celebrities and fugitives, it's still easy for private citizens to go to ground. And this is what Stuart and Debbie both do. They drop out of sight.

Gradually I start to realise: they don't trust me.

Why not?

I'm a journalist. Nobody trusts me.

Not even my mother, who repeatedly makes me promise that no, I am absolutely not going to write a story for the papers, no matter how often I repeat myself.

Why would I do that, Mum? Why would I tip off the press that I'm Stuart's brother? Why would I invite them to start trawling through my personal life?

And so I sit at home tracking developments via news websites – the *Guardian, Daily Mail, Sun* and later in the day, *Evening Standard.* This is how I learn on 24 June that *Police Search East Tilbury Marsh Land*, as the hunt for Danielle's body continues. Divers are now searching lakes and ponds and ditches in the marshland around her home in East Tilbury.

The police are no longer looking for Danielle.

They are looking for her body.

The *Missing Persons* case is now a murder investigation.

The following evening I read on a newspaper website that the suspect is a self-employed builder in his 40s. Having been questioned for almost 60 hours he was bailed until 22 August.

Apparently the suspect told reporters, *It's nothing to do with me. It's all a big mistake.*

Meanwhile, Essex Police issue the following statement:

Essex Police: Press Release – Have you seen Danielle?

26 June 2001

Police are appealing for information about 15-year-old Danielle Jones, from East Tilbury, Essex, who has been missing since setting off for school on the morning of Monday, 18 June.

She left home on foot to catch a bus to St Clere's School at nearby Stanford-le-Hope, but did not get aboard the bus and failed to arrive for classes. She was seen at about 8am on the morning of her disappearance, walking along Coronation Avenue, East Tilbury.

Her disappearance is out of character and her parents and police are concerned for her well-being. Danielle is white, 5ft 7ins tall, slim and has long blonde hair and blue eyes. She wears a dental brace.

Anyone with information is asked to contact Essex Police, telephone 01245 452207 or email us: danielleinfo@essex. police.uk

Danielle is pictured wearing school uniform and also in casual clothes. There are also pictures of her taken from a family video. Large photos are also available.

So now Stuart is suspected of abducting *and murdering* the missing girl.

I tell myself again to calm down, that there must be some mistake, that this will all blow over in a couple of days when they realise they've got the wrong guy. I push away a terrible thought, but it keeps coming back.

Is he guilty?

It doesn't seem possible. To the best of my knowledge, he has never been involved in any sexual crime.

But if that's the case, why do the police suspect him?

I start to wonder: is he capable of murdering a 15-year-old girl? And not just any girl, but his own niece?

I find myself unable to sleep properly, and acutely aware of the fact that I live alone. Waking in the middle of the night I have the feeling that someone or something is in the room. I get up but don't switch on the light. Instead, I stand in the darkness or sit at my desk, trying to understand what is happening.

Another week and I start to feel unstable, insecure, *haunted*. I drink heavily, trying to blot out a creeping sense of dread and confusion. The glib bachelor life doesn't feel so good any more. I don't want to be lonely. I don't want to feel haunted. I don't want to feel crazy. And so I sleep with a woman for the wrong reasons, in an attempt to block out my fear and vulnerability. When I tell her about the phantom presence and ask if she can sense it too, she is kind and understanding, but it's obvious from her expression that she is concerned for my mental health.

I tell myself to calm down and get a grip, but every night as I lie in bed alone I feel it again, this sense of someone watching, and waiting.

Is this actually happening, or am I creating this phenomenon? Is this just a manifestation of some deep-rooted and unexplored shame, some sense of guilt through association?

Is there any meaningful difference, if it seems real to me?

I have to act. I can't live like this. I must translate these feelings and intuitions into concrete actions in the daylight world, the rational world.

The *real* world.

But how? Where would I start?

Who will listen to me?

Wednesday 27 June 2001
9 days since Danielle's disappearance

I log on to BBC News to find *Home Video of Danielle Released*. Not the video itself – stable broadband streaming is still years away – but a still image taken from a grainy VHS clip. It shows a shy blonde girl in a grey sweatshirt, nursing a pet rabbit in her arms like a baby.

She looks closer to 13 than 15.

A couple of days later two members of Steps – Danielle's favourite pop group – film an appeal for national TV, imploring Danielle to call her parents and asking anyone with information to come forward. That afternoon Essex Police announce that a text message was sent from Danielle's mobile phone several hours after she went missing. But they refuse to discuss its contents, or who received it, or whether it indicates Danielle might still be alive.

On Saturday 30 June over 400 volunteers, mostly locals, join 60 police officers in a fingertip search of fields and marshlands around East Tilbury and Coalhouse Fort, a disused Victorian artillery fortification that I know from childhood. Back then it was an eerie place, full of echoing subterranean chambers and foul odours, a place that only the most daredevil kids would explore – kids like Stuart and me.

My sense of impotence and uselessness is complete. I find myself an unwilling voyeur, locked out of a public process that consumes most of my day's mental and emotional energy. Hundreds of total strangers are now more intimately involved, working harder to resolve the question of my brother's culpability, than I am.

And no matter how often I push away these feelings with sex and booze and drugs, the invisible presence keeps coming back. I try to pretend otherwise, but I keep waking up in the middle of the night, unable to shake off the feeling of being watched, being judged. Is my subconscious playing tricks? Or is this a supernatural presence?

One night I stay up drinking into the wee hours, sitting by a living-room window bathed in moonlight, waiting for a sign. After all, that's what my mother had done. I remember how she told me as a child: *You have to listen carefully and wait. It doesn't come when you're looking for it. You just have to wait.*

And so I wait, and wait some more. And then the darkness seems to stiffen and grow more dense, the space charged with energy. I pour myself another glass of red wine and decide to address the presence I now feel watching me from the shadows.

I think I know why you're here, I say.

The air in the room seems to shift and soften as I stretch out, waiting for an answer.

The night sky is already lighter when I wake up on the sofa surrounded by empty bottles and sticky glasses, and laugh at my own stupidity. I'm such a fool, spooking myself like this.

The next few nights, I sleep fine.

But just when things are starting to calm down, I jump awake. There's an intruder in my room, watching from the darkness. And for once I'm stone cold sober.

Ah, that's the problem. Goddam sober brain, playing tricks on me.

I get up and go to the kitchen for a glass of water, and stand barefoot on the tiled floor in the darkness trying to understand ... *what, exactly?* Not so much a presence as a mood, like an emotional cloud, an overwhelming sadness that hangs in the air. For a moment I think about turning on the TV or playing some music, anything to dispel this atmosphere. But that's not the answer. Instead, I enter the front room and stand by the moonlit window.

I try to rationalise. This bleakness that trails me: is it mine? Am I projecting it onto my surroundings? It doesn't seem to be *my* sadness. This is a kind of melancholy I barely recognise. Is it being communicated *to* me? I don't want to believe so, but it's getting harder to avoid the obvious. I don't believe in a creator God or an eternal soul. But I do believe that death is not the end and that a life terminated unjustly, in chaos and confusion, will almost certainly manifest some kind of psychic resonance in the material world.

Perhaps the strangest thing is that I don't feel at all threatened, standing in the dark with this invisible companion. Whoever or whatever is watching from the shadows, there's no malevolent intent. Rather, I have a curious feeling of being implored to speak, to utter some word of acknowledgement. To accept this reality. Which, I know, will then require me to act on it.

I'm being given a chance.

With cold tears streaming down my face, and even though I feel like I may be taking the first step towards losing my fucking mind, I speak.

Okay, I say into the darkness, I will try. I will do my best.

I realise there's only one person I can share this with, someone who thinks in similar ways and believes in similar things. Someone who might take me seriously.

I call Celia in London and she listens while I tell her about the mute presence in my apartment. About the bargain I've entered into.

You understand what I'm saying?

For a long time she's silent and I wonder if she, too, doubts my sanity.

Of course, she says. I just don't know why you sound so surprised. What did you expect?

Can I come and stay with you?

That's probably a good idea.

8

Quidenham, 1970–71

Nobody we know has a car, because nobody we know can afford one.

Like those legendary colour TVs we keep hearing about, cars are for senior policemen and head teachers, factory managers and door-to-door salesmen, men with moustaches, tie clips and elbow patches. Men whose thumbs click retractable stainless-steel ballpoint pens.

Not for the apron-and-overall, cap-doffing, pencil-licking classes like us.

For us, being driven in a car still feels like a small miracle. How many cars have we been in? Maybe half a dozen. But only on special occasions, as when our mother takes us up to London on the train for our annual visit to a popular tourist site – the Zoo or the Tower, that kind of thing – and we'll take a three-minute taxi ride from Fenchurch Street to the tube station.

Last year, my first at grammar school, I was playing football when the nylon studs of a boot gashed my knee and the head-master had to drive me to the hospital. I was worried I'd bleed all over his polished grey leather and gleaming walnut, but Mr Smetham gave me a towel to hold against the wound and told me not to worry. Despite the throbbing pain and smell of warm blood, that ride to the emergency room in his Rover Mk II was like floating on clouds.

But this is easily the biggest and most luxurious car I have ever been in, perhaps the biggest I've seen, a Daimler Sovereign. The way it corners in broad, sweeping arcs, the horizon sliding silently back and forth across the windscreen, it feels more like a yacht than a car.

Up front, his hair silky from last night's shampoo, Stuart sits like a prince alongside our chauffeur, a polite but distant young teacher with a toff's accent and a tobacco-coloured corduroy jacket. I'm on the back seat alongside my little sister and mother, all of us dressed in our best clothes as if for Mass, only we don't really go to Mass anymore, not since Stuart and I left our Catholic school. Only our little sister is still enrolled and she leaves in a few months, so there's really no need to keep up pretences. Especially given our mother's recent divorce, *an effing cardinal sin, a defilement of the effing sacrament.* I know this because sometimes when she's busy cleaning the fire grate or peeling potatoes and she doesn't realise I'm there, she mutters these very words, interrogating them contemptuously under her breath.

No, we're dolled up because this is a special day. We're excited, chattering with Stuart about his new boarding school, riding along to wave him off as he starts his new life out in the Norfolk countryside. The school has sent this young teacher in this big car to collect us all, to show us how well they're going to look after him.

Loaded into the Daimler's cavernous boot is the new blue trunk with the brass corners and padlocked clasp – my sister and I are jealous that Stuart is now the first of us to have his own key to anything – packed with all the things Mum bought him recently using a special grant, one she'd wangled out of social services. She's clever at that sort of thing, working the system for her kids. Occasionally she will tell us as much, before quickly warning us never to repeat her words. Over the last few weeks she has gradually packed his special blue trunk with his special blazer and raincoat and wellingtons, his special shirts and socks and underwear, his jackets and ties, jumpers and trousers and shoes and plimsolls, all brand new, along with the football boots and shirts and shorts and other sports equipment he'll probably never use.

Never been much of a team player has Stuart, although during the hottest days of our endless summer holidays he will sometimes indulge me for an hour or so, both of us stripped to the waist, lean bodies slick with sweat as we sprint and twist across patchy grass on the rough field at the end of our street, shoulder-barging and body-checking each other as we battle for control of my football.

After a while though, he'll become frustrated – as much by my taunts as my dribbling skills – and with an explosive curse he will lunge feet first, chopping me down at the knees. Then we'll get up and face off, and after some pushing and shoving and kicking we'll wrestle each other to the ground in a writhing struggle for dominance, getting grassburn on our peeling pink shoulders, teeth bared, grunting through saliva bubbles a kind of hissing laughter, before throwing a couple of half-weight punches and then hands up, *okay okay okay*, declaring a truce.

We never push it too far, for we know it's not worth making a real fight of it. There are kids out there who genuinely hate and want to hurt us – we save our hard-knuckle fists for them.

Now well into the third hour of our journey, the magic has worn off and the chatter died down and we've all grown bored of this long floating silence. Worse, my tedium is starting to give way to resentment, because if I'm honest, part of me is glad he's going, that he'll finally be out of my way. Edging into puberty, I'm more self-conscious than ever of my puffy hooded eyes and thick lips, my spotty round cheeks and thin straight hair. His beautiful heart-shaped face only highlights my deficiencies. If girls look at me it's with pity and scorn, while Stuart's cherubic looks and milky skin can still get them gooey-eyed and fawning.

The teacher pulls off the motorway ramp to plunge down an unmarked cambered grey road and we find ourselves gazing into a windscreen of blazing golden green, as we glide through tunnels of sunlit woodland, past tiny white cottages with thatched roofs and rose gardens. We have never seen roads like this, fairytale countryside like this. We come from low flat estuary marshlands, a place of reeds and gorse and craggy hawthorns hemmed in by dockyard cranes and power station chimney stacks, far from these leafy canopies and sylvan glades.

As the Daimler slows to walking pace for a series of tight S-bends, and we roll across dinky stone bridges over delicate silver streams, I'm thinking, *Oh, this is what they're talking about in all those wanky poems we have to read at school, all that toss about babbling brooks that sparkle out among the fern.*

Then we follow a long mossy stone wall until we swing through a pair of open iron gates, up a drive that winds across a vast carpet of lawn, finally cornering a clump of ancient trees before easing to a stop with a ratchet of handbrake and crunch of gravel, to find ourselves looking up at a broad-fronted white house, more like a mansion than a school.

Here we are, says our driver. Eccles Hall.

We climb out as the headmaster Mr Tuohy strides up to greet us, all smiles and spectacles and long bony hands, accompanied by a couple of older boys, who are told to remove Stuart's trunk and hump it up to his dorm. After a round of toe-curling introductions where my mother gushes her thanks, Mr Tuohy leads us on a quick tour of the school, which despite its verdant setting seems less impressive once we get beyond the tennis courts, especially when we come across a classroom building that is clearly a tarted-up wartime Nissen hut, spidery rust peeking out from its whitewashed edges. After inspecting the art room and science lab, both of which smell damp and musty and faintly of farmyard animals, the headmaster suggests we all *repair to the conservatory* for afternoon tea and a chat.

My sister and I gobble up all the sugary biscuits while Stuart looks around, eyebrows knotted, his expression quivering between apprehension and pride. For weeks now my mother has been preparing us for this moment, painting a picture of this posh school and the tremendous opportunities it will afford, this great adventure our brother is about to embark on.

The logic goes something like this: having passed her 11-plus exam in the 1940s and won a scholarship to Palmer's Girls grammar, by far the best local secondary school, my mother had her heart set on the three of us following in her footsteps. Having passed my own 11-plus exam and won a scholarship to Palmer's Boys, I am set. Stuart was meant to follow me into Palmer's, where we'd continue to look after each other. But despite being a bright kid, he failed the exam and my mother's dream fell apart. Instead, he was enrolled in St Cedd's, a Roman Catholic boys school in not-so-nearby South Ockendon, with a so-so academic record and a reputation for harsh discipline. Unsurprisingly, Stuart bucked against the system, confronting teachers who tried to control him and playing truant. Worse, already on the cusp of being expelled, he recently got into trouble with the police, although my mother refuses to discuss it or explain what he did. But there are rumours among our friends that he shot another kid with an air gun.

Normally, this wouldn't be such a big deal. Getting shot by some little bastard with an air rifle hiding in the bushes? That's an everyday hazard for kids in Poet's Corner, whose streets are named for Titans of English literature: Dickens, Thackeray, Kipling, Shaw and the less familiar Cowper, on whose Avenue we live. I've already been shot twice, once in the buttock and once in the torso, each lead pellet leaving a large purple and yellow bruise. But Stuart shot some kid in the forehead at close range. Could have blinded him, they say. Maybe even killed him. Hence all the fuss. Nine times out of ten the law would have let it ride. Instead, the police began talking about prosecution, approved school, a criminal record.

So that was the end of Plan B.

But my mother, ever resourceful and swift to action, dug around until she found this residential school for 'bright but maladjusted' boys, mostly the offspring of foreign diplomats and civil servants, well-bred kids from loveless families. And while parents normally paid a small fortune to offload their sons, the school also had a placement system for smart lads from the worthier end of the working class. Our mother had won Stuart a place, managing against all odds to revive her dream of a superior education for her fiery younger son, in a cultured and nurturing environment.

That was the idea, anyway.

But now, with the biscuits all gone and our hushed voices fading into the conservatory's lofty ceiling, this place feels unspeakably cold and alien. The headmaster's smile is frozen as he looks at his wristwatch.

It is time for us all to leave, except Stuart.

Out on the drive, standing by the Daimler's open doors, we say our goodbyes and start sobbing. My mother, my sister, myself ... and even Stuart, the toughest of us all, a kid whose tears are as scarce as diamonds.

None of us will say it, but we all know why.

It feels wrong to leave him here. It goes against everything we've been taught about looking after one another. The only safety and security we've ever known was as a unit, huddled together, sticking up for each other, and now we're deliberately unravelling that. Mr Tuohy puts a long, bony hand on Stuart's shoulder, sensing the need to hold him down.

And then it's all over, and we're gliding down the drive again, the gravel crackling and crunching beneath the tyres, as my mother dabs her eyes and reassures us.

Don't worry, she says. It's alright, there's no need to cry. It's all for the best, it's a good thing, really. It's a lovely school. He'll get a very good education.

She sniffs, and sighs, He'll be happy there.

*   *   *

Crushed.

His new word, like his new attitude, is scornful and dismissive. Unwilling to brook the slightest argument. That's how he sees himself when he returns for the summer holidays.

I sneer back, *You what?*

He illustrates with a theatrical gesture, snatching an invisible rock from the air and pulverising it in his fist, scattering imaginary dust into my eyes with a flick of his wrist.

Crushed, he repeats. Meaning, *Argument over, you lost.*

I want to slap him. He wasn't like this before. His special new school was supposed to make him calmer, friendlier, more disciplined. Instead, it has only reinforced his sense of being special and superior. If anything, he's more smug and arrogant than ever, and I decide I hate him.

Even more shocking, he seems to believe he's superior not only to me and his sister, but even to Mum. While he hasn't yet tried out his new word on her, there's a subtle change in the way he talks to her, some sense of grievance and forbearance.

This is what happens, I tell myself, when you rub up against snotty rich brats in some poncey private school out in the countryside.

Later, when the summer holidays are over and we're all back at school, I try it out. In the middle of a some trivial playground dispute I make a snappy remark, and before my rival can respond I throw the hand gesture and blurt out triumphantly: *Crushed!*

The kids around us whoop and howl at this stroke of genius and start mimicking the new put-down, throwing invisible dust in each other's faces.

It doesn't matter whether it's true or not.

There's no comeback.

This tiny word, this sneering gesture, how can they generate such power?

We need all the power we can get, my brother and me. We have a host of predators stalking us along the streets of Tilbury. Perhaps because we're Catholic, perhaps because we hit somebody's cousin, or maybe just because I'm a Jap cunt and he's my brother, a variety of thuggish kids are always looking to crack our heads.

A couple of years ago I was kicking my ball on the field at the end of our street, when a rain of iron fists spattered me from behind, too fast to counter, pounding my head until my vision blurred, beating the air out of my lungs and pummelling me to the dirt, and then shoes and boots stomped me and battered my head this way and that until, with my terror and willpower fading into darkness, I heard my mother's voice in the distance, shouting, *Oi, you leave him alone!* They scattered like rats – a gang of five or six – and there she was, helping me up, wiping blood from my lip and turning my bruised face side to side in her hand.

Why did they do that? she demanded, outrage mixed with anger.

What? Uh, I don't know.

Don't lie! You must have done something to them.

Mum, I didn't even see who it was.

It was those Scatton kids and their mates, she says. Little bastards. No point going round their house, their parents don't give a shit.

She puts her hand on my back and walks me home to clean me up. Of course, I don't tell her, but I know exactly why they'd attacked me.

I'd heard them grunting *Chink* and *Jap Cunt* as they stomped on my back and kicked me in the face.

Sometime after this I was walking down the road with Stuart when we spotted a couple of the Scatton brothers. They didn't see us until it was too late. Our retribution was swift and brutal. We left them cowering and trembling, faces swollen and bloody, shirts ripped open. We told a couple of their friends to tell their mother what had happened and why. And that next time, they wouldn't walk home. They never bothered either of us again.

But then Stuart goes away to his posh boarding school and another person comes back in his place. Someone cold and sneering and arrogant.

Crushed.

Worse, he has taken to showing off one of his many new treasures, his battery-powered pocket calculator. Since mathematics is my weakest subject and even a slide rule strikes me as fiendishly complex, this gleaming slab of futurism is close to an act of sorcery. Of course, he takes great delight in flashing it around, this electronic wonder. He tells me it's a miniature computer like the kind they used to put men on the Moon. When I scoff, he says it's basically the same thing, an electronic circuit board that renders binary calculations in decimal form.

But you, he sneers, you wouldn't understand that.

Crushed.

That does it. I sneak into our bedroom later and dig around in his precious blue trunk until I find it. Then I slip outside and walk a few blocks to a stunted little road named Shaw Crescent. I sit on the kerb, feet either side of a cast-iron drain, and with a cheap petrol lighter I slowly and ceremoniously burn one corner of it, watching with satisfaction as molten blobs of smouldering plastic drip through the grate and into the sewer. It feels like an unholy act, like torturing some tiny helpless creature to death, but I force myself to keep going. When the lighter gets too hot to hold I place the blackened and twisted remnant on the kerb, take a hunk of broken paving slab, and smash it until there's nothing left but plastic shards and a tangle of soldered fragments and tiny blue diodes. With a scuffed toe, I nudge these pieces into the drain and watch them sink below the oily black bubbles.

Of course it's obvious that I'm the culprit, and I know I'll pay for my actions. But I refuse to confess, even when my mother bends me over an armchair and beats me with a piece of three-quarter-inch dowel until it snaps, leaving angry purple stripes across my backside.

No matter how painful the punishment, nor how much it pleases him, I refuse to give Stuart the one thing he wants – a confession. Why? Because a confession will mean an apology,

and there is absolutely nothing in this world that can make me
say sorry.

Not now, not ever.

Crushed?

Fuck you.

Tilbury, 1971

One morning I wake at dawn and slide out of my bunk bed.
Silently, I open my tin tray of watercolours and put the brush in
my mouth to load it with saliva and then mix some green and
brown. The day before, in some *Beano*-type comic, I'd come
across a *super jolly jape* I could play on my younger brother.
While he's still asleep in the upper bunk, at the perfect height, I
will carefully paint spots all over his angelic face. When he
wakes up, I'll look at him in shock and tell him he must have
caught some terrible disease. Of course, he'll tumble as soon as
he wipes his face, but for one perfect moment he'll stare at
himself in the bathroom mirror, confused and terrified.

And I will laugh and mock him.

After checking his eyes are firmly closed, I lean forward with
the brush and gently apply the first spot on his cheek.

His fist hits me so fast and hard that it knocks me flat on my
back, the watercolours flying across the room. Before I can even
think about getting angry I'm laughing, and then Stuart is laughing too. The black eye, I'll tell myself later, was almost worth it.
And for a while, as we're growing up, it's just normal rough and
tumble. No big deal.

But gradually the tenor will grow darker.

Stuart and I, we don't play Cowboys and Indians. Even as
kids we know that's old-fashioned stuff for pansy boys, a load

of Milky Bar Kid bollocks. We know there are no good guys in white hats. We play secret agents and superheroes, hunting and killing spies or evading cosmic assassins with superhuman powers. If captured, we play out torture and humiliation, dispensing slow evil to each other, taking turns to writhe and scream and plead for mercy. And then, after some life-or-death struggle, one of us will be thrown down a well or off a cliff, or strapped in a car and pushed into a lake.

At this point our arms are thin and boyish, our fists carry little real weight or power. We both want hands that are hard and powerful like the Old Man's, that land like lumps of lead. But we're not strong enough yet. So for now, all our energy goes into our bikes.

Adults and kids, coppers and priests, everybody in Tilbury has a bike. Bikes allow us all to navigate this thinly populated but sprawling flat town with its swathes of open grass and low-density council estates. Our mum has a ladies' bike and our grandad has an old man's bike. Men like Jack Sharkey hook twangy metal bicycle clips around their ankles to prevent their dungarees getting tangled in the chain. Slow and methodical, they cycle in pairs to their jobs in the docks or the factories with a roll-up hanging off the lip and a pair of canvas saddlebags slung over the back wheel, maybe a metal basket on the front holding gloves and goggles, or a little metal shelf behind the saddle for hand tools wrapped in oilskin. They fix chunky battery-powered headlights on their handlebars, or connect dynamo-driven lamps to their front forks. Their bikes – built for comfort and stability, regularly inspected and lubricated – reek of safety.

Our bikes are different. Stripped to essentials and built for maximum flash and speed. One summer, using aerosol paint stolen from a local car repair shop, I spray my bike metallic candy apple red. A couple of nights later someone steals it from my front garden and I simply start all over again. Stuart and I are expert mechanics, building from scratch. We scour junkyards and rubbish tips to find a racing frame, the lightest possible. A coat of paint, silver or yellow or black. Add a slim wheel on the front for speed and a fat tyre with chunky tread on the back for traction and grip. The saddle, leather with springs for comfort, can be cannibalised from older models. Then add gears, nothing fancy, three or five at most, and adjust chain tension, popping out the greasy links with an electrical screwdriver to take up the slack. We fit tiny lightweight mudguards, just big enough to prevent dirty water splashing into our eyes, and chrome racing pedals with yellow plastic reflectors. We only need one brake, on the rear wheel, with new rubber blocks in the calipers, one-eighth of an inch clearance, ready to bite into the tyre wall at lightest dab of the lever. No lights or bells, dead weight.

And always, the cruiser-style stag handlebars. The wider the spread the better, with black rubber handle grips. Some kids like tassels swinging from the ends, but to us that looks totally *wafty*. Not at all *cushty*, which is what you want.

We ride standing on our pedals whenever possible, freewheeling in frozen perfection, arms wide and legs straight like ski jumpers. We slalom across each other's path and jump our machines up and down the kerb. As we pedal, we swing our bikes side to side under our hips, swaggering as we ride. We watch our shadows racing beneath us, and we like the shape our hair makes as we flick it metronomically. We bawl out pop songs as we ride, inserting rude words we're not supposed to use.

Wild thing
You make my dick spring
You make everything
Grooovy ...

Sometimes we're chased by the feral dogs that roam this town, seven or eight mangy strays that have formed a pack and now strut down the middle of the street, heads high and growling, daring locals to try their luck. There are no animal services to round them up, but nobody seems too worried because, apart from the odd bite, they're not really a problem. Not for adults, anyway. By the age of 10, most kids this end of town have been bitten at least once and we're no different. Still, the dogs will only attack if they catch you alone – you're safe if you also run in a pack. Otherwise, grab a big stick before they reach you, or find a car and climb onto its roof.

Besides, our wild dogs are kind of famous. A few months ago a television news team came down from London to do a story about them. The presenter said it was such a shame that their owners had abandoned these poor mutts. We laughed. Nobody had ever *owned* these dogs. For us, as with most people we know, dogs are vicious and stupid and dirty, full of fleas and disease, not to be trusted. Apart from guarding property at the end of a steel chain, we can't understand why anyone would keep one.

As well as these scabby mongrels, we ride with one eye out for the bullies who roam this corner of Tilbury. Tony Hardcastle is the worst, only 17 but already built like the proverbial brick shithouse, his massive 16-hole DMs perfect for kicking us to the ground, his fists the size of oven mitts, a crop-headed two-bob villain whose biceps strain the short sleeves of his gingham Ben Sherman, leering at us with teeth like broken tombstones and one cloudy blind eye forever gazing at some unseen horizon, an injury rumoured to have been inflicted by his long-dead father in a drunken rage. Hardcastle loves to terrorise smaller kids and then make vile remarks about what he'd do with our mothers, who'd all love to take a length from him, apparently. One time, Stuart glares up at him and says when he's bigger, he's going to find him and kill him. Hardcastle squints at Stuart with his single blue eye, spits at him and mutters *Poxy little runt* as he wheels away laughing. But I know Stuart means it, and Hardcastle is too thick to understand what just happened.

And then one day, I'm not interested in bikes anymore, not even the insane bone-juddering slalom down Gun Hill. Instead I lie in a darkened room listening over and over to The Stones' *Let It Bleed*, trying to understand lyrics that promise a very different kind of thrill. That's the real difference between Stuart and me, the music. While he still chirrups along to pop songs on the radio, I'm fascinated by Their Satanic Majesties. Hoping for communion by osmosis, I have taped a colour poster to my bedroom wall, showing the band in eyeliner and candy-coloured satin shirts, hands wrapped around each other's heads and necks and shoulders.

My mother is horrified.

They look like poofs, she says. They look like a bunch of druggies.

Secretly thrilled, I say nothing: I want to look like a poof and a druggy, too. Dolly birds love that kind of thing, I've seen the way they gape at The Stones on the telly.

By this time, I am 13 or 14 and painfully shy. I have inherited the Old Man's hair – thin, straight, limp, and already receding from an oversized forehead. Since I flat out refuse to let her trim it anymore, my mother's last bowl cut has now evolved into a lopsided combover with a jagged homestyle fringe. In desperation, I try to bleach it a lustrous blond, but in my haste I rinse out the chemicals too soon, resulting in a brittle copper thatch. Kids point at me in the street and cover their mouths. Beneath this terrible, half-abandoned hairstyle, my face is a greasy blob, the cheeks covered in blackheads and fat pimples with cream-coloured heads.

To make it worse, Stuart still has his beautiful Disney kid features, thick lashes and dark flashing eyes, button nose and silky skin. He also has our mother's lustrous black mop, the strong hairline signed off with a cow's lick. Even his teeth are perfect, a miracle given our Irish heritage.

Girls flock to him, though he appears oblivious. On the rare occasions when I dare talk to them, these same girls laugh at me. Standing next to him I feel more ugly and weirder than ever, but I'm also protected, because he always has my back. And I need his help, because there are too many cowardly pricks in this town just dying to have a pop. People like Tommy Clark from Grays, who comes up with his little gang while I'm sitting with my friend Jimmy in the State Cinema, minding my own business waiting for the film to start.

I'll be waiting for you outside, he snarls. I'm gonna do you, cunt.

Why?

No reason. He doesn't need one. He's going to fill me in, that's all the reason he needs. When the lights go down, I nudge Jimmy and we sneak out. I half-run to the bus stop rather than take another hiding for nothing.

Then there's this fiery brat called Ginger Gordon, who likes to feign punches whenever he sees me on the street, and laughs as I flinch and try to walk around him, eyes to the ground. My friends Jimmy and Stanley and Andy, they'll help out if they get dragged into it, or step in and even it up if it's two-against-one. But otherwise they stay out of fights where they're not directly targeted. I can't blame them. They have their own enemies.

By this time, neither Stuart nor the Old Man are still around, not in any meaningful way. The Old Man has long since been expelled and excommunicated, reduced to sofa surfing around town or crashing in bus shelters, while Stuart spends months at his fancy boarding school, returning only for school holidays, ever more convinced of his innate superiority.

Meanwhile, my latest nemesis is a kid called Macklin, only a year older but significantly taller and heavier, a bull-necked, bucket-headed kid, with a booming bass voice and a helmet of dark, coarse hair. Macklin likes to spit in my direction and call me *woman*, which in Tilbury is the worst insult anyone can hurl. And since I let him get away with it, it must be true.

And then one morning, I'm bigger and more masculine than a week ago. Maybe it's all those long hours sprinting after a football, or maybe just hormones, but the puppy fat has begun to melt away and my biceps and shoulders are expanding, while the Old Man's cheekbones have started to jut out. After a *straightener* outside the Toot, Macklin stops picking on me.

Shortly after this, having tried and failed for almost six months, I finally get served a pint in a local pub, the Anchor. For me and Jimmy, after months of swigging bottles of Olde English cider while sitting on the swings in the Daisy Field, this is exciting news. We quickly learn to skip the Anchor in favour of the Toot, where drinks are much cheaper.

The Toot is what everyone calls the Working Men's Club and Institute, part of a network of social clubs that sprang up in the nineteenth century, catering to the newly mobile industrial workforce. The idea, based on union principles, was to provide recreational facilities for itinerant working men and their families, membership of one club granting admission to any other. In a place like Tilbury, largely built by Irish immigrants and the sons of surrounding rural areas, these working men's clubs – the Toot, Scruttons, the Irish, the Railwaymen's Club – are woven into the social fabric.

My generation had grown up looking forward to the annual coach outings organised by these clubs, trips to amusement parks and piers and beaches in Walton-on-the-Naze or Clacton-on-Sea on the Essex coast. Every summer we'd stuff our faces with hot dogs, toffee apples and candy floss, and then make ourselves nauseous riding on roller coasters or the Big Dipper.

Now, as we creep up on adulthood, these social clubs provide a stepping stone from the local youth club scene to adult entertainment. While a local band plays Top 40 covers, we boys strut around the dancefloor pretending to ignore the local girls, or sit at tables eyeing them over pints of cheap gassy beer like Watneys Red Barrel or Double Diamond. Our lives are so closely intertwined with the social club phenomenon, in fact, that my mother currently supplements her Family Allowance working as a barmaid at the Railway Club. Some evenings I'll even drop by to say hello and she'll treat me to a fancy soft drink, a Britvic orange or a Schweppes lemonade. But since I'm only 16, she refuses to serve me a pint, which is why I usually slink off to get one a few hundred yards up Calcutta Road, in the Toot.

On any week night there are maybe 40 people in the Toot, twice as many on weekends. On a big night, a Bank Holiday or Christmas Eve, there can easily be 200 – entire families, three generations, plotted up at the tables lining the carpeted lounge area, three or four drinks lined up around the ashtray, laughing and shouting in a fug of cigarette smoke, while little kids chase each other up and down the aisles. The men drink brown ale or light and bitter, maybe a lager top. Ladies sip stout or port and lemon or Babycham, while nippers guzzle watery orangeade and younger teens have shandy. Kids my age hang around the sprung dancefloor, nursing pints their parents have turned a blind eye to, or dance faux-nonchalantly, staring into the middle distance, to the local band's version of *Bus Stop* or *Lady Madonna*.

*   *   *

The first couple of times Stuart comes home for the holidays, we fight like brothers. But as we get older and bigger, we fight more like thugs. From bitter experience and our father's seafaring tales, we have learned never to reason with an angry male. The best strategy is to attack first with blinding rage, in a flurry of punches, kicks and headbutts, using any weapon to hand. By our mid-teens we see the world as vicious and unpredictable, always ready to attack and dominate us, so we must remain vigilant, on a hair trigger, ready to go from nought to ballistic in a split second.

And so we learn to circle each other, tossing out the occasional threat or menacing glance. We know we cannot live much longer under the same roof – we share the same explosive temper, the same instinct to rush headlong into violence. If we no longer fight, it's not because we have mellowed or grown more stable. We no longer fight because we recognise in each other the strength and speed to inflict lethal damage.

Like most brothers, we remain fiercely loyal. But unlike most, we share a hostility and rage learned before we could talk, a throbbing menace that echoes all around us in this town, which has anger and brutality in its DNA. It's not that people from Tilbury are savages. For the most part, they are decent and honest hard-working people, who nurture their families with kindness and civilised values. But for every household headed by someone like our grandfather Jack Sharkey, a simple man of modest appetites, there is a vicious predator lurking on the corner – someone like Alec Campbell, spewing bile and lashing out at any slight, real or imagined.

*   *   *

Sometime early in 1972 I stop going up to N17 on Saturday mornings to watch Tottenham Hotspur. The thrill of losing myself in the roaring mob, chanting and clapping in martial rhythm, the mad terror of cascading crowd surges on the terraces, the running fights outside the ground, all that has started to lose its charm. Instead I spend long hours with Jimmy in his bedroom, smoking cigarettes and listening to Lou Reed, David Bowie and The Doors, trying to decipher lyrics, analysing esoteric moods. Soon I'll become obsessed by the Pop Art retro-futurism of Roxy Music, and shortly after that I'll start delving into the frenetic syncopation and fiery howling of James Brown, the loping streetwise cool of The Fatback Band.

But my brother isn't getting into music. He's still feeding off the reckless thrill of combat, getting into fights and leaving a wake of petty destruction. Does he ever kiss any of those girls who seem to follow him around? Who knows? He is secretive, deceitful, distant. Perhaps I should have expected as much. Already I've pushed him away many times. Years later I will wonder: would things have turned out different if I had taken an interest, pulled him closer? What might have happened if I'd been less self-absorbed, less arrogant and hostile?

The problem is that I'm so desperate to survive – which means exuding toughness and eliminating any trace of weakness, especially intimacy – that I have no room for him, or anybody else. This is how we've been raised, with the sense that we must plunge forward and never look back or wait for others to catch up. Self-doubt, even self-reflection, is asking for trouble. There is no time for second-guessing, especially now that I'm determined to escape this place, and soon.

All of this, combined with the attitude he brought back from Eccles Hall – his own arrogance and disdain – has broken our brotherly bond and driven us apart.

And then, one summer day, we get into a stupid but typical fraternal spat at the foot of the stairs. It erupts into punches, and then I'm halfway up the stairs, a couple of steps above him, in a position of advantage, punching down. There's a flurry of blows and he takes something from his waistband and lifts it to strike me. I see the blade and kick out at him, my trainer hitting him in the chest. He comes at me again. Desperate to knock him off balance so I can escape, I kick out again, but this time he plunges the eight-inch hunting knife into my shin.

The shock is so great I don't even feel the wound, just the warm blood spurting down my leg inside my bell-bottoms. As he stands urging me to come at him, ready to stab me again, our mother pushes him aside to get between us, giving me the chance to dart behind her and out the door, and run down the street. When I stop and pull up the leg of my jeans there's blood spurting from a jagged two-inch wound halfway down my shin, parallel to the bone. My Converse high tops are ruined, but I'm lucky the serrated blade has cut along rather than across the strands of muscle, without severing any arteries or tendons. I limp a few hundred yards to my friend Andy's house and tell his mother Eve some pathetic lie about catching my leg on barbed wire, and she cleans and dresses the wound for me. At dusk I return home warily, to find my mother has confiscated Stuart's knife. She tells me this as if it's supposed to be punishment enough and an end to the matter. There's no apology, no justification.

Though years have now passed since the Old Man has lived with us, his brutality has desensitised us. Nobody ever mentions the stabbing again, like it never even happened.

* * *

One cold foggy night that winter, I bump into Stuart outside the Anchor, where we both drink pints of lager, despite the fact that I am still only 16 and he is 14 months younger. When I ask where he's going, he says he's on the lookout for Ginger Gordon, the redheaded kid who makes a habit of hitting and threatening both of us. Gordon is no bigger than me, but like most of the local neanderthals he's not interested in a fair fight, and relies on his little gang to back him up.

I tell Stuart that I've just seen Gordon and his pals barely an hour ago, leaving the Toot.

You saw him at the Toot?

Yeah, I say. You're safe as long as you stick to the Anchor.

Nah, I'm gonna put an end to this bollocks, for good.

Oh yeah? How you gonna do that?

With a cold smile, Stuart unzips his black leather bomber jacket and pulls it open to show me what he has tucked inside: a foot-long, stainless-steel axe, its blade gleaming with bright menace. I can tell by the way it sits against the nylon lining that it must weigh 10 pounds, maybe 12.

Let him start on me tonight, says Stuart. He'll get a face full of this.

You hit someone with that, you'll kill 'em.

That's the fucking idea.

Stay in the Anchor, Stuart.

See you later, Al.

Later I'll learn that Gordon had indeed started trouble when he exited the Toot and found Stuart leaning against a wall. He'd sneered and threatened to cripple my brother, a standard Tilbury threat. But then Stuart drew the axe and lunged at him with some lunatic roar, swinging for his head, and Gordon took off as fast as humanly possible and never looked back. I don't know if Stuart had genuinely tried to hurt him, or merely wanted to scare him.

But once again, despite my misgivings, it works like a charm. Apart from dirty looks, Gordon never bothers either of us again. We are learning all the wrong lessons.

9

Thursday 5 July 2001
17 days since Danielle's disappearance

This morning my mother calls me in Paris and says the police want to speak with me. Would it be okay if she gave them my number?

Of course, I say. In fact, tell the police I *want* to speak with them, so maybe I can get an idea of what the hell's going on.

The next morning I get a call on the landline from someone claiming to be a detective. I'm wary, because there's always the possibility that my mother has been duped. Ten years earlier I'd sat at a desk in the *Daily Star* and watched as a news reporter, pretending to be a police officer, conned an unsuspecting punter into revealing personal information over the phone.

So now it's my turn to be suspicious and evasive, wary of this disembodied voice claiming to be that of Detective Superintendent Keith Davies. I listen rather than speak, keeping my answers terse and lean.

Yeah, that's me, Stuart's brother. How's Paris? Oh, very nice. Wasted on the French, haha.

He speaks in a warm and affable manner, eminently reasonable, exactly as I'd expect of some crafty hack. I notice the slightly lengthened vowels, the vaguely rural diphthongs. An Essex accent, but different from my own customised Estuary English.

I'm thinking, *Colchester? Maybe one of the villages around there?* But then I become aware that he's not asking the questions a tabloid reporter would ask – about growing up with Stuart, how I feel about the case, how it's affecting me and my family. Instead, he's *telling* me that he has been spending a fair bit of time with my brother lately, getting to know him quite well, actually.

He's a good-looking bloke, isn't he?

I stop pacing the room and press the cordless phone closer to my ear.

Go on, I say.

Yeah, quite handsome. And full of charm. Everyone says how charming he is, what a character. He loves to crack a joke, doesn't he?

Beneath the matey tone he is clearly implying that my brother's persona is a carefully constructed facade. It's an insight that hits home. That's exactly what Stuart's like – too jovial by half. I remember the nagging doubt I'd always felt about his breezy manner – avuncular, you might call it – even while basking in its glow.

Now I know this is not some sly hack trying to blag a few quotes.

DS Davies says he'd like to talk to me in person about my brother. Is there any chance I could come to London in the next few days? He doesn't want to sound pushy but this is important. There's a missing 15-year-old girl who hasn't been seen for almost three weeks.

And you believe Stuart's got something to do with it?

I'm sure of it, he says. But what I want to know, Alix, is what do *you* think?

What I think, although I don't say it, is that his use of my first name is a little too chummy, a little too forward. Is there an angle I'm missing? Am I being played? Paranoia crackles in the air. Perhaps Stuart is listening in to the call, and this is just a ploy to fuck with his mind.

You see, Stuart? Not even your brother believes you. Might as well take the deal and plead guilty. Sign here.

I'm not sure, I say. Maybe.

Have you spoken to him about it?

Not yet. I've tried calling several times but I haven't been able to get hold of him.

Strange. I don't think he's got a lot of work on right now.

Yeah.

Well, I've got some information I'd like to share with you, but I'd rather not do it over the phone. I can come and meet you in Paris, if you like.

No, I say, I'm coming to London next week. We could talk then.

Oh well, I wouldn't have minded a trip to Paris, but whatever works for you.

I tell him where I'll be staying in Holborn and we fix a date so he can *drop by and have a little chat.*

Damn, he's slick.

*   *   *

In the days before leaving Paris I check online for the latest updates. On the first day of July, Essex Police announce that their hunt for the missing teenager is now focused on *a blue Transit-type van, seen in the area on at least two previous occasions.* Both times, apparently, the male driver was seen parked and talking to teenage girls.

Stuart, I know, has a blue Ford Transit.

The police must know it, too. So what's the point of putting out this information? Are they simply trying to rattle him, or do they believe there might be another blue Transit van out there, with another male driver talking to teenage girls?

A few days later I'm sitting at a table in a flat just off Kingsway, having a cup of tea and a chat with DS Keith Davies. A sandy-coloured man with a crop, his rusty facial hair is neatly trimmed into a raffish goatee that looks barely code-compliant. His sports jacket and check shirt with tie and slacks combo looks like something you might find if you googled 'business casual for plain-clothes detective'. Within seconds, it's clear that his patient and soft-spoken phone manner is the user-friendly interface for a relentless determination.

He asks how I'm holding up.

I'm fine, I say.

His cool hazel eyes flit around the room, consuming every detail.

Yes, he says. You seem to be alright. No worries then?

Of course. That's why we're here, isn't it?

I know your mum's upset. How are the rest of your family taking this news?

Well, I say, as you can imagine, most of them are very disturbed. But my main concern is keeping my daughter's name and photo out of the papers. It's bad enough that she'll have to learn about it someday, but I really don't want her school friends to break it to her before we explain it, her mother and me. Or worse, have the tabloids write some shitty story about the *other* bridesmaid, the lucky one who narrowly escaped her evil uncle's clutches. I'm resigned to the idea that sooner or later they'll come for me.

I don't think they're really interested in you, says Keith Davies.

Well, I've already had half a dozen messages on my answering machine, mostly from *The Sun*.

They've got a job to do, you know that.

Indeed.

So, would you say you actually *know* Stuart?

What do you mean?

Okay, let me put it this way. How *well* do you know him?

He's my brother, we grew up together.

So you know he's been in trouble with the law, that he's been to prison many times?

Of course. I've visited him in prison many times.

Do you know *why* he was in prison?

Yeah, mostly burglary, theft, stolen goods.

Did he tell you that?

I suppose so. Can't remember. Maybe my mum? I was living in London by then, he was in Tilbury. He's always lived there. Why?

So you don't know about Stuart's history of sexual violence towards underage girls?

What? No. He doesn't have … I think you've got the wrong …

The first time he went to prison, in 1977, do you know what that was for?

Yes, handling stolen goods. He was working with a gang who were burgling local people's houses, stealing televisions and hi-fi equipment.

No, he says, in the tone a parent might use with a child who claims the Earth is flat.

No?

No, that's not it at all. Stuart was convicted of beating up a 16-year-old girl and stealing her purse. He hit her so hard that he left her with two black eyes. And then he sexually assaulted her before running off.

What?

That's a fact. And that's just the start of it.

For the next 10 minutes or so I fall into some kind of trance as he explains the ugly brutal crimes my brother has been accused of down the years. Some that he had been convicted of, others he'd managed to walk away from. None of which I'd known about.

Stuart used to live with you at one point, right?

What? No, never. Why do you say that?

Are you certain? You never shared a flat in the East End? Stepney, or Whitechapel?

No, definitely not. Who told you that?

I thought you lived there at one point. Victorian red-brick building, big courtyard?

Yeah, that's where *I* lived, not Stuart.

Tell me about that.

Grove Dwellings, in Whitechapel. I was at art school. Most of us were. We squatted in these derelict buildings that had been condemned, but then we formed a housing co-op and got a local government grant. Completely rebuilt the place as community housing.

When was that?

Uh, I moved there in the late seventies and moved out in … what, 1985? But Stuart never lived there with me, he was always …

But as I'm saying these words, they catch in my throat.

Of course.

Long-sunken memories float up to the surface. Yes, he *was* there for a brief period. Not living with me, but as a short-term resident. Somehow I managed to get him membership of the housing co-op and temporary tenancy of an empty flat for a few months, before it was gutted and refurbished. He'd lived there with Debbie.

I look at DS Davies, wide-eyed.

How the fuck did you know that?

After Stuart was arrested, he says, and his photo appeared in the papers and on the telly, numerous women came forward claiming he had either assaulted or stalked or harassed them. All of them said this had happened when they were 14 or 15 years old.

Numerous?

We're still working through the complaints, taking statements and trying to verify the timeline to make sure they're credible, but we're talking about something like 15, maybe 20.

Twenty? *Holy fuck.*

Could be more, he says.

And what about Grove Dwellings?

One woman said he'd taken her to an old Victorian brick building in the East End, near Whitechapel station. She didn't know the street, but she felt sure she could find it if we drove around. It took us about an hour, but gradually she started to get her bearings, and as we were driving along Adelina Grove she said, *That's it.*

For a long time I sit there, letting this sink in. I helped him get a flat, got my friends to support his membership and vote him in, helped him and his girlfriend move in, and according to an old diary entry I'll find much later, even cooked dinner for them.

And yet, when his girlfriend wasn't there and I wasn't looking, he took a little girl there and abused her?

My stomach is starting to churn when another thought comes to mind. I already know the answer, but I ask anyway.

Is she dead?

He sighs and looks at me for what seems like forever.

At this point, he says, almost certainly. But we have to hope she's still alive and act accordingly. You never know.

And you're sure that it was Stuart? I mean, I know it looks like it *must be* him, but could it be someone else?

DS Davies shrugs and turns his palms up.

Stuart is the only real suspect we have, he says, and that's not because we're blinkered. After all, no matter what I think of him, no matter what I've dug up on him, I've still got to prove that he's done it in order to get him convicted. There's no point in me going after him without good cause.

It's not just because he's an easy pinch, then?

Not at all, quite the opposite. Because as I say, I've still got to find and provide the evidence that will prove he's done it. Nobody's going to take my word.

It's just so hard to believe that he could ... Fuck, this is so horrible, I don't know what to say.

He tightens his mouth and nods slightly.

What was it like, growing up with Stuart? Your dad wasn't really around much, is that right? Not a very nice bloke, either.

Did he tell you that, Stuart?

We spoke to your mum, remember? She told us a little bit about your early life, you and Stuart and your sister. But I'd like to hear it from you, if you're willing to share it. Your side of the story. It might give us some clue about how to talk to him.

So I tell him about school, about how Stuart was always so beautiful, how I secretly loved him because he seemed to shine, because his voice was so pure and unselfconscious when he sang.

He's a good looking bloke, isn't he?

How we were fiercely loyal to each other.

And full of charm. Everyone says how charming he is, what a character.

How we grew apart and then he started going to prison, and I would visit him in prison because I didn't care – I was still kind of proud of him, proud of the way he held his head high and mocked the system.

He loves to crack a joke.

10

The Ship, 1973

I can no longer see my father's face. When I try to recall his features all that comes to mind is a passport-size black and white head shot, stapled to his worn and faded merchant seaman's card. A 50-year-old memory of an image that was already two decades old. A tiny photograph of a 25-year-old sailor, posing earnestly for an official document, long before he disembarks at Tilbury and meets my mother. My father, but not yet my father.

The Old Man, as we siblings refer to him.

The Other Thing, as our mother calls him.

Whenever I recall the first time I saw that photo, I still feel the shock it sent through me, seeing him as if for the first time in all his stark malevolence.

I know this man. That thin black hair, greased and scraped back, those high pale cheekbones. I know that icy gaze, plunging into me.

Of course I know him. As I look at this photo the Old Man is sitting beside me, head back and drink to his lips, watching me from the corner of his eye. I have known that piercing gaze since I could sit upright, the ever-present lightning flash on my childhood horizon. But now, fixed between the real thing and the photograph, I realise how frightening he must appear to others, how his annihilating glare can electrify any space with menace, penetrate any psyche. Even in collar and tie he looks outraged, burning to pluck insult from an offhand remark, ever ready to pounce.

Be warned. If your gaze and his connect, you are never looking at him. Even if only for a split second, even staring out from this tiny photograph with its spidery hairline cracks, he is always looking at you.

And you had better look away right now.

Local people seldom ask me about the Old Man, because we all know the score: big fish in a little pond. If his name comes up, they talk about how nice he looks, always so smart and well-dressed. They never slag him off. His faults are legendary, but he still exudes some air of mystique. Even my mother, who will no longer say his name and almost spits whenever she refers to him – and then, only to say how worthless and cowardly and selfish he is – even she hasn't managed to obliterate all trace of awe. Listening to her, I hear the echoing voids in her story, all the things she's leaving out. Her unspoken words only magnify his presence-through-absence, his nautical voodoo.

Sometimes I wonder if she knows what I'm thinking.

Yeah, you hate him now, and you won't even say his name, but you loved him once. So what magic did he work on you, how did he charm you into falling in love with him, into being his wife?

And I look at the photo again and realise: *I can have eyes like this.*

Already, I know my eyes are abnormal. From day one the kids at school have mocked and taunted me about my hooded eyelids, which make me look Asiatic and therefore alien. Now, for the first time, I can imagine my gaze as a weapon. I may not get respect, but I will have deference. I will magnetise women and terrorise men, staring down and striking terror into anyone whose eyes meet mine.

I'm still underage, barely 16, but I am drinking with him. It's a sunny afternoon and we're sitting in the saloon bar of the Ship, in the shadow of the docks. He has bought me a pint, or perhaps poured some of his beer into a glass for me. We are talking idly about what kind of work I should be looking for, although for him there's no job on Earth worth a cup of cold piss. Apart from his own, of course.

*　　*　　*

Where is Stuart?

I'm no longer sure. If it's term time, he's still away at Eccles Hall, his fancy school in Norfolk. If the summer holidays have started he's lurking around Tilbury, although I wouldn't know where to find him. We don't spend time together anymore, not since we started attending different schools. Besides, I don't like the way he behaves with girls – he's too arrogant with them, too rough. He pretends he's only playing but then he'll put a girl in a headlock or twist her arm. Jimmy's little sister, who at 14 is just a year younger than Stuart, tells me she's scared of him because of the weird way he behaved recently towards her.

Weird how?

He's a bit of nutter, isn't he? Bit of a bully. He said he wanted me to go out with him and I said no. So he grabbed me and bent my arm right up my back. And then he started biting my neck, giving me love bites. Well, you know my Old Man, he's like your Old Man, he'd kill me if he saw that on my neck. Anyway, he saw Jimmy coming along the street and he run off.

Sorry, I say. I'll have a word.

I don't know what's wrong with him, she says. It's not like he needs to force anyone to go out with him. All the girls fancy him anyway.

Yeah, I say.

He knows it, too, she says. He's a cocky git. My brother Peter told me he was talking to him outside the Toot one night and Stuart said, *Watch this*. And he clicked his fingers at these two girls and they come running across the road to see what he wanted.

He's such a fucking show-off.

Oh yeah, she says, full of himself. And he's got the gift of the gab.

Perhaps this is why, even though I know Stuart has few friends in Tilbury now – after all, for most of the year he lives 100 miles and two counties away – I make no effort to spend time with him, no attempt to console him or revive our own friendship.

Anyway, if he ever saw me talking to the Old Man, or even heard about it, Stuart would be furious. I can't even mention him without Stuart's jaw clenching, his eyes narrowing, his speech reduced to a feral grunt. My brother still hates him with an incandescent purity that leaves me feeling weak by comparison.

Similarly, I know my mother would be feel betrayed and humiliated if she learned I had been talking to The Other Thing. Worse, she might even report him to the police, because several years ago she went to court and got an exclusion order that categorically forbids him from contacting or even approaching any of us.

And so I keep these interactions secret. Even though they would be shocked and outraged, I can't help but be fascinated. Stealing sideways glances, I wonder if I'm staring into my future. Is this what lies ahead, my grim genetic destiny? Or can I use my head – as he is always telling me I should – in order to cheat fate?

These questions dog me so hard that I always find ways to stumble into him at his various haunts, accepting his invitation to sit and talk, so that I can glance at his clean-shaven profile, his nicotine-stained fingers, the tiny dark blue feather in his hatband that picks out the icy blue of his eyes. During these illicit moments I scrutinise his features and gestures, the shape of his hands and ears and nose, noting differences and similarities, parsing the gifts and curses of ancestry. And as he sinks deeper into drunkenness I note the gradual smearing of mood, the boozy bonhomie sliding through sour resentment and into volatile paranoia. Talking to the Old Man is an anthropological field trip, a psychological case study: an attempt to understand his worst behaviour in order to preempt my own.

I have contradictory theories: he is fearless, adventurous, dangerous. But he is also cowardly, weak and pathetic. He squanders whole days of his life sitting in bus shelters, on park benches, on the steps of public buildings, drinking cheap plonk – sherry or cider or fortified wine – surrounded by unshaven men in dirty, threadbare clothing, men who smell faintly of urine, men with scabs on their brows and cheeks and noses, the tell-tale wounds of blackout drunks who collapse face first.

Somehow the Old Man never does this. Somehow he always makes it back to wherever he stays, somewhere he can wash and shave the next morning, somewhere he keeps his clean clothes. He never seems to puke, at least not on himself. Unlike his crusty circle of broken drunks, his shirts are always fresh, his shoes always polished, even when he's slumped in the corner of a bus shelter, eyes half-closed, a bottle of VP sherry between his feet and a stump of cigarette ash smouldering between his fingers.

I have to hand it to him. Most of the time he has these clowns eating out of his palm. They gather around him like a cult, rapt, as if his word is law. He is not merely the King of Drunks, but a kind of avatar, the God of Drunks in human form, come down to earth to lead his slurring and staggering flock to a higher plane of inebriation, one where they can get shit-faced all day every day, while still maintaining impeccable hygiene and carrying off a raffish style. In him, they see hope and glory, they see how they too can terrorise and neglect wives and children, piss away rent and food money, sleep off their hangovers in public spaces, yet still emerge the epic heroes of their own boozy, blurry, self-pitying mythology.

Because I know this man but don't understand him, because he both horrifies and fascinates me, and because having been expelled from grammar school I'm not sure what to do with my life, I have begun to wonder whether I should emulate his one great daring choice and go to sea. My half-baked logic is that by following in his wavering footsteps I'll spot the obvious wrong turn he took long ago and sidestep it.

And so I say, I'm thinking of joining the Merchant Navy.

Glass halfway to his lips, he looks me over as if I've just announced my enrolment as a police cadet.

You? You want to go to sea?

Yeah, I thought maybe, you know. Get a ship.

I'm half-hoping he'll wrap an arm around me and walk me over the railway bridge and we'll breeze past security at the dock gate and stroll across concrete plains under the looming gantries until we reach that 20,000-ton Scandinavian cargo ship. Together, we'll walk up that gangway and he'll introduce me to some white-whiskered sea dog who looks just like Captain Birdseye, and after they clap hands on each other's shoulders and shake, he'll say, This is my son Alexander, I'm sure ye'll have a berth for him, right?

Instead he takes a long drag on the butt of his Senior Service and crushes it into the yellow plastic ashtray, then brushes tiny flakes of ash from his tie and exhales a lungful of smoke through his nostrils.

He says, Well first you need to be 18, that's the minimum age now. But I don't rate your chances.

Why not?

Containerisation is why not. No need for a bunch of galoots to lug stuff out the hold anymore.

But they still need crew members, don't they?

Most ships today, you've a crew of 10 maximum. Aye, 10 men, ship the fucking size of Parkhead.

But *you* still get work.

Son, I've been at sea for 30 years. I'm a chef. You know the most important man on the ship? It's no' the fucking captain. Captain can't even set sail without a chef.

I don't mention how my mother has told me about the many times he'd held up ships waiting to sail, captains fretting on the bridge with the tide going out, while he roused himself from a bench somewhere, half-empty bottle in hand. Or how the ship's chef holds the keys to the liquor chest, and so of course every hand wants to stay in his good books. How I can see why he'd think himself the most important man on board.

Instead I say, Maybe I'll get lucky.

Sure, and maybe you'll win the fucking pools.

So I just go into the docks and ask?

He reaches inside his jacket and takes out a wad of papers and brown leather that turns out to be his swollen and battered wallet, along with a small black notebook and his old faithful – a six-inch sharpened steel nail file. Then he digs around some more and pulls out his Merchant Navy card, tossing it on the table with exaggerated nonchalance.

You'll need one of these, he says, indicating the card.

I stare at the photo stapled to it, at his fearsome gaze staring back at me. Along with his maritime credentials there's another card, white and blue, embossed with a seal, his name written in capitals on the front. He watches me carefully as I pick it up and examine it. Inside there's some dense French text and a grid with a list of items, checked off and dated with a fountain pen.

What's this?

That's my Cordon Bleu certification, he says, preening. That's fucking gold dust, that. There's barely a handful of ship's chefs anywhere in the world with that qualification.

This sounds to me like his typical exaggerated bollocks, but I nod respectfully.

What does it mean?

It means I can cook for presidents and kings in a five-star hotel. For the Pope. For 60 Scouse bastards on a fucking banana boat to Belize. No difference tae me.

He laughs and throws back a gulp of bitter. His Adam's apple, a lump of thyroid cartilage the size of a walnut, goes up and down in his gullet like a yo-yo.

His dress sense is classic early-sixties Rat Pack: dark lounge suit, white shirt, slim tie, trilby at a jaunty angle. Though he'd never admit to something so effete as copying another man's look, he undoubtedly models himself on Sinatra. They share those pale blue eyes, the same high forehead and thinning dark hair. The same lean and wiry physique. Greyhound build, the Old Man calls it. And like Sinatra, after a few drinks he will get up and sing. But after a few more he will scowl, and then he may well hit people. And while his singing voice is nothing special – a resonant but limited baritone – his fists are lightning fast and rock-hard.

He drains his glass and gets to his feet.

I need the head, he says.

Dust motes swim in the sunlight as it cuts a hard diagonal across the bar. A dreamy piano chord and loping bassline fill the air, announcing that someone has dropped a tanner into the jukebox and selected *Satellite of Love*, one of my favourite songs at this moment. Though still a virgin I know about hookers and drag queens and dope dealers, thanks to long evenings spent with my pal Jimmy, listening to Lou Reed records in his bedroom. Whenever the Old Man mentions New York, I try to imagine the people described on *Transformer*. I want to be part of it, this New York of fabulous freaks, and I wonder if maybe that's why I'm here in the Ship, listening to this tune.

Maybe it's a sign, I tell myself.

The Old Man comes out of the head smiling, arms out Gene Kelly-style, and does a little soft-shoe shuffle to Lou Reed, right there in the middle of this half-empty, sun-drenched saloon bar. He points to his temple.

Up here for thinking, he says.

He points to his shoes.

Down there for dancing.

He does a couple more steps, a twirl, and then stamps his heel down and grinds it into some invisible enemy face.

He slumps in his chair, nods smugly and takes a deep drag on his snout. He only smokes untipped cigarettes, what he calls *proper snout*. Anything with a filter is *burd snout*. If he runs out and needs to bum a smoke and someone offers him *burd snout* – Embassy or Guards or Rothmans, for example – he'll inspect it scornfully before breaking off the filter and flicking it into the gutter. Then he'll scowl and mutter some dark curse as he fires up the broken end. His steel pocket lighter is a cheap butane model with a dodgy valve. I remember standing with him in a bus shelter one time, just after he'd refilled it. As he cupped the snout with his free hand and snapped the lighter, a tongue of blue flame shot up into his face, singeing off his left eyebrow. It was one of the rare times we shared a laugh.

Up here for thinking, down there for dancing.

Dopey slogans, dive bar philosophy. He's full of this shit.

And yet, as well as a gaze so ferocious it could petrify a Doberman, he has this raw presence that seems to trigger an instinctive response in others, the way a herd of antelope at a watering hole will stop drinking and look up in unison when they scent a big cat upwind. This dark charisma is reinforced by his idiosyncratic speech pattern, a brutally efficient hybrid of Glaswegian, Cockney and New York dock slang, peppered with nautical and military jargon, rank blasphemy, Gaelic, Arabic and Swahili terms, and snatches of torch song lyrics. When he's on a roll what emerges from his mouth is a stripped and greasy, blunt and muscular marine poetry. This seafaring drunk has hammered out his own lingua franca, which he enunciates in a withering, snarling growl. A couple of years earlier, even before Bowie started ripping off Lord Buckley for his Ziggy vocabulary, the first time I heard the phrase *talking jive* was when it fell from the Old Man's lips.

As in, *So I'm half-cut at the dossers' bar in the Anchor trynae get a round in, flagging a 50, when this inbred cloon who wouldn't know Tynemouth from Timbuktu, this raggedy-arse imbecile comes up tae me and starts talking jive about some bent gear back at his drum, telling me he wants me to go take a shufti. So I say, Do I look like I just fell out a fucking tree? I tell him, You see this, pal? That's my weak mitt and it'll break your jabbering jaw, so pray to God it lands first, cause this one? That's my good hand, and it will fucking kill ye stone dead. Now get tae fuck.*

I knew this story was grossly inflated but still, I tell myself, there's literally nobody else in the world who speaks quite like this. Despite getting most of his secondary education at the end of a strap, this seafaring culinary worker, this bar-brawling, wife-beating, foul-mouthed fabulist has fashioned his very own vernacular, stunted and irregular perhaps, but uniquely and perfectly fitted to his personality and worldview. It was my mother who taught me to read and write, who first made words fun to play with, but it's my father who lives and breathes linguistic alchemy, whose gutbucket prose shows me – the grammar school boy – how to cut through the era's class-conscious syntax and diction. Listening to him, the air itself is charged with defiance and I can taste liberation. The vast serpentine beast called English can be wrestled to the ground, choked to death, stripped for hide and meat, and its skin and bones worn as ornament.

For this reason alone, despite his many grotesque faults, I hold him in awe.

The Ship, 1974

One evening I'm in the saloon bar of the Ship, standing at the bar with Jimmy and a couple of other lads. Someone nudges me from behind, a reckless move in a Tilbury pub at the best of times. I turn to find the haughty, mocking, powdered face of Steve The Duchess, a flaming old queen who pencils in his shaved eyebrows and wears crimson lipstick. A former merchant seaman who works behind the bar when he's not necking industrial quantities of gin, Steve has decided somewhere along the line that the best defence is attack, and now embodies just about every queer cliché imaginable. And it works. Nobody dares confront him about his lifestyle. Even the most bigoted hard men leave him alone, because Steve may be wiry and camp, but he can go to town if need be.

And even more fearsome than his ability to throw a punch is that filthy mouth of his. If you mock his purple eye shadow, or his fitted shirts undone to the sternum, or his chiffon neckerchief knotted to the side or his jangly bangles, Steve will give you a mouthful, ending with something along the lines of, *Sweetheart, you're not man enough to satisfy me with that tiny scrap*, or *Call that a cock, I've seen more meat on a chicken foot*, or *Darling, I'd bend you over and fuck your brains out, if you had any*.

Steve nods, looks over my shoulder and says, Someone you know?

I turn to peer through a gap that gives onto the public bar, on the other side of this L-shaped boozer.

Behind me, Jimmy says, Is that your old man?

His back is turned, but I can tell it's him from the trilby and the way the faces around him look up in awe. He's holding court as usual.

Fuck, I thought he was banned.

Yeah, says Jimmy. But *you're* banned, too.

Yeah, but he's been banned like five or six times.

Maybe he apologised. Wanna go round and see him?

What? No, fuck him.

At closing time I step outside, expecting to find him under the lamppost on the corner, waiting for me. And there he is.

We shake hands and he holds out his pack of Senior Service.

I hold up my pack of Bensons and say, Thanks, I'll have one of these.

We're standing under the lamppost smoking and talking, when this guy comes up on my right and starts in on the Old Man. Friendly at first, but invasive.

Hey. Hey. *Hey you*. Big man. Didn't you say we'd get a drink? Hey you. Wanna get a drink or what?

The Old Man says, Aye, in a minute.

Let's go then.

I'm talking.

Yeah, I can see that, and I'm talking to *you*.

Aye, I know, and I'm talking to my son here.

The Old Man says this while looking directly at me, ignoring the drunken galoot.

Now the guy is really pissed off.

Hey. *You*. D'you hear me, he says, his tone getting ugly. *I'm talking to you.*

The Old Man has taken out a nail file and is scraping under his nails with the tip. I know where this is going. His nostrils are flared, a bad sign.

He says to me, softly, You going to take care of this, or am I?

Did you hear me? the guy says, chest out, swaying slightly.

I turn back to the Old Man and give a small shrug.

Do you fucking hear me? I'm talking to you!

Can you take care of him?

I nod.

Okay, then.

I turn to face the guy, who is now shouting and jabbing his finger at the Old Man, but ignoring me, probably because I'm 17 and he's at least mid-forties, a good two stone heavier.

Okay, I say, placing my palm on his chest. Leave it out, mate. We're talking. Give us some room, eh?

He doesn't even look at me.

Listen, I say. This is my dad. We're talking. Leave us alone, will you?

He slaps my hand away and pushes an index finger into the lapel of the Old Man's jacket. The Old Man wobbles but doesn't even look up from his kerbside manicure.

I said *I'm* fucking talking to *you*, ya fucking ignorant …

He doesn't see me take a half-step sideways and pivot. He

doesn't see the right hook I send crashing into his jaw. His head snaps backwards at a weird angle and the rest of him follows in a fluid arc, landing with a rubbery thud.

He's not moving.

Maybe it's a lucky shot, or maybe he's so drunk a child could have floored him, but either way, I feel a surge of pride. Okay, so I sucker-punched him, but I'm impressed by my own brute strength. I just knocked out a grown man with a single shot.

Then all at once, looking down at this sad drunk sprawled on the pavement, eyes closed and mouth open, I feel sick. Maybe he's a father too. Maybe his son is somewhere nearby. How would he feel if he came around the corner now and found his father lying on the pavement outside this stinking boozer, spark out? Especially having been KO'd by a cocky teenager with a stripy tank top, permed hair and platform shoes.

No' bad, says the Old Man, blowing on his fingernails as if he's done the dirty work himself. Okay, he says, let's get outta here before the law shows up.

As we walk away I notice the Old Man looking at me sideways, mouth turned down. He nods slowly. I know what he's thinking.

You're just like me, after all.

I stare straight ahead as pride and shame swirl through my veins, no way to confront him, no way to correct him, no way to prove him wrong. But when I replay it in my mind the following day, I realise the Old Man has conned me. The other guy had spooked him and the Old Man was desperately trying to hold it together, trying to hide how frightened he was.

All that bullshit about, You gonna take care of him or am I? He was bluffing.

11

Southwark, Saturday 7 July 2001
19 days since Danielle's disappearance

Staring into the darkness, I'm waiting for whatever is out there to take shape and emerge. Waiting for some kind of sign. Did I imagine I could leave this behind in Paris?

I sit up and lean back against the wall.

It's fading now, but still faintly present, some kind of mood that lingers at the edges of the room. A feeling that just a few moments ago was hovering over me as I slept, close enough that I jumped out of my dreams to sit bolt upright – startled, wide-eyed, catching my breath.

To find nothing.

Just white noise roaring under the darkness and the hazy sodium light seeping through the curtains.

Celia stirs, props herself up on one elbow. I can feel her gaze on my face.

What's wrong?

Nothing. I just …

Pushing herself up to sit beside me, she stares into the darkened room, listening. She leans her temple on my shoulder, reaches into the crook of my arm. Her touch is warm and earthy. It grounds me and I exhale.

It's the girl again, she says.

Yeah, maybe. I don't know. Maybe I'm just imagining …

Are you scared?

I don't know. It doesn't feel ... *vengeful*. You know what I mean? Not *angry*.

What does it feel like, then?

Just kind of ... *sad*. Like, just an overwhelming sense of sadness.

D'you think you might, you know ... could it be projection?

Fuck, I don't know.

Some camomile tea?

I'm okay.

Let's go back to sleep.

Yeah.

We cling to each other and slide back under the white noise into the darkness, into slumber. Our dreams are shattered by the staccato burst of Celia's landline. She throws back the duvet and clambers over me, muttering, Who the fuck is *this*?

The red numerals on the clock radio read 2.52 a.m.

We both know it can't be for me, because I would never give out this number. And it can't be her parents or one of her siblings, because they would call her mobile.

She lifts the receiver and says, Hello?

There's long moment of limbo until she flicks on a small table lamp and we're surrounded by her art books and photography monographs, stacked on her desk, her shelves, the floor.

Who is this? she says. *Hello?*

I hear the buzz of a voice on the line, but can't tell if it's male or female.

Celia says, What do you mean, *Who am I?* You called *me*. At three o'clock in the morning.

I mouth at her, *Who is it?*

She shrugs and mouths, *Some woman.*

The voice buzzes again.

Oh, I see. Well, my name is Celia Mulenga. No, I'm not with a newspaper. No, not television, either. Sorry, who am I talking to? Well, I just told you my name, why can't you tell me yours?

I'm thinking, Who is this weirdo? Why is Celia being so polite?

Just as I realise and reach for the receiver, she says, Okay, goodnight, and hangs up.

I think it was your mum, she says.

What did she say?

She wanted to know who I was and why I called her earlier.

Oh, of course.

While Celia was out running an errand that afternoon and my phone was charging – more than 12 hours ago – I'd used her landline to call my mother. But when I heard the generic BT answering service, I'd hung up without leaving a message. She must have dialled 1471, the automated callback service. But why do that at three in the morning? Why ask about newspapers? Had the press been hassling her?

I take the phone from Celia and call my mother.

No answer. This time, I leave a message.

Hi Mum, it's me. I'm staying at Celia's place, you just called here. Anyway, I don't know why you're calling at three in the morning, but I hope you're okay. Please call me back and let me know what's going on.

We wait. No answer.

I call again, leave a similar message. We wait another ten minutes. Fifteen.

No callback.

Eventually we get back into bed and turn out the lights, but I can't sleep. In fact, I know I'll still be lying on my back and looking up at the ceiling when dawn comes.

Christ, I think. Guess I got a sign after all. Not the one I was expecting. The paranoia has now created a feedback loop, howling and screaming and engulfing everyone remotely connected to this hateful story.

*   *   *

We wake up late. After a breakfast that's really lunch we take the Northern Line to King's Cross, where we pick up our rental car, a grey Vauxhall Astra. Celia feeds a selection of her homemade mix tapes into the cassette player as we cruise through empty City streets and onto the A13, following it along the Thames and into Essex, towards Stuart and his pregnant wife Debbie. Despite having called both his home and mobile numbers five or six times, leaving a message each time, I still haven't heard from him. So I'm on a suburban safari, to track him down and confront him directly.

Though she hasn't said as much, I know Celia is concerned about my state of mind. It doesn't help that I keep jumping up in the middle of the night, startled and confused, unable to say precisely what spooked me. And while I won't admit it, I share her concerns. As confusion and doubt creeps in from every direction, the situation seems to be slipping out of control. I need to try and pin down the truth.

I need to get Stuart's version of events.

At first I'd assumed it was all some terrible misunderstanding, that he'd been unfairly targeted because of a few ancient and largely irrelevant crimes. But since talking with DS Keith Davies a few days ago, I realise how little I really know about my brother: Stuart has been deceiving me for decades. Having always fancied myself as the smart, sceptical type, I'm shocked to learn I could have been so gullible.

How did I get it so wrong?

For years now I'd thought of Stuart as someone who'd matured with age, a once-troubled boy who'd finally gone straight and settled down. Yes, he had been violent and aggressive as a kid – we both had – but like me, he'd grown out of that phase. Yes, he'd been a thief and served multiple prison sentences, but that was long behind him now. Over the years our family narrative had evolved to fit this new and more palatable image. Stuart, we all tacitly agreed, was a non-violent offender whose worst crime had been burglary. He'd served his time and – what's the cliché? – paid his debt to society. He had never hurt anybody, never committed any crimes of gratuitous or sexual violence. That was our collective misunderstanding, the story we'd slowly come to accept and believe.

Which is why even now, as I drive down the A13 towards a confrontation, I still cling to the hope that this might be nothing more than a series of weird coincidences, that the police might yet find his alibi checks out. But I also know that if DS Keith Davies was telling the truth – and there's no reason he would have lied – then Stuart is a far darker character than any of us ever imagined, a brutal and dangerous predator, a violent paedophile.

Worse, he may be a murderer.

My brother.

These two narratives go to war in my head: the one I'd always clung to and *want* to believe, and the horrific story I'd heard barely 48 hours earlier from a senior Essex Police detective, who at this very second is out there somewhere, searching for a missing 15-year-old girl.

*　　*　　*

Celia snaps her gum and grins.

What you thinking about, Fairy Boy?

Her nickname for me. As in precious about clothes and grooming, cares too much about feelings.

Oh, just wondering how long it'll take.

What's that?

For you to walk home, Celia.

Ha, Sharkey's got jokes.

How can I tell her the truth? That I'm wondering about me and my brother, about DNA and genetic inheritance. Wondering which of us is closer to the Old Man: the teetotal ex-con with the quiet suburban life, or the boozy rake with the fancy clothes? Wondering about that time, many years ago, when a vicious row with a girlfriend got physical and I slapped her back, leaving her with a black eye. Wondering how I could ever have raised my hands to a woman, something I had sworn to my mother I would never do. Wondering at how deeply I had suppressed that memory, and if there are others, even more shameful, about to bubble up. And worst of all, wondering whether there's a latent predator in my psyche, just waiting to be triggered. What exactly makes someone a killer?

Nature, nurture?

Both?

Forty minutes later we pull up at Grays station, where my childhood friend Andy Hollington is waiting for us. Bluff and cheery, with a grey-blond goatee, Andy's annual highlight is Glastonbury, always on or close to his birthday, and he wears the standard Glasto mashup of raver casual and hippy jester. When I'd called to say we were coming down to look for Stuart, he'd immediately said he'd come up from Southend to join us. I'm glad he did. Not that I expect trouble, but it's always good to have an old friend by your side when stepping into the unknown. And we're definitely entering uncharted territory right now.

We drive into town and pull up across the road from Stuart's house. It looks deserted: curtains drawn, sealed off from the world, a house in denial. But then, given its location at the corner of two roads – living room windows facing the street, open to passers-by or snooping journalists – I'd probably draw the curtains myself. Especially if I'd been accused of abducting my teenage niece.

Using Celia's phone I try Stuart's home number once more, then his mobile. Both calls go straight to voicemail.

By now I've managed to get Debbie's mobile number, so I try that.

No answer.

We get out and look around. The empty street looks like the set of a sci-fi movie, where aliens have abducted the residents of these red-brick and pebble-dashed houses. Yet I can feel that tingle everyone has felt at some point, that unmistakable sense of being watched. Behind those net curtains Stuart's neighbours are lurking, eager for a glimpse of the suspect.

I walk up the path, knock at the door and listen.

I knock a second time, then a third.

Nothing.

I step into the front garden and try to peer through a razor-thin gap in the curtains, but all I can see is the corner of a chintzy sofa in a darkened room. If he's home, he's hiding. Perhaps round the back, in the kitchen that overlooks the garden, or maybe upstairs in one of the three bedrooms. Either way, there's nothing left to do but get back in the car and go see some relatives, to ask if they know what's going on.

We drive a few miles to my Aunt Ruby's house and sit and drink tea in her living room. My mum's younger sister by a couple of years, she is a gentle soul, now in her seventies.

Yes, she says, it's terrible, isn't it. Really awful.

Aunt Ruby has heard about Stuart on the news but doesn't know anything apart from what she saw on the telly. She says she'll call her son, my cousin Eric, though she doesn't think he'll have any idea where to find Stuart, either.

We never really see him, she says. He keeps himself to himself, doesn't he.

It feels odd to be searching for my brother and unable to find him. For years I always knew where to look – either in prison or at home. Stuart was the permanent fixture, always right there, wherever you last saw him. I was the elusive one, always moving, shifting, changing lanes. And now the roles are reversed, leaving me baffled. If he's innocent, surely he needs as much help and support as he can get? And if he's guilty but trying to convince people otherwise, why would he behave in such a suspicious manner?

I don't understand his logic. Why is he hiding?

Aunt Ruby calls Eric at his work and hands me the phone.

Hey, Eric. Alright mate?

Alright, Alexander? What you doing at my mum's then? Not like you to pay a social visit.

No Eric, you're right. Actually, I'm looking for Stuart, only he's not answering his phone. You don't have any idea where he might be?

Sorry mate, I don't have a clue. You tried him at home, of course?

Yeah, I say, just been round there. No answer. Can't get Debbie on the phone either.

Yeah, wish I could help. But if you do speak to him, tell him to watch his step.

What does that mean?

Well, I was talking to some fellers at work and there's a rumour going around there's some *real nutters* out there, driving around Grays looking for him. And he's in real trouble if they catch him.

Although I know the answer, I ask, Why's that?

They say he's a nonce, mate, that's why. He's fair game. All I can say is I hope you find him before they do, Alexander. These are dangerous people. They won't leave it at a good hiding, they're gonna hurt him seriously if they catch him.

Celia and Andy look at me expectantly, but I don't want to say anything in front of Aunt Ruby – she doesn't need to hear this. We finish our tea and say our goodbyes.

Yes, I tell her, I will try to get down more often. I promise.

*   *   *

We're in the car fixing our seat belts when I explain what Eric just told me. I can see from Andy's reaction that he knows more.

What is it, mate?

He says, I was wondering whether to tell you. I heard the same thing the other night down the pub.

What's that?

Bunch of geezers driving round, tooled up, looking for him. Blokes with teenage daughters, girls who recognised Stuart on the telly because he's approached them on the street. I wasn't sure if it was just pub talk, so I didn't wanna say anything.

Maybe this explains why Stuart has gone to ground. His phone number, widely advertised locally on business cards and flyers and promotional T-shirts, would be readily available to anyone who wanted to make a threatening call. Maybe he knows that violent men with weapons are looking for him.

The sun is low behind us and the sky a fiery red as we follow the A13 east towards Southend, to drop Andy off. We're halfway there when he suggests we spend the night at his place. There's a spare bedroom, and after all, how often do we get to see each other these days? We could get some fish and chips. *Sarfend, innit?* And there's a great boozer just a few minutes' walk from his place called Sunrooms, we'd love it.

We spend the evening drinking in Andy's favourite pub, a welcome respite from trying to find my brother. Who, I realise now, may be a fugitive.

And not for the first time.

*   *   *

When we get back to Celia's place the next day, the BBC evening news shows footage of Essex Police divers emerging from a manmade lake near her home.

They're looking for her body.

The news report also shows a small army of local volunteers combing the wild grassland nearby, walking shoulder to shoulder in a long ragged line, heads down, poking the ground with sticks or kicking at clumps of grass, hunting for any trace of the missing girl: an earring, a necklace, a hairband.

I vaguely recognise the area. These are the salt marshlands and mudflats that lie between Danielle's home village of East Tilbury and the tiny hamlet of Mucking, about a mile and a half north, bordered to the east by the Thames. I used to roam these fields as a child, sometimes with Stuart. This area was once known for its quarries, supplying the gravel, chalk and lime for London's post-war housing boom. In return, London sent its garbage, filling the gaping holes in the earth with trash, rendering the air thick with flies and the stench of decay.

A generation ago these fields and landfills were adventure playgrounds for me and my brother, our childhood stomping grounds. As kids we splashed and dived in those muddy waters.

On our way home we would pluck handfuls of fat gleaming blackberries from the spider-webbed thickets lining those stony footpaths. Today this area is known as Thurrock Thameside Nature Park, a designated environmental Site of Specific Scientific Interest, complete with Visitor Centre – a family destination with footpaths, bridleways and cycle routes to explore.

But in the summer of 2001, with Danielle Jones missing and her parents clinging to the last vestiges of hope, it is still a sprawl of brackish marshland and ancient woods – knotted with hedgerows and fringed with reed beds, pocked with trenches and ditches and manmade lakes. In other words, a labyrinthine sprawl of hiding places, a maze of potential crime scenes.

Although I'm aware that it is difficult terrain, I have no idea how much muddy ground will be paced and trampled, how many brambles and bushes will be hacked and slashed, how many pits and quarries will be plumbed, how many derelict barns and disused silos will be breached and scoured. This boggy marshland covers 650 acres, more than a square mile. Roughly the size of the City of London, this is ground zero in the search for the body of Danielle.

A search that will become the largest in British criminal history.

12

Tilbury, 1975

The most recent photograph I have of me and my brother is in an obsolete nonstandard format, 3¼ by 3½ inches, clearly taken on a cheap camera. But perhaps because it was printed on Fujicolor Crystal archive paper, it is still in decent condition. On the back, in biro: *August 1975*.

In this full-length shot taken outside our council house in Darwin Road, I am 18 and he is 17. I stand on the left, Stuart on the right. We both have flared jeans and I'm wearing a tan-coloured Stirling Cooper duster coat pulled back to reveal a navy bowling shirt, while Stuart has a black leather bomber jacket over a white shirt. We're smiling at the camera with our arms around each other's shoulders. At this point he's still the smaller, cuter one. I'm three inches taller, with a longer face and wider forehead. My hair is dyed matt black and blow-dried into a blocky quiff, a style that required me to kneel in front of the tumble dryer with a nylon brush for 15 minutes, since I could never quite get the same lift with my feeble hand-held hairdryer.

Stuart's hair, however, is naturally jet black and full of bounce and shine and curl, falling untutored in an elegant centre parting and flicking up and away from his boyish brow to reveal a cherubic smile. He points across his own torso at me, thumb up and index finger extended cartoonishly, as if to indicate that I am The Man.

Apart from the formal shots taken at his second wedding in 1996, I think it may be the last photo taken of us together, smiling and fraternal. I feel a mix of emotions whenever I take it out and ponder it, as I do from time to time. Our newly reconstituted family has just moved into a brand-new council house and we both have jobs that pay us enough to buy our own clothes. We look so happy, so hopeful – if not winners, at least survivors.

Almost half a century has passed since this carefree moment.

Looking at this photo now, I wonder who took it. Was it my girlfriend from that time, Cindy? Perhaps our mother? Whose idea was it, and why? Did we both just happen to be outside the house, or did we come out and pose the shot? What happened immediately afterwards? It looks as though we might be ready to go somewhere together, but that strikes me as unlikely.

For brothers, we never did fraternise that much.

*   *   *

By now my mother has found a boyfriend, a tall, mild-mannered man called Gerry Parker. A few months before the photo with my brother is taken, I'm getting ready for work when Gerry appears in the kitchen. I know he and my mother have been dating, but this is the first time I've known him to stay overnight. I try to mask my surprise, and he tries to hide his embarrassment. Realising I'm in a hurry because I'm running late, Gerry offers to give me a lift to work.

Technically, I'm an apprentice diesel fitter. In common parlance, I'm a grease monkey, my days spent in the pit beneath Scania, Volvo and ERF trucks with enormous diesel engines – Cummins, Gardner, Rolls-Royce or Perkins – changing oil and air filters, cleaning or replacing fuel injectors, checking tappets, lubricating axles and suspension racks with a grease gun. Soon

I learn how to handle the arc welding kit and start to make excellent overtime bonuses by coming in on Sundays to weld coupling plates, the so-called fifth wheels, onto new tractor units.

*   *   *

One Saturday night I'm out with my friend Mick Dyson and his brother-in-law, a guy with the unlikely name of Tony Moroni. After a few beers in the Stella Maris, a seaman's hostel and social club on Dock Road, we decide to head down the road to the Ship, which is cheaper and full of our mates. As we leave the Stella and step onto the pavement, three young couples are entering. I barely register them as they brush past, but behind me somebody snarls:

Watch where you're fucking going, you chinky cunt.

At first I wonder if someone is talking to me, but I look back to find Mick squaring up to one of the men, who apparently has bumped into him. For the first time I realise they are Asian, maybe Chinese. Their dates look like local girls. Tony pushes one of them and suddenly a lot of chests are being puffed up. Then it all kicks off, with Tony and Mick throwing punches and the other guys swinging back. At this point it doesn't really matter who started it, or that my friend Mick is a racist wanker – a fact I have frequently forced myself to overlook. I wade in to even up the numbers. There's a lot of silly punches thrown, few of which connect. It's a festival of teenage posturing, prancing back and forward in the middle of the road, fists up, shouting, *Come on, then! You want some? Come on!*

Out of nowhere, I get punched in the face and it hurts. Eyes shut, I throw one back and feel a jolt of pain as my knuckle connects with skull bone. The girls start squealing as the fight turns serious and blows begin to land. And then somebody jumps on my back and pulls my hair, jerking my head back violently. Instinctively, I throw a punch backwards over my shoulder and hear a loud thwack.

As if a switch has been flipped, everyone freezes and stands gawping at the guy behind me.

Only when I turn around, it's a girl.

Like everyone else, she is frozen and open-mouthed. A thin red line appears over her eye. A drop of blood oozes out, and rolls over her swollen eyelid. She looks up as the blood runs into her eye, then swoons and buckles at the knees, sinking to the floor.

Her friends rush towards her.

Fuck, says Mick Dyson.

Let's go, says Tony Moroni.

They start running. I follow.

A few blocks later, breathless in a dark alleyway, we hear the two-tone police siren wailing *nee-nah nee-nah* through the balmy night air.

Split up, says Dyson. Just go home.

I know my mother is already in bed as I creep up the stairs like a thief. I get undressed in the dark, open a window and smoke a cigarette. Then I get into bed, thankful to have made it home without getting caught.

Twenty minutes later there's a loud knock at the front door. I hear my mother go down and answer it. After a brief discussion, she calls me. I pull on my jeans and go downstairs to find two policemen standing in the living room, braced for action.

My mother says, What have you been up to?

I shrug and frown, *What?*

One of the policemen says, Were you at the Stella Maris tonight?

No, I've been in my room all night.

Don't lie, says my mother. I just heard you come in.

Well, says the copper, someone hit a girl outside the Stella about half an hour ago and you fit the description.

My mother snaps, You hit a girl?

No!

The copper says, What happened to your hand?

All four of us look down at my right hand. It is bruised and swollen, the skin torn around the middle knuckle.

And so, in the early hours of Sunday 13 July 1975, I am charged with two counts of Actual Bodily Harm.

At the station I ask the arresting officer what description I was supposed to fit.

He smiles and says, The girl said, I don't think he was, but he looked Chinese.

And you knew that was me?

He shrugs, like, *Who else?*

Up until now I've been working all the overtime I can get for almost a year, putting away £10 or £15 every week. Having recently married and had a baby, one of my older workmates – a diesel fitter nicknamed Maffy – is selling his bronze TVR 1600M, a ferociously powerful sports car with a lightweight fibre-glass body. The offside wing needs some work where he had a prang, but it still runs like a beast. He wants £1,000 – I have nearly £800 put away. But after consulting a solicitor, who advises me that my only chance of avoiding jail time is to seek a jury trial, I end up spending the lot on a QC to represent me when I appear in court a few weeks later.

My trial lasts less than an hour. First, the arresting officer describes being called to the scene, taking a description, arriving at my house, and noticing my scuffed knuckles. After the plaintiff is sworn in, the prosecution asks her to identify her attacker and she points to me. Under cross-examination, she describes the fight and explains to my QC that, yes, she had jumped on my back and pulled my hair. But that was only to stop me from hitting her friend.

My barrister asks, Do you think the defendant meant to hit you?

I don't know, she says, but he definitely hit me. That's how I got the cut above my eye.

My QC is halfway through his next question when the judge interrupts him and turns to the witness.

I need to clarify something, says the judge. Could you please repeat what you just said to counsel?

She repeats her words.

Please, says the judge, think carefully before answering. Are you saying that you are uncertain whether the defendant meant to hit you?

Well, she says, his back was turned to me, so I can't say for sure that he definitely meant to hit *me*. But he definitely meant to hit *someone*.

And with that, the judge, who is certainly not going to allow any mistrial or appeal to arise from this case, dictates my QC's job to him.

The charge of Actual Bodily Harm, the judge explains, requires *intention*. If the main witness cannot be certain that the blow was intentional, there is no case to answer.

My barrister puffs his cheeks, nods and humbly agrees. The judge says the first charge is dismissed. And since the second charge stems from the first, that too is dismissed.

Barely 50 minutes after entering the dock, I walk from the court an innocent man. I will never again spend time with Mick Dyson or his extended family. And although my defence has cost me all the money I had saved to buy Maffy's TVR, it's the best investment of my young life.

What I cannot know is that, long after this tawdry episode has faded from memory, I will recall this day as I read about Chelmsford Crown Court in the news.

My brother Stuart will appear in this very same courtroom 27 years later, charged with the abduction and murder of Danielle Jones.

13

Paris, Wednesday 11 July 2001
23 days since Danielle's disappearance

As the train pulls into Gare du Nord, I feel nauseous. While going home is normally a welcome retreat from horror and weirdness, it has started to feel almost cowardly, a flight from the real. In Paris, I live in a bubble. Nobody here has heard the nightmarish story of Danielle Jones and her disappearance, a story that makes national headlines in the UK almost every day. I still haven't told my friends in France about the maelstrom at the centre of my life, or the terrible revelations of the last four weeks.

Even my daughter in London still doesn't know what is happening in my life – and by extension, her own. Keeping this secret makes me feel as if I'm hiding my own guilt and shame, rather than my brother's. I try telling myself it's not my fault, but I'm unconvinced.

Then again, how would I begin to explain such a grotesque situation? How do I tell friends that my younger brother is the prime suspect in the abduction and murder of his 15-year-old niece? How do I explain to my 13-year-old daughter that her Uncle Stuart has almost certainly kidnapped and murdered a girl roughly her own age – and yes, I mean *that* Danielle, the *other* little girl at Stuart's wedding. How do I explain that police believe he groomed Danielle and entangled her in some kind of sexual relationship, and then killed her? How many friends should I tell? Should I ask them to refrain from telling their own friends, people I don't know? How much detail will they need, how many questions should I answer? Will they believe me when I say I knew nothing of Stuart's double life as a serial predator? Will they look at me sideways, wondering if I share his psychological traits? Will they now recall flippant remarks and wonder what I *really* meant? Will they reframe my artfully rakish persona as something far more sinister and quietly cut all ties with me?

For years I had refused to be judged by others, telling myself I didn't care what people thought of me, that I had my own yardstick for what was correct and acceptable. But the events of the last four weeks have called everything into question, especially who I think I am and where I'm going. At last, I'm worried about being judged. Even though I didn't commit this crime, I know it will radically alter how people see me and how I perceive myself, casting shadows over my past and future. I have been plunged back into things I'd thought forgotten, forced to confront a history I thought I'd escaped. There I was, living in Paris and hanging out with my new friends, the hip media figure who could fraternise with artists or criminals and feel at ease in either world, never needing to evaluate his moral standing. Now those assumptions have been overturned and my glib attitude seems increasingly out of tune. If the police are right, my brother – a serial predator, hiding in plain sight – has not only abducted and killed a teenage girl, but also disposed of her body in an unknown location.

Maybe I should wait to see what happens. After all, I tell myself, there is still a slim chance that he is innocent, still a sliver of hope that this nightmare will miraculously resolve itself, that Danielle might turn up safe and sound. But I'm also aware that

the longer I wait to explain what's happening, the more duplic-
itous I will appear when the news finally breaks, and thus the
more my behaviour will seem to resemble his.

And so I must confront yet another sickening irony: like
Stuart, I am now living a double life, guarding my own dirty
little secret.

*   *   *

Back in Paris I pick up where I left off, scouring British news
websites morning, noon and night. A couple of days later the
BBC reconstructs Danielle's last-known movements for its
Crimewatch show, in the hope of jogging memories and eliciting
tips from the public. Tony and Linda Jones also appear on the
programme, appealing for assistance. The show draws a huge
response, with hundreds of people calling into its phone lines
with leads and information. But two weeks later there is still no
trace of Danielle.

Towards the end of the month Celia arrives to spend a few
days with me. We visit art galleries and tourist attractions, and
try to pretend that life is something like normal. But still I get no
response whenever I call Stuart or Debbie – even though I know
they have both been in touch with my mother. I start to wonder
about Stuart's mental health. If by some chance he is innocent,
does he have the strength of mind to withstand the constant
pressure of being the prime suspect? If not, what will he do? Of
course, he is definitely avoiding me, but is he the type to abscond?
Will he become a fugitive, leave the country?

By way of distraction I turn to finalising the summer holiday
with my daughter that I've been planning for months. After
flying to Kuala Lumpur I will rent a car and we'll drive to a
cabin resort in the Malaysian rainforest. Then we'll head to the
east coast for a week on the beach.

Of course, Fiona has heard about Danielle's disappearance. By now there can hardly be anyone left in the UK who hasn't. The case is a national sensation, with constant updates in the press and on TV news. Whenever I speak on the phone with her mother – at this point, every couple of days – we agree it's almost miraculous that Fiona has not yet realised that the prime suspect is her Uncle Stuart. Jane has even overheard Fiona and her girlfriends discussing the case, but still our daughter hasn't joined the dots – almost certainly because Stuart and I have different surnames. Fiona has met Stuart twice, but only briefly. Once when she and Danielle went with Stuart and Debbie to have their matching bridesmaids' gowns fitted, and then a few weeks later at their wedding. But Fiona was only eight years old, so it's unlikely that she even registered Stuart's surname. And now, five years later, she doesn't seem to recognise him from the grainy photos in the news.

It feels almost callous to be flying halfway around the world while my brother is on bail, suspected of an atrocious crime. But with Stuart refusing to answer or return my calls, and proving mysteriously elusive when I'd driven to Essex to confront him in person, there is not much more I can do to help the police investigation. Besides, Fiona has been looking forward to this holiday for weeks, and cancelling now will only confuse her, or even arouse her suspicions.

I call her mother to ask, You don't think we should cancel?

No, says Jane, I think it would be good to take her away for a couple of weeks while all this is going on. Have you spoken to your brother yet?

He's still not returning my calls.

That's strange, isn't it?

Maybe not. Maybe he knows I've been talking to the police. They want me to go and speak to him, see what I think.

Do you believe he's guilty?

Looks that way to me, but I'm not sure. That's why the police want me to talk to him, observe him, see if he's acting guilty.

Do you really think you'd be able to tell?

Oh, I'll know the second I look him in the eye. He can't hide something like that from me.

*   *   *

A couple of days later I'm getting ready to run some errands when the phone rings.

Heard you were looking for me, he says.

Where have you been? I've been trying to get hold of you for weeks.

Yeah, he says. Sorry about that. The police had my mobile for a while and then we had to stop answering the home phone. Too many reporters calling, all hours, day and night. It was really upsetting Deb, so in the end I unplugged it.

Fucking journalists, I say.

Hanging's too good for 'em. Anyway, what can I do you for?

Nothing, I say. Just wondered how you were getting on.

Yeah, okay. All things considered, you know.

Well, I'll be coming back to England for a few days at the end of the month before going on holiday with Fiona. Be good to see you?

Oh yeah, where you going?

Malaysia, we're going to visit the rainforest.

Oh, very nice. Can't take me with you, can you?

Uh?

Smuggle me in one of your suitcases?

Oh, right.

Nah, just it'd be nice to get a break from all this stuff. Doin' me head in.

Right, I say. Yeah, must be quite stressful.

Oh, mate. It's been a madhouse around here. But it's Debbie I feel sorry for.

Yeah, how is she?

Yeah, it's a real worry, what with her expecting the baby any minute now.

Of course, I say. Anyway, I was thinking of coming down and paying you a visit. It'd be great to see you before we fly out – you know, catch up. There seems to be a lot of confusion going around, people saying all this stuff about you. I'd just really like to get your side of it.

Yeah, not much to tell, really.

Well, it'd be good to see you anyway. You know, been a while.

Yeah, alright then. Not sure that Deb will be up for it. She's pretty shook up right now.

Oh, I understand. Just you and me, then.

Yeah, alright.

We agree to meet me at his house the following Thursday.

Rayleigh, Thursday 2 August 2001
45 days since Danielle's disappearance

When I leave home at 8 a.m. this morning, the latest UK news has not yet appeared online.

So I have no idea that while I'm sitting on the Eurostar to London, bracing myself to confront my brother, Danielle's parents are holding a press conference at Rayleigh police station.

Asked by a reporter about her state of mind, Linda Jones fights back tears as she addresses the assembled media.

I really do not think she can be alive anymore, she says. We would have heard from her. We have to have that little bit of hope – but I don't really think she's alive anymore.

Husband Tony tells the press he has cancelled their planned family holiday on the Greek island of Zante, due to start the following Monday.

By the time they are wrapping up, I'm riding the tube to Jane's place, where I will stay for the next few days before leaving with Fiona for Malaysia.

Later that afternoon, I will take the train to Grays and meet up with DS Keith Davies, before going to visit Stuart.

By the time we say goodbye a couple of hours later, I know that my brother is guilty.

Grays, Monday 6 August 2001
49 days since Danielle's disappearance

The following Monday, on the day they had originally planned to fly to Greece for their family holiday, Tony and Linda Jones join police officers to distribute 1,500 leaflets to the public in and around the Grays area.

Danielle has now been missing for exactly seven weeks.

Stuart is still out on bail. He does not join in the effort to distribute leaflets about his missing niece, the teenage girl he would pick up from school in his blue Transit van.

The girl he would address in text messages as *Sexy Legs*.

Malaysia, Wednesday 8 August 2001
51 days since Danielle's disappearance

I fly out with Fiona from Heathrow. Within 48 hours we are staying in a wooden bungalow deep inside Taman Negara, Malaysia's largest national park and one of the world's oldest tropical rainforests. We have no newspapers, television, radio or internet. Planning this trip three months earlier, I had no idea how thankful I'd be to find myself totally cut off from the outside world, unable to follow the case even if I wanted to. A few days later we drive to the coast and check into a beach resort. Despite feigning nonchalance I remain constantly alert, eavesdropping on the people around us, careful to avoid any English tourists. I make a point of scanning loungers and tables for discarded British newspapers, snatching them up and disposing of them before Fiona might find them.

Two weeks later we return to Kuala Lumpur. Finally I can leave my sleeping daughter in our suite and sneak down to our hotel's business centre and get online, where I find the following report in the *Telegraph*:

Saturday 18 August 2001, *Daily Telegraph*

Missing Danielle's Uncle Re-Arrested

The uncle of missing schoolgirl Danielle Jones was arrested yesterday on suspicion of her murder and was being interrogated by detectives last night.

Stuart Campbell, a 43-year-old builder, who had been questioned previously over the disappearance of the 15-year-old, was arrested at his breakfast table at 7:15 am. He was driven 30 miles to Harlow police station where he arrived with his head covered by a blanket.

Police deliberately chose a location some distance from where Danielle vanished to minimise the risk of protest from local people. As Essex police questioned him throughout the day, a force spokesman said: 'It is very unusual to hold a man on suspicion of murder when a body has not been found. We fear the worst.'

Campbell is married to the sister of Danielle's father, Tony. A police liaison officer was keeping Mr Jones, 40, and wife Linda, 41, informed of developments at their home in East Tilbury, Essex. They were reported to be 'very upset', and their distress was made worse by the fact that a member of their own family was being questioned over their daughter's disappearance.

Mrs Jones has said she fears that her daughter is dead.

Campbell, who has protested his innocence, was first arrested on suspicion of her abduction five days after she vanished and was released on police bail.

Police said they expected to continue questioning Campbell, whom they did not name, and were prepared to hold him for up to 96 hours without charge.

Inspector Alan Cook of Essex Police said: 'This has been a very difficult investigation. We are eight or nine weeks into the investigation and we fear for the worst. We have not found Danielle or any of her belongings and we must continue the search.'

Of course, I say nothing about this to Fiona, who is still sleeping when I return to our room.

For a long time I just sit and watch her, until finally switching out the light.

*   *   *

After breakfast I make some excuse about a forgotten credit card and leave Fiona in the room while I go back down to the business centre and trawl news websites for the latest updates.

There's a report that a woman has come forward claiming to have seen a girl matching Danielle's description at approximately 10 a.m., barely two hours after she disappeared. According to the witness the girl was sitting in the passenger seat of a dark blue Transit-type van driven by a white man in his late 30s, with a strong build and neat, short dark hair. The van was headed away from Grays towards Lakeside shopping centre.

The same Lakeside shopping centre where Stuart had taken me just a couple of weeks ago. Had we driven past the site where he disposed of Danielle's body?

Had he used me as unwitting cover to check the crime scene?

I'm still struggling with this idea when I come across a heartbreaking piece by Tracy McVeigh in the previous weekend's *Observer*, headlined *Village Haunted by Missing Danielle*.

According to McVeigh, East Tilbury has been traumatised by Danielle's disappearance. While neighbours and locals have rallied round the family, distributing leaflets and posters and joining police on fingertip searches, there's a mounting sense of unease that a dangerous killer could be roaming the area.

With the investigation entering its third month and police making little headway in finding Danielle or identifying her abductor, villagers are increasingly concerned for the safety of their own children. This has just literally ripped this village apart, says one local woman.

Fear hangs over the place. School children are being walked to and from bus stops.

Without actually naming him, the report points directly towards Stuart Campbell, and then quotes Inspector Alan Cook, who describes the investigation as frustrating and very strange.

It's like you have a 5,000-piece jigsaw, he says, and we do not even have half of the puzzle. We are seriously lacking that golden nugget which will take us forward.

Finally, the report notes that Tony Jones can no longer face going to work at his dry-cleaning business.

He has taped a handwritten sign on the door: *Sorry, I have had to close.*

London, Wednesday 22 August 2001
65 days since Danielle's disappearance

Fiona and I arrive at Heathrow at 4.10 p.m.

After dropping her at home I go to Celia's place. Using her iMac, I get online and read that, after seeing his photograph in the news media a number of women have recently come forward, and based on their statements and items seized during the search of his house, police have now charged Stuart with several new offences, some of them historic.

Investigators now believe that he has molested or attacked at least 30 victims over a 20-year period. He is charged with seven offences unrelated to Danielle Jones, including taking indecent photographs of children, the assault and unlawful imprisonment of an underage girl, and the indecent assault of two other girls. He is also charged with illegal possession of 916mg of amphetamine and 92 tablets of Pemoline, another stimulant drug.

Celia listens patiently while I list the evidence and charges. I tell her that I'm furious, that I want to confront Stuart and tell him enough's enough, he has to tell that poor girl's parents what he did with her body.

We've got to put an end to this, I say. If he were here right now, I would beat the fucking truth out of him, or kill him trying.

The next morning I call DS Keith Davies and leave a message on his answering machine. I tell him how angry I am and ask him to call and arrange for me to see Stuart in a prison cell, so I can confront him.

Later that day and the next, I call Stuart again, to see if I can straighten out this twisted story. Once again, my calls go straight to the answering machine.

Once again, Stuart doesn't call back.

The following morning Celia flies out to Orlando for a family holiday with her sister and brother-in-law and their two young daughters. They will take the kids to visit Disneyland and the Epcot Center. She gives me her hotel number and says I can always call her if I need to talk.

Paris, Thursday 30 August 2001
73 days since Danielle's disappearance

This morning I phone my mother to ask if she has heard from Stuart since we last talked. But the instant she picks up she tells me, Wait, there's someone at the door.

On the line I hear two men greeting her in a familiar tone: Hello, Molly.

Since her phone is in the hallway right by the front door, their voices are shockingly clear as they identify themselves as detectives. I can tell from her tone that she's too nervous to tell them I'm listening in.

They've come to discuss my brother's latest bail application. They explain that Stuart's new bail conditions, stemming from the latest wave of charges, mean that he can no longer remain in Essex, which would leave him close to – and able to interfere with – witnesses and potential crime scenes. So he has given our mother's address as his residence while on bail.

By the way, says one of them, you're a grandmother again. Did you know? Yeah, Debbie had a baby boy at seven o'clock this morning.

I hear the other one saying that he doesn't think it's a good idea for Stuart to come and stay with her:

The press will get the address, he says, and they'll come knocking.

And there's a real risk, says the other, of someone trying to attack him.

Even though this is a blatant attempt to influence, even frighten her, I know it's also true. Both my cousin Eric and my friend Andy have told me there are some *real nutters* out there determined to hurt Stuart, people related to some of the women now accusing him of sexual assault.

My mother tells the detectives, Excuse me a moment, I just want to finish this call.

When my mother gets back on the phone, she is close to tears and asks me what she should do.

Mum, you should do whatever you think is right. Whatever you choose to do, I'll back you either way.

I want to let him stay here with me, for Debbie's sake.

Well, I think you should think about yourself first.

I'm torn between warning her to stay clear of her son, and telling her to follow her heart. As a mother, she wants to help him. And of course Debbie will also want him out on bail, so he can see his newborn baby. Perhaps Debbie still believes he is innocent, despite all the evidence seeming to point to his guilt.

Then I hear my mother explaining to the police that she has to go now, because her oldest son is holding on the line, calling from Paris.

Oh, that's him on the phone right now?

Yes.

Would that be Alix?

Yes, that's right.

The detective asks if he can speak to me and she passes him the phone.

Hello, Alix? This is DS Andy Harvey. I understand from my colleague DS Keith Davies that you've spoken to Stuart recently?

Yes, that's right.

And Keith says that you believe he is guilty?

I know it. He was lying to me.

Well then, I'm sure you can understand why we don't want Stuart staying here, because as we explained to your mum …

Yeah, I heard you. And I agree with you. But I want my mother to make her own decision.

I can hear the other officer in the background, explaining the most recent charges, which I can tell Mum hasn't fully absorbed yet.

I hear her asking, *What other young women?*

Then DS Harvey explains to me how he sat in on last week's interrogation and is now certain beyond any doubt that Stuart is guilty:

If Stuart was innocent, he says, surely he'd say something more than just, *No comment.* That's all he said, *No comment.* He must have said it 40 or 50 times. If that was me, if I'd been wrongly accused, I'd be going up the wall.

That's exactly what I've been saying. He doesn't strike me as an innocent man who's been wrongly accused. Quite the opposite, in fact.

I tell DS Harvey about the weird conversation we'd had in his van, and how Stuart had told me the police were playing mind games. And how, when I asked why he thought that, he'd told me the police were trying to break him down.

So I said to him, But if you're telling the truth, what's to break down?

Precisely, says DS Harvey.

I feel torn, I say, because yes, he's my brother – but I'm absolutely sure he's guilty. He has been lying to me, impersonating a reasonable sort of bloke. That's what he's been doing all these years, and I've finally tumbled him, the bastard.

Tumbled.

As the word leaves my mouth I notice how odd it sounds, and then I realise why. It was one of the Old Man's favourite terms.

Jesus, I think. *What a time for him to show up.*

DS Harvey says my mother wants to speak to me again and puts her back on.

She's crying.

She says, If I don't let him stay here, where else can he stay?

He's a big boy, Mum. He'll find somewhere to stay.

Can't he stay with you for a while?

Mum, I live in France. I'm pretty sure he can't leave the country while he's on bail.

No, I suppose you're right.

Of course, what I want to tell her is, No, he can't stay with me, I don't want him anywhere near me right now.

Instead I say, Don't worry, Mum. It will all be okay.

Through her tears, she says, Be nice to Debbie, won't you?

Yes, I say, I'll be nice to Debbie. But I'm going to tell her I don't want him staying with you.

Of course, I know that I'll do nothing of the sort. Debbie has just given birth, so I wouldn't want to upset her. And she clearly isn't interested in my opinion anyway. In the three months since Danielle disappeared, Debbie has yet to answer or return a single one of my dozen or so calls. I've even tried calling her mother, asking her to get Debbie to call me.

Response? Nothing.

I still have a handwritten note from the time:

The conversation with Debbie's mum was a weird one. She said she didn't want to talk on the telephone. They're all clearly worried that I'm going to write something about all this. They're very paranoid about it all. And perhaps rightly so.

Well, says my mother, maybe you can avoid talking about that, let Debbie make up her own mind.

Mum, I can't even get Debbie on the phone, let alone have a conversation with her.

The problem, she says, is that you're a journalist. Debbie and her parents are scared that you want to write about it for a newspaper.

Oh, so my suspicions were correct.

Mum, I say, why would I want to write about it for a newspaper? I'm trying to keep a low profile so Fiona doesn't learn that her uncle is suspected of murdering his niece. Seriously, are they totally stupid, these people?

They just want to stay out of the papers. I think that's why they've gone down to Hastings, to get away from the reporters.

Why Hastings?

Oh, Debbie said her parents have got a place down there. Is it Hastings? I forget. Somewhere like that.

Ah, she just let the cat out of the bag.

Later that day I call Debbie, expecting to leave yet another politely restrained message on her machine. To my surprise, she answers:

Oh hi, Debbie. Congratulations! I heard this morning that you'd had the baby.

Thanks, she says. How did you know?

My mum told me.

Oh, I wonder how she knew?

Um, I say, apparently the police told her.

The police told her? I wonder why they wanted to tell her …

I can feel her paranoia bristling down the line. Has Stuart told her that I can't be trusted? There's a long pause while I wait for her to talk. She doesn't ask any questions about my life, what I've been doing, how I might be dealing with this bizarre situation we've both been thrust into. I wonder, not for the first time, how much longer I can bite my lip.

Anyway, I say, just wanted to make sure you were okay.

Yeah, I'm fine.

And the baby's doing well?

Yeah. Ahh, he's lovely.

And you, how are you holding up?

Yeah, I was just going to have a lie-down, as it happens.

Okay, I won't keep you.

Yeah, I just didn't want it getting in the press tomorrow morning.

Oh, yeah. Right.

Christ. This is what she's worried about?

Her 15-year-old niece is missing, her brother's daughter,

*presumed dead, murdered by her husband – and all she can say
is that she doesn't want her name in the papers?*

So, do you know what you're going to call him?

I think probably Simon. Yeah, Simon Joshua.

Nice.

Well, I better go. I need to lie down.

Alright, well, congratulations again.

Thanks, she says. And maybe see you one of these days.

Yeah, I hope so.

Bye.

Bye.

Maybe see you one of these days?

Is she thinking about the trial?

14

Tilbury, 1975–77

My appearance at Chelmsford Crown Court in August 1975 marks a shift in attitude. Looking back at that whole experience – the fight and subsequent trial, and my narrow escape from the teeth of the British criminal justice system – I realise how close I'd come to wrecking my life before it had really begun.

And so I start looking around for a way out of Tilbury. I befriend a married couple called Pete and Viv, young teachers who also work part-time at the local youth club. They treat me like a smart and funny kid, as opposed to a beery yob. So instead of running around Tilbury drinking all night and getting into fistfights outside the chip shop, I spend evenings at their flat while they cook pasta and make salads, and then we sit around listening to records and talking about books and art, and drinking wine and even smoking the odd joint. I show them my drawings and we discuss rock music and street fashion. Although barely five years older than me, they both seem incredibly sophisticated. They have studied literature at university, and can quote poets and philosophers. Aside from the Old Man, Pete is the only person I have ever met who has been to New York. Eventually they tell me that I should stop wasting my life and go to art school. Vivien gives me a Thames & Hudson book by Eric Newton called *The Arts of Man*, my first step on a fumbling path towards an understanding of art history.

On their advice I start making drawings for a portfolio, apply to an East London technical college, and gain a place on its Foundation in Art and Design course, the one-year primer course required before starting any degree course in art.

Meanwhile in late 1975, outside a local secondary school, Stuart has honed in on a short, dark-eyed 15-year old schoolgirl called Jennifer Freeman. By the time of their wedding in June 1976, Stuart is 18 and Jennifer has just celebrated her 16th birthday.

She is already six months pregnant.

Sensing my scorn, Stuart asks my mother's boyfriend Gerry to be his Best Man. I'm happy to be overlooked for this honour. Though I don't say it outright, my entire family knows that this wedding seems absurd to me, conceived in desperate haste and doomed to collapse.

Still, I dutifully dress up for the ceremony at Grays Registry Office, and raise a toast at the reception, a few hundred yards down the road, in a small function room above a pub called the Railway Inn. My mother and Gerry meet most of the cost, and do their best to instil the ceremony with some sense of decorum. But sitting at the head of the table next to her cocky young husband, hands resting on the prominent bulge under her bridal gown, Jennifer looks exactly what she is: a small, frightened and embarrassed child.

Their daughter, christened Jennie-Lee, will be born in August.

I don't attend the christening, because by this time my world had been turned upside down by yet another book from Pete and Viv's library, a battered paperback copy of Kerouac's *On the Road*. Shortly after the wedding I strike out to hitch hike through France and Spain, with an idea that I might even make it to Morocco before returning to start my art school studies.

Meanwhile in Tilbury, things start out reasonably enough.

My mother and Gerry help the young couple furnish their tiny terraced house in Grays, granted by the local council in record time thanks to the imminent arrival of their child. But shortly after they move into their two-up two-down on London Road, Stuart is made redundant from his factory job. He quickly finds another – as a sales assistant on the floor of an electronics store in Grays High Street called Rumbelows – but the pay is lousy and there is no overtime, not like the factory job, where he'd worked all the hours God sent. Now he is barely making enough to cover the rent and feed his family.

And it's not like he's wasting money on himself. Stuart doesn't drink, gamble or do drugs. He's not a druggie like his big brother.

Everyone knows that.

But with things so tight, he gives in to temptation. A couple of serious criminals approach him and convince him to pass on the addresses and phone numbers of Rumbelows customers who've recently purchased expensive TVs and stereos. A few weeks later Stuart will call those customers from the store, just to make sure their new goods are working properly. Of course, this means he can easily ascertain when these customers will be at home to answer the phone, and when they'll be out. He passes on this information, and the gang breaks in to steal the new electronic equipment, plus any cash or jewellery, and later sells the stolen goods.

And of course, Stuart gets a cut.

He was struggling to pay for nappies and baby food. He was desperate.

What would any father do? That's right, whatever it took.

Can you really blame him?

That was the story I heard, anyway.

My mother explains that Stuart will plead *Not Guilty* in the hope of working out a deal, maybe appearing as a prosecution witness against the gang in return for probation. True, he'd already had a few scrapes with the law as a kid, but he doesn't have a proper criminal record, so there's little chance of a substantial prison sentence. Probably a suspended sentence, maybe two months inside if the judge gets out of bed the wrong side. Nothing too serious, that's what we're told.

As the case trundles towards trial my mother and Gerry help out with Stuart's rent, because of course Stuart is now unemployed again, leaving him and Jennifer and the baby living on a weekly pittance from Social Security. As an art student on a county grant of £10 a week, I have nothing to chip in. Not that Stuart would take my money even if I had some to offer. He knows I have always disapproved of his marriage.

Who knows, I think, maybe this could be a good thing? Maybe he'll get probation and straighten himself out, find a better path.

Maybe raise his sights a little.

While Stuart is awaiting his trial date, I'm finishing my one-year foundation course and starting to apply for BA courses. But having squandered much of the academic year on sheer hedonism, making only sporadic efforts to complete assignments, my portfolio is thin to the point of anorexia. Consequently, I fail to bluff my way into a Bachelor's degree.

Instead I trigger Plan B, and swiftly re-enrol at my technical college for its Diploma in Art and Design, a three-year vocational course specialising in graphic design. And then, in the first week of September, just as I'm getting ready to resume college, I wake up in my Whitechapel squat to find a letter on the doormat.

It's from Stuart.

The return address is B Wing, Her Majesty's Prison, Aylesbury. *He's in prison.*

Wait, did my mother tell me about his trial? She must have. She always tries her best to keep us all in touch with each other, to maintain what's left of our familial bonds. Maybe she told me but I simply forgot? I can't remember. Come to think of it, I can't even recall what he'd been charged with.

Handling stolen goods, something like that? Conspiracy to break and enter?

Meanwhile, not only has he been tried and convicted, he's already locked up.

And I have no idea for how long.

Even more confusing, I'm not even sure who he thinks he is writing to.

His letter opens, *Hiya Al.*

I think to myself, *Who the fuck is Al?* Nobody calls me Al, not anymore.

Even as a child I'd never liked kids calling me Al, especially not with that estuary accent that made it sound more like *Owl.* Worse, it was the name that our mother had called our father, at least in their exquisitely rare moments of domestic calm.

Al was the Old Man's name, not mine.

I'd long since chosen a much better name, inspired by Muhammad Ali. Realising I could absorb his name into my own, I'd started spelling my name Alix in the early 1970s. One day in summer 1975 I took my birth certificate to an old-school ink shop on Dock Road, its walls plastered with sketches of swallows and anchors and hearts and topless hula girls, and paid a tattooist named Harry Potter £2.50 to tattoo ALIX on my left shoulder, beneath an Ace of Hearts.

Classy, all my mates agreed.

And so by the time I receive Stuart's first prison letter, there is practically nobody else in the world who still calls me *Al.*

I remember thinking it was a ploy, an appeal to our lost

childhood. A hint of flattery, but also a way of bringing me down to earth, reminding me not to get above my station.

The tone of his letter is cocky and unrepentant, although there are hints of vulnerability. He tells me that it's okay that I haven't written yet, *because I know not too many people know where I am. In fact, not too many people have noticed I've gone.* He says he'll send a Visiting Order as soon as he can, and even though he has addressed the letter to my Whitechapel squat, he hopes we're all keeping well down in *Tilbury on the mud.* The breezy tone, the awkward humour, it's a clear attempt to put a brave face on a miserable lot.

The saddest lines concern his baby daughter: *Jennie-Lee had her first birthday on Saturday 26th August (last Saturday). I was sick as a dog because I could not be home with her.* But he moves on swiftly to his imminent appeal, asking that I wish him luck, before signing off:

Love,
Stu (The Man) xxx

I learn from my mother that he's in prison for four years.
Four years.

For trying to put food in his kid's mouth. It seems so unfair. Still, he has the appeal coming up, so he could well get his sentence reduced. And anyway, there's no way he'll do the full four years. Time off for good behaviour and a bit of luck, he'll serve about half, isn't that how it works? I think so.

Yeah, just over two years, as long as he keeps his nose clean. Be out in no time.

Can he do that?

Maybe not. If someone tries to bully him, I know he'll fight back.

*   *   *

And so I do the right thing, writing back in an effort to keep his spirits up. I tell him about my band and how we've written some songs and we're going to book some time in a recording studio and make a demo, which we'll hawk around the record companies in search of a record contract. That's the El Dorado, the record contract – that's all I want. That's why I decided to go to art school in the first place, so I'd meet arty chancers just like me, kids who like music and fashion and want to be famous. Pete and Viv had assured me that was where I'd find them.

I write and tell Stuart funny stories about my life. Like how six months earlier I'd been in bed with Cindy drinking red wine when we rolled over and I fell out and landed on a wine glass, getting splinters of broken glass stuck in my right thigh, just above the knee. And how it had healed up just fine until the other day, while I was pulling on my underwear and felt a jolt of pain as the briefs snagged on my knee. How I'd looked down to find a half-inch shard of curved glass poking out beside the original scar like a sardonic memento.

I take the train from Marylebone to Aylesbury – sometimes alone, sometimes with Cindy – and catch a bus to the prison. A few weeks later he writes again, thanking me for coming.

This time he calls me Alix.

Sorry to hear that you woke to find a piece of glass protruding from your leg, he says, before telling me he's hoping our mother will bring his daughter Jennie-Lee on her next visit.

I think to myself, *protruding?* My brother's too smart to be in prison.

He asks me to get him a radio, *because when I'm locked up, all I can do is sing to myself because I'm not much good at making conversation to myself ... Well, what I'm trying to say is that it's driving me barmy.*

He assures me he'll include another VO with this letter, and signs off with the news that he will take his English O-level that morning.

While I know what he did is wrong, it strikes me as a terrible injustice, this story of a young father locked up for trying to provide for his wife and child.

My kid brother, still a teenager, is being persecuted for trying to be a good parent. Separated from his wife and baby. They could have given him probation, even a suspended sentence. Twelve months inside would have been harsh.

But no, they gave him *four years*.

*　　*　　*

When Stuart next writes to me, in late October 1977, his tone has changed again. My mother has written to tell him that his wife Jennifer has moved out of their house and into a new council flat. By now I know that Jennifer is seeing another local guy, although my mother has sworn me to secrecy. We don't dare tell Stuart, she says, in case the pain causes him to do something reckless.

And so we play dumb, even though I suspect he knows we're hiding the truth.

Anyway, he writes, *Mum is going to come up and see me and bring up my daughter. I haven't seen her for four months and I'm scared stiff now because when I see her she probably won't know me. She never did like being picked up by strangers so I only hope she doesn't cry when I pick her up because I don't think I could take that.*

He wishes his wife would visit him, but accepts there is virtually no chance of that.

After all, he says, Jennifer hadn't even informed him that she was moving house, which is why he stays up half the night depressed and worrying. But then he moves on to what he calls *brighter things*. Over the last few weeks he has taken up weight-lifting and started competing in local amateur competitions, winning several certificates.

He also says that he will take his English O-level exam on the 14th of the month, which I can only assume means that it was cancelled a few weeks earlier, when he'd first mentioned it. And then there's the catering course he just signed up for, and which he hopes could lead to a career as a chef. Given how deeply Stuart still hates the Old Man, the idea that he might follow in his father's footsteps bewilders me.

Still, I tell myself, any trade is a good trade.

Finally, he asks again, *Did you manage to get a cheap radio? I hope so cause I'm cracking up now I'm in a room on my own. Especially when there's nothing to draw or paint. It seems that weight training is fast becoming my life.*

After saying that his appeal should be coming up soon, he signs off.

HMP Aylesbury, November 1977

Why am I doing this? I know it's criminal. I know it's dangerous. I know it could fuck up my life. But I have to do it.

Why?

To prove that I'm fearless, that I'm the *big* brother. To show how much I value our bond. To make it clear that Jack the Lad brothers like us, we don't give a fuck about your rules. Because he needs to get messed up and because he'd do the same for me if we swapped places. Because I don't know what I'm doing with my life, so I might as well do something reckless that gives me a thrill and makes me feel alive.

Something I can boast about later to my art school mates.

By now I'm a crank connoisseur. As a street drug, amphetamine usually comes as a white powder, although it can be pink, blue or grey. Pink and white speed are generally the best, followed by the pale bluish kind. The grey shit is horrible dirty gear. And since any powder is always cut several times – glucose or powdered milk or baby laxative if you're lucky, crushed aspirin or warfarin if you're not – it's a risky business unless you know the dealer.

I don't have a source for powder. But I do have a regular supplier of amphetamine tablets called blues. Carl deals out of his Victorian tenement squat right across the courtyard from my own. Like me, he has tepid dreams of rock stardom and critical acclaim. Like me, he listens to arty punk bands and spends his days reading Genet and Sade and Pynchon and Burroughs. Like me, he writes pretentious lyrics for primitive rock songs. Despite or because of our similarities, we snipe behind each other's backs, the narcissism of small differences.

Carl's price varies depending on availability, but they're usually two for a pound, or twelve for a fiver. Thirty for a tenner. Which is what I buy every fortnight, thirty pills. In other words, I'm taking Stuart a third of my weekly stash. So I wrap five pills in a scrap of Kleenex and tuck them into the waistband of my boxers, gambling the guards won't detect it when they pat me down on the way in. I decide to consciously forget that I have drugs on me, reasoning that if I don't even know I'm carrying then I won't feel any fear, and won't emit the paranoid energy that might trigger a strip search.

My magical thinking does the trick and I make my way into the echoing Visiting Room with the heavily made-up girlfriends and wives, the anxious and resentful mothers. We sit waiting as the prisoners enter one by one to join loved ones at metal tables, chairs screeching on the vinyl floor, while the solitary guard in a white shirt and clip-on tie leans against the wall, scanning the room for inordinate touching or the passing of contraband.

When I visit Stuart in prison, what exactly are we doing? Looking back, I can't recall any shame. Indeed, we are proud of ourselves. We are defiant. Our mood is one of celebration. But what are we celebrating? The sheer fact of survival? A brotherly bond? Our scorn for authority? The dumb beauty and prowess of youth?

It's all of those things but something else as well, something I can never quite define. He's celebrating something he hides from me, and I'm celebrating something I can't explain to him. Best I can tell, we're celebrating reciprocal cool. We feed off each other, creating more than the sum of our parts. Even though we don't need to spend time together – after a while, we *can't stand* to be together – we still talk *about* each other, reflect each other and admire our own reflections in each other. I'm the arty punky one, he's the baby-faced rogue. Thanks to me, he has an aura of funky bohemian. Thanks to him, I have a whiff of seductive danger. Each of us the other's buzzing and flickering neon halo: it's our tacit agreement.

Stuart enters like a young god in convict garb – a baggy shirt with fine blue stripes, black trousers and elasticated plimsolls, no laces. He swaggers across the room with the rolling gait of the undefeated, chin up, head back, hovering over his surroundings, aloof and smug and untouchable. Is this a front for me? If so, it works. I feel a shiver of pride.

That's my brother. He takes no shit from anyone. And nor do I.

His chair screeches and we greet each other in our clipped, customary way.

Alright, Al?

Not bad. You alright, Stu?

So he's calling me Al again, and I'm calling him Stu. *What is this thing where we truncate each other's names into little more than a grunt?* As if anything more generous might be construed as sentimentality – and therefore weakness.

Yeah, he says. Can't complain. Place is a shit hole, screws are a bunch of back and fronts, but yeah, okay.

It's hard to hold eye contact. Every few seconds, he glances around or looks back over his shoulder. Not at anything particular, I realise, more a conditioned reflex.

You put on some weight.

Bit of muscle, yeah.

Weightlifting?

Nothing else to do in here.

Guess what? Got you that thing we talked about.

He looks around slowly, then back at me, a gleam in his eye that shows he understands.

You got it here?

Yeah, I say. When you're ready, under the table.

Yeah, no rush, he says oh-so-casually, glancing back at the screw, who has turned away from us and is carefully watching a couple at the back of the room. Kissing is banned to prevent mouth-to-mouth transfer of plastic-wrapped drugs, which an inmate could then swallow and retrieve later from the toilet bowl. But holding hands, intertwining fingers, stroking forearms, that's allowed – the guard's only job to ensure nothing gets palmed from visitor to inmate during all the fussy touching and stroking. And since there's no physical contact between me and Stuart, we're not on his radar.

We have all the time in the world.

Nonchalantly as possible, I slide my fingers into my waistband, edging the small package into my fist. Still talking casually, we both lean in. Left arm resting on the table, I slide my right hand beneath it, the speed pegged between index and middle finger.

Okay?

Stuart glances back over his shoulder. The screw is still turned away.

Eyes locked on mine, almost imperceptibly he extends his left arm under the table.

I'm trembling, and not just because I have smuggled illegal drugs into a prison and am now passing them to an inmate, two serious crimes. But also because I'm speeding out of my box. In fact, I've been speeding for several days, and I'm still wired from this morning's coffee.

Beneath the table, my hand is shaking.

It's only now that we realise we're fumbling around blind, trying to judge from posture where to find each other's hands. Can we even reach each other beneath this table? Are we sitting too far away?

I feel a tug on the tissue paper.

Got it?

Uh huh.

I'm about to let go when Stuart grunts in exasperation. I feel the tissue tear and the bundle come loose. We stare at each other, wide-eyed and frozen, as the pills *clack clack clack* on the vinyl floor and go skittering around, the hard-edged sound cutting clean through the ambient chatter and murmur and burbling of babies.

Fuck.

The screw *must* have heard it.

But no. We glance sideways and he's still watching some crop-headed ginger bloke who's furiously kissing the back of his girlfriend's hand.

None of the cons or visitors have noticed, either.

We continue to stare into each other's eyes, vibrating now with barely contained hysteria, lips pursed to suppress any give-away burst of laughter.

A few more seconds and we look down to locate the goods. With the edges of our footwear we slowly scrape the pills back under our table. I knock my cigarette pack to the floor, scooping up three pills as I retrieve it.

The guard? He has clearly decided we're not worth his time.

Stuart nudges the last two pills towards me with the toe of his plimsoll.

As long as you don't bend down too quick, he says, it'll be fine.

After several agonising minutes, I have recovered all the pills and somehow rewrapped them in the tattered scrap of Kleenex. This time, I go for gold, placing my hand on the table, palm down.

Ready?

He gives the tiniest nod. Eye on the guard, I choose the moment.

Go.

As I pull my hand back he reaches forward, and in one smooth motion palms the speed into his waistband.

We smile, exhale. Mission accomplished.

Will they search you on the way out?

Oh yeah, he says, always. But it's just a rub-down for weapons. I'll tuck this under my balls before then.

As I walk back across the courtyard with the wives and girl-friends and mothers, I can't help smiling. Now I have the answer to my question.

Committing serious crimes in prison and walking out a free man?

That's a hell of a drug, right there.

Whitechapel, 1978

Stuart writes a brief note from HMP Aylesbury B Wing thanking me for my recent letter and including yet another VO, dated 13 February and valid for 28 days. After wishing me luck in my pursuit of a record deal, he turns to what is fast becoming his sole interest.

I've been making a few records myself, he says, *but of a different kind. Yeah, you've got my number, weightlifting. I'm now Bucks county champion and a South Midlands champ, how's zat!*

After a snide reference to our sister – *Mum told me that Sinéad actually got a job!* – he ends on a pitiful note.

I'll sign off now as I can't think of anything constructive to write.

On Saturday 23 March 1978, *Saturday Night Fever* is released in the UK and becomes a box-office smash hit, sparking a nationwide craze for disco. The following day, still cut off from popular culture, Stuart writes to me again. At the foot of his letter is a drawing of a Teddy Boy leaning against a lamppost and smoking a cigarette – a reference to the story I'd told him on my previous visit, about how on Sunday mornings at Brick Lane market, marauding gangs of Teddy Boys have now started to attack anyone wearing punk rock styles. I'd learned this the hard way a few weeks earlier, when a pair of 40-something Teds left me cowering under a market stall with lumps on the back of my head from the kicking they'd dished out.

Less than a year into his sentence, the mindless monotony of prison life is already taking its toll on Stuart, his once-breezy tone replaced by a sour and resentful voice, not just boastful of his weightlifting achievements but now blatantly racist.

He thanks me for coming up with Cindy to visit him because, *it really did make me feel human again, it's not every day I get the chance to see two 'white' people. I was just getting used to seeing miles and miles of blacks as far as the eye can see (or should I say 'spear can throw'?) Anyway, you know what I mean – plenty of bloodclots in here.*

This strikes me as a disturbing twist. Until this point I'd never known Stuart to spout such brazen racism. Oh, his natural talent for mimicry had always lent itself to copying the cheery bigotry of many of the era's social club comedians, with their grotesque parodies of West Indian accents and their ugly Rastus-and-Eliza routines. But this seems worse. This sounds personal.

I worry about this shift in attitude, which seems to indicate a slump in his mental state. Especially when I read his closing lines.

I know that the contents of this letter probably sound pretty moronic but you can understand that there really isn't that much I can write about as one day is more or less the same as the next, all of which means a lot of nothing, which is exactly what I do.

Worse, that tiny glimmer of light at the end of the tunnel is rapidly fading.

Until now my brother has only ever been incarcerated in a series of institutions for Young Offenders. Although currently housed in an under-21s prison, he has just turned 20 and will soon be re-categorised as an adult. This means he's perilously close to being locked up with the old lags, the hardened thugs and truly deviant cons in places like the Scrubs or Wandsworth. Sometimes I wonder if he has given any thought to this, or whether he has already accepted the effortless slide into a convict lifestyle, and a lifetime spent in and out of jail. And yet I feel unable to talk to him about it. He's so cocky and nonchalant about prison, it feels faintly ridiculous even to express concern.

That's simply not what we do, discuss our feelings. Especially not our fears. We have to grit our teeth and set our jaws and throw ourselves headfirst into danger. That's what we've been taught ever since we could walk. That's how we've survived. That's what works.

That's all we know.

Anyway, it's not as if I have things mapped out, either. I'm literally stumbling through art school on speed and hash, dropping the odd tab of acid, guzzling Holsten Pils, and crashing on a third-hand mattress in a grimy cold-water tenement with jerry-rigged electricity. I'm wearing flea market clothes and fantasising about becoming a rock star with my amateurish arty punk band. Though I do have standards. Unlike some of my peers I stay away from heroin, at least. I'm not going to die of an OD, not me.

But that's as much of a plan as I can muster.

Whenever I visit Stuart and work up the courage to ask if he feels miserable or lonely, the answer is always the same.

Nah, he says. Don't worry about it, I'll be fine.

He smirks and shrugs it off.

What you gonna do? It is what it is.

*   *   *

Stuart writes to me on Thursday 22 June 1978 from a new prison: HMP Grendon. Although just 15 miles from HMP Aylesbury, Grendon is a very different place: the only adult prison in the country to operate wholly as a therapeutic community, a radical penal experiment built around the principles and practices of psychodynamic group therapy. Inmates must specifically request a transfer, and then pass personality and intelligence tests which have been compared to entrance exams. Finally, in order to gain admission they must agree to undergo regular group therapy.

In return, they spend far less time banged up in their cells, and enjoy a far greater degree of autonomy over their daily schedules. The system is self-regulating: anyone who disrupts the tranquility of the unit can be voted out by the other inmates and returned to a regular prison.

Outsiders often see Grendon as a cushy number: more freedom, a milder regime and a dedication to mental health that provokes scorn even inside the penal system. Their colleagues at HMP Aylesbury mock Grendon's prison guards as *nannies* and *bleeding hearts*. But there's nothing soft or cosy about the daily group therapy sessions where inmates must admit, analyse, debate and take responsibility for their crimes, examining their own motives and actions in a bid to understand and break out of damaging psychological patterns.

This seems like a truly hopeful sign. If Stuart has volunteered for therapy and communal responsibility, maybe he's finally getting his act together. I know we both have a hair-trigger temper, so I'm reassured by the idea that he might be addressing that issue. Maybe now he'll take stock and find some direction for his life, instead of constantly running into trouble. Maybe the brighter, more playful side of his personality will resurface.

But then I receive his first letter from Grendon Underwood. In the top left-hand corner, he has drawn a fat black spider dangling from a web, like something from a creepy horror comic.

When I come home, he writes, *I'm getting a set of weights and I'll show you some quick and easy ways to put some meat on yer ol' bones before someone starts kicking sand in your face every time you go to the beach. Ha! Ha! Ha!*

By this point, either my mother or I must have finally bought Stuart the cheap radio he has been asking for, because he now has access to music. And although he still hasn't seen this year's biggest film, *Saturday Night Fever*, he has plugged into the disco craze via mail order:

> Sent away for a book from Lester Wilson (the man who taught John Travolta to dance, WOW!) so I can learn some new dances, though Lord knows why! I can already do the Disco Duck, Walk, Drive, Hustle, and Swing and a few more, as there's not much else to do in here ...
>
> Love,
> Stuart xxx

Next to the three kisses he has drawn an arrow, pointing to them. And next to that, a question mark – apparently asking whether kisses on a letter to his brother are appropriate.

*   *   *

Later that same month I quit my Dip AD course. Having been expelled from my grammar school for fighting and stealing, I have now flunked out of art school after one year, thanks to my focus on hedonism and music. I'd thought I was ready for art school, but the sheer volume of ideas and theories and facts has been like trying to drink from a firehose. Especially since all artistic roads seem to lead back to my own psychological problems.

The truth is that I'm afraid to take a cold hard look at myself, afraid of what I'll find. Or perhaps that I'll find nothing at all. Whatever the case, I'm always running away from myself, always propping myself up and masking my issues with alcohol and drugs, unable to achieve anything like stability. Like my little brother I prefer to put on an act, pretend it's all a joke, using forced humour to stave off and disguise a deep-rooted sense of inadequacy.

But amid all this gloom there's finally a silver lining. HMP Grendon seems to have done the trick, and Stuart will be out of prison soon. Having served two-thirds of his sentence, he is now eligible for parole. And let's face it, he should never have been locked up in the first place. He was a teenage father and they broke up his family. And while he was rotting in jail, his wife left him for another man.

What an outrage. He was struggling to pay for nappies and baby food. What would any father do?

That's right, whatever it took.

Who could blame him?

Tilbury, 1970s

Sometime in the late 1970s, I have a hazy recollection of being in the kitchen of Darwin Road when my mother handed me a Sunday tabloid and pointed to a report about a murder trial.

Read that, she said.

Why?

Just read it.

The report detailed the trial of a Scottish woman who had killed her husband, stabbing him to death with a kitchen knife. The woman had argued self-defence, claiming her husband was an abusive drunk who had beaten her for decades. After a relatively short trial, she had been found guilty of manslaughter.

The dead man's name was John Campbell.

Is that …?

Yes, my mother said. That's the Other Thing's brother, Johnny. The one we went to stay with when you were just little kids.

I had a dim recollection of that damp and musty prefab in the Glasgow suburbs. Of that nauseating sense of homesickness, of accents I couldn't understand. Of listening to Uncle Johnny laying into his wife in the next room. Of the Old Man pleading with my mother to return, using his pet name for her, *Wops*.

The jury had heard that John Campbell was an abusive drunk who had beaten his wife and children for years. One night he arrived home staggering drunk as usual, and she had gone to the kitchen to make tea. But when the water was boiled, he snatched up the kettle and threatened to scald her. Terrified, she seized a kitchen knife.

You wouldn't dare, he sneered, lunging at her.

With that, she rammed the knife into his heart, killing him instantly.

My memory of reading that report is hazy now, but I seem to remember that the judge directed the jury that it should convict the defendant of manslaughter only, and then gave Mrs Campbell a two-year suspended sentence. However, I recall with vivid clarity what my mother said as I finished reading the piece, and placed the newspaper on the table.

Two years suspended? If I'd known that, I would have done it myself, years ago.

Kind of sad though, I said. For the kids, anyway. Dying like that.

Sad? The bastard got what he deserved.

Yeah, I suppose you're right, Mum.

Suppose? Pah. I should have done it myself.

15

Paris, Friday 7 September 2001
81 days since Danielle's disappearance

I call my mother to say I'm going to make Stuart tell the truth about what he did with Danielle, even if I have to beat it out of him. But before I can speak, she says the police have been around to her flat again. This is their third visit and she is starting to get anxious and upset about it. They have even been to the Hertfordshire pub where, at 68, she still has a part-time job.

Don't worry, I say. I'll talk to them, tell them to back off.

Have you spoken with Debbie?

Yes, I congratulated her. And no, I didn't say anything to upset her. Mind you, she *should* be upset.

What do you mean?

About her husband killing her niece, that's what I mean.

He didn't do it!

What are you talking about, Mum? Of course he did.

No, she insists. I don't believe he did do it. Debbie says she is certain that Stuart is innocent and that's good enough for me. She's his wife. If anyone knows the truth, she does. She lives with him and she's a smart girl.

A smart girl? I take a deep breath.

Well, she says, I think he's telling the truth. And I want him to come and stay with me.

What? Are you crazy? You told the police you didn't want him using your address.

Well, I changed my mind.

Yeah, it's too late now. You signed a document denying his application.

No, because I spoke to Stuart's lawyer and after she explained what's been happening, I went to court and told them I wanted to, what's it called …?

I hear paper rustling as she unfolds some document and then reads aloud.

… to countermand my statement denying use of my premises as a bail house.

Oh my God. So what did his lawyer tell you?

She told me the police are lying.

What do you mean?

She told me Stuart didn't go to prison in 1991, that's a lie.

The police can't lie about a criminal record, Mum.

Well, she told me that he hadn't been to prison for rape or sexual assault or anything like that. And she said there are no recent cases of molestation or whatever it was, and there are no women coming forward, that's a lie too. There's nothing in the lasts 10 years. And she said Debbie was right, he hasn't been charged with the murder. The police just want to hold him so they can force him into a confession.

Mum, the police can't just lie about things like that. It's illegal.

Her voice hardens as she says, That's what his lawyer told me, and that's what Debbie told me, too. And I believe *them*, not the police.

My mind is reeling.

Mum, what are you talking about? It was in the newspaper. It was on TV. It's all over the internet. *He was charged with murder.*

Well, the papers were wrong then. Debbie says he was arrested but he hasn't been charged with murder and Stuart's lawyer said she's right.

After we hang up, I stand staring down at the cobbled courtyard, unable to process the conversation I've just had. Is there any chance at all that Stuart's version of events might be true? Have the police been manipulating me? Is it possible they're trying to frame him because they don't have a real culprit?

Or am I getting misinformation from my mother?

And if so, where is she getting it from?

Is everyone living in denial?

What the fuck is going on?

*　　*　　*

A couple of days later DS Keith Davies gets back me. He apologises for not replying sooner, explaining that he has been on holiday. He reminds me that I left an angry message on his answering machine just over a week ago, saying that I wanted to go and have it out with Stuart, and asking to get me into a cell with him, alone.

I explain to him that since then I've had conflicting information, and now I'm really confused. According to my mother, who says she heard this from Debbie and Stuart's lawyer, either the police have not yet filed murder charges, or the charges have been dropped.

Help me out here, Keith. One side or the other must have the facts wrong. And I'm caught in the middle. Perhaps the murder charge has been dropped or downgraded to manslaughter, is that possible?

Absolutely not, he says. Whatever Debbie or Stuart or any lawyer might be saying, I can assure you the murder charge has not been dropped and is still on file. However, Stuart wasn't charged with murder when he was *most recently* arrested, so perhaps that is where the misunderstanding has arisen.

Okay, I say. Maybe that's all it is, a misunderstanding. But what about this story my mum says she got from his lawyer, that Stuart has never been charged with abducting young girls?

Again, I don't know where this is coming from, but he definitely has convictions for false imprisonment and sexual assault.

Recently?

I can't quote his entire criminal record off the top of my head, but I can categorically state that Stuart spent eight months in prison on remand awaiting trial for the abduction of a minor.

And when was this?

In 1991, and you might not know about it because Debbie told her family – and probably yours – that he was away working in Manchester. Through a technicality, when he went to trial the most serious charges were dismissed, and after pleading guilty to false imprisonment, he was sentenced to time served plus two and a half years suspended. Which meant he walked free from the court.

But I don't understand, Keith. Why would Debbie still be supporting him now?

Debbie, you've got to remember, keeps changing her mind. One minute the relationship is definitely over, and the next ... well, let's not forget she's just had a baby and her hormones will be all over the place. But as time wears on, maybe things that she knows and has kept quiet about, or things that she's turned a blind eye to, they'll start to eat away at her and she may yet change her mind again. But for the time being, she's managed to convince herself that he's innocent.

So my mum and me, I say, we're not the only ones swinging back and forth?

Not at all. And that's entirely understandable, especially in the early stages of a prosecution. Quite common among family members, in fact, even when all the evidence points one way.

And you have no doubt that it's Stuart?

Correct. I am absolutely convinced that Stuart is guilty of the murder of Danielle Jones and I am determined to see him tried, convicted and imprisoned for his crime.

No other suspects?

Stuart is the only real suspect we have. And as I say, I've still got to find and provide the evidence. Nobody's going to take my word.

Alright. Thank you for answering my questions.

Not a problem. So, can we talk about the message you left me? You sounded pretty angry and said that you want to help me out.

That's right, I say. But there is one more thing. I've got to ask you to speak to your colleague, DS Andy Harvey. If I'm going to help out – and I want to do that – then DS Harvey has to let up on my mum. She's an elderly woman. He can't keep turning up at her flat, or visiting her at work, which obviously embarrassed her.

No problem. I'll talk to him and ask him not to do that again.

Thank you, I appreciate that. So tell me what I can do.

Well, as you know, Stuart is presently on remand in Chelmsford Prison.

Right, so you want me to visit him. Can it wait till next week?

There's no hurry, he's not going anywhere. And there's no doubt in my mind that Danielle is dead. But Alix, we need to clear this up for Lin's sake. I was with that woman today and what she's going through? It's awful, I'm telling you. She can't sleep, she can't eat, she can't even *grieve*. So I want you first and foremost to find out what happened to Danielle so that Lin and

Tony can have some closure. And personally, I want to find the evidence to prove he killed her, so that he's convicted and sentenced.

Well, I'll be back in London soon. In fact, I've already booked my ticket for the last weekend in September.

Okay, I will find out the visiting procedure for HMP Chelmsford and let you know the details.

Great, let's speak next week about arranging the visit.

Sounds good.

Until then.

I hang up and slump back on the sofa. It feels surreal to sit in this Parisian apartment while replaying the conversation of the last 20 minutes.

My brother in prison, charged with murder. His criminal record, involving abduction and sexual abuse of minors.

His wife, a new mother. The son he has yet to see – and may never even know.

The half-truths, confusions and lies that have riddled this story from the start.

And tangled up in all that, the simple pleasures of life: holidays, birthdays, children.

So many things that will never be the same again for so many people.

But especially for Tony and Linda Jones.

16

Tilbury, 1979

If I walked the streets of Tilbury long enough I would invariably find the Old Man drinking with his cronies in a bus shelter or on a park bench. One afternoon, in my rush to catch the London-bound train arriving on the station's far platform, I ran around a corner and almost fell over him, sitting on the steps, drinking with two pals. After a second of shock, he stood up and clasped my hand as if greeting a visiting dignitary.

Hey you two, he said. Say hello to my son, Alexander.

His pals looked up and nodded solemnly. One was swigging from a small bottle of aftershave. He held it out and I shook my head. Then he offered it to the Old Man, who scowled – he still had some standards. Anyway, he was holding a bottle of Olde English cider, sorted.

Stumbling into these encounters I was fascinated by the group dynamic, often passing an hour just watching and listening, trying to understand. Did he hang out with these shabby drunks for their company? Because nobody else would tolerate him? Or maybe he loved being the centre of attention, the sharpest and most sophisticated inebriate in town?

Equally fascinating was his self-mythologising. I often heard him claim he could converse in a dozen languages. Gradually I came to realise this meant he could curse in Gaelic, order drinks in Spanish and ask for the toilet in Swahili – but not much more.

Still, his geography was far better than average, and he had stories for days. Like the one about being on shore leave in Calcutta, walking along a backstreet one bright sunny day, when he sensed something odd about his surroundings. And how he stopped in the middle of the road, looking around at the locals, wondering why they were staring at him, when all at once he noticed their stubby grey fingerless hands and it hit him like a freight train.

He had wandered into a leper colony.

He'd never run so fast, apparently.

Perhaps he felt he was educating these poor bastards, who sat gazing up at him while he narrated, boasted and pontificated. With his wisecracks and tough talk and occasional dance steps he certainly entertained them, made them feel smarter and braver and happier than they really were. He made their plight seem reasonable, their sins forgivable, their thirst only natural.

But by the time I'd enrolled in college I was no longer trying to understand him, and any shred of sympathy or filial respect was long gone. Although we never said as much, our random and stunted exchanges were becoming an embarrassment to us both, underscoring our ever-greater distance from each other. There was no meaningful relationship to be formed with this ageing semi-vagabond, who spent most of his waking life drunk and spouting grandiose bullshit. Worse, I knew this was a man who hit women. And since I was now an adult, that fact took on a new gravity. Where once I'd harboured a trace of admiration, now I felt little more than pity. Despite all his talk about being a fighter, he wasn't really a tough guy at all. Not anymore, anyway. I knew that from the incident outside the Ship, where he'd manoeuvred me into cold-cocking a complete stranger in order to save himself from humiliation.

The most memorable of our encounters was a mild summer day in 1979.

Back in Tilbury for a brief visit, I saw him coming down the street towards me, maybe 20 yards away.

I stood and smiled, but he didn't respond.

Of course, I thought. It's those stupid sunglasses he's wearing.

Oversized chrome-plated wraparounds, they looked so incongruous on him that I wondered if he was wearing them as a joke. Especially since he was also carrying a battered white plastic bag.

The Old Man with a white plastic bag?

Would Sinatra be seen dead like that?

The fuck he would.

I stood waiting for him to recognise me, to smile. But he kept walking, and had almost passed me when I spoke.

Hey, how you doing?

Huh? Oh, it's *you*. How are you, son? Are you back from London now?

Just visiting.

Aye. How's your studies going?

Yeah, not bad.

I pointed to the plastic bag in his hand.

What's that?

That is fresh leeks and onions, son. I'm off to make a wee bite. Have you eaten?

I'm not hungry, thanks.

Well, d'ye fancy a walk with me? I'm staying with a pal just over there on Fielding.

Yeah, why not.

Years had passed since he'd last been to sea and he was now probably unemployable. Lack of income had led to a steep decline in personal appearance. While his shirt was clean, the collar was badly frayed. His suit was pressed, but the elbows sagged and his trousers had that weary sheen. He was smeared with the patina of failure – thinner than I'd ever seen him and visibly weaker, the stains on his fingers a deeper shade of ochre.

He looked sick.

And he was sporting these ridiculous, enormous sunglasses with fake chrome frames, their chunky arms dotted with circular cutouts. Couldn't he see how dumb they looked, these Vegas-era Elvis shades that clashed so badly with his Rat Pack style?

Perhaps they were hiding an injury, maybe a black eye? As we walked I tried to peer behind them, but they were closely fitted to his face. I didn't want to embarrass him, but I had to know.

So, what's with the shades?

Aye, what about them?

Bit flash, aren't they?

You think so.

I'd say so, yeah.

I need something to protect my eyes.

Why's that?

From the light.

I looked up at the overcast sky and back at him.

The sun isn't even shining, I said.

He stopped and turned to me.

My liver is fucked. Ye satisfied now?

Sorry.

I still didn't understand, but knew better than to ask again. It was enough information for now: fucked liver equals bad eyes, ergo Elvis shades. Only much later would I learn how chronic alcohol abuse often causes cirrhosis, impairing the liver's ability to purify toxins from the blood. In severe cases, the liver becomes a useless lump of scar tissue, so the blood gets tainted with toxins, which damage sensitive parts of the body, such as the retina. This is why late-stage cirrhosis can lead to severe eye problems, even blindness.

We walked at the Old Man's pace to a pebble-dashed council house on Fielding Avenue. The legal tenant, a friend of his, had *gone away for a couple of months* – almost certainly to prison – and left the Old Man and another drunk to look after the place.

I wondered if he'd forgotten, or whether he'd ever known, that his ex-wife, my mother, had been born on this street. What would he say if I mentioned it? Something scornful. Scorn was his default mode whenever he had any amount of alcohol in him. Which was any time of the day or night, if he could help it.

He hooked the key string from the letter box and opened the door. I followed him down the hall, the only sound the tick-tock of a fake walnut clock on the living-room mantelpiece. As we passed I caught a glimpse of the ancient catalogue furniture, wooden arms and legs heavily scratched, cushions dotted with cigarette burns, spots of grimy foam.

Thin yellowish curtains diffused the kitchen's grey light. At one end, the standard cast-iron stove, enamelled periwinkle blue, door ajar to a bed of cold ash. Two rust-spotted chrome chairs with primrose plastic seats framed a Formica table. There was no fridge, but on a shelf stood several cans: baked beans, frankfurters in brine, condensed milk. The Old Man took off his fake chrome sunglasses and placed them on the table with his plastic bag.

Cup of tea?

Not right now, thanks.

He reached into a cupboard, took out a plastic colander that held five or six small potatoes and placed it on the table.

I'm making a vegetable soup. You can help if you want.

Okay.

Here, he said, handing me the wooden handle of a paring knife, ancient but well honed. While he filled a saucepan under the tap and poured iodised salt into it, I took a potato from the bowl and started peeling it over the newspaper he had placed on the linoleum floor.

What the fuck are you doing?

I looked up at him, dumbfounded.

He stooped to pick up a three-inch strip of potato peel and held it in front of my face, pointing with a nicotine-stained finger at the underside.

That is *food*. You're wasting good *food!*

What?

Give me that, he said, taking the knife and potato from me. Watch. Like *this*.

He skimmed the potato's surface with a feathery touch, stripping a fine curl of peel, half as thick as the chunk I'd lopped off. Then he flipped the potato in his hand and did another side, and then once more. He held it in front of me, naked, smooth and glistening. Then he turned and held it over the pan, slicing the waxy flesh into the water.

Okay, I said. Got it.

He handed me the knife again, and I took another potato and started peeling, keenly aware of being watched. He made a noise somewhere between a sigh and a cough.

No?

Leave it, he sighed. I'll do it.

I can –

Give it to me.

Okay, I said, standing up. I better get going anyway.

Aye.

Good to see you.

Oh, aye.

Take care, then.

Yeah. You too. See ya later, alligator.

I left him bent over in that cheap plastic chair, slivers of peel curling from his hands and spiralling onto the newsprint, fine and effortless. He didn't look up.

I let myself out and walked back up Fielding Avenue wondering how a life could become so sad and small. For a second I felt empty, almost lost. And then I remembered those ridiculous sunglasses, and had to smile. He was literally *blind drunk*.

That fractured moment in a stranger's grubby kitchen was the first and only time I ever tried to make food with my father, the chef.

And the last time I ever saw him.

17

Paris, Sunday 23 September 2001
97 days since Danielle's disappearance

My friend Dominique Green, a film and TV producer, invites me
to lunch at her apartment on avenue Ledru-Rollin. Over a bottle
of red wine we discuss the recent terror attacks on America – the
term 9/11 is not yet the standard shorthand – and how rapidly
the world is changing.

My corner store no longer sells beer, I tell her. The kid behind
the till says it's *haram*.

What do you expect? Local resentment, that's the price of
gentrification.

Gentrification? I'm working class.

Alix, don't be ridiculous. You're a gadabout English journalist
who bought a fuck-off apartment in an ethnically diverse
Parisian neighbourhood. You're a yuppie now. Embrace it.

I guzzle more wine while Dominique prepares lunch and eyes
me carefully.

So, she says, apart from having to buy your beer at the supermarket, poor lamb, how are you?

I open my mouth to speak but the words won't come out.
Instead, I pour another hefty glass while I ponder the question.

How am I? Where would I even start?

*Well, you see, Dominique, it's like this. I'm almost certain that
three months ago my brother killed a 15-year-old girl called*

Danielle Jones, his own niece, and that he murdered her because of some sexual intrigue. What do I mean by that? Well, I'm not sure, nobody can be certain, but either he'd been having sex with her and she threatened to tell his heavily pregnant wife – who, by the way, has since given birth to a son – or maybe he assaulted or even raped her and killed her afterwards. Or maybe he tried to initiate sex with her but there was a struggle and he killed her accidentally and then panicked.

That's what the police told me, that they don't believe he set out to kill her ... but I don't know, maybe they're telling me what they think I want to hear. Whatever happened, he dumped her body somewhere and now he pretends to know nothing about her disappearance, despite having shown an unhealthy interest in her from a young age. So far nobody can say with any degree of certainty what happened because she disappeared on 18 June and here we are on 23 September, which is 14 weeks later, and she is still missing and police have been searching local fields and wasteland with hundreds of volunteers, and diving in lakes and marshy water for months. And her parents are on national TV in England, crying and shaking, and Stuart has been arrested on suspicion of her murder and apparently his only comment is 'No comment' and he's still in prison on remand and the police want me to go and speak to him to see if I can get him to say what he did with the girl's body.

Oh, and even though this murder is national news in the UK, my 13-year-old daughter still hasn't realised that the man charged with the murder, the scowling, dead-eyed brute on the front of all the papers, is her Uncle Stuart, my kid brother. Crazy, right? And so for weeks her mother and I have been living in dread of the moment when she puts it all together, or maybe one of her friends finally points it out, and she realises that she actually knows the dead girl. Not only knows her, but that she and Danielle were twin bridesmaids at Stuart's wedding, with matching pink satin gowns and bouquets. And recently I learned that my brother is a violent sexual predator who has stalked and imprisoned and assaulted and taken indecent photographs of teenage girls before, and has a criminal record stretching back three decades, which he somehow managed to conceal from his own family, as well as Danielle's. But also, Dominique, because the police have not yet recovered a body there's still the tiniest trace of doubt, which makes it all even more difficult to process. Because without a body, nothing is final, nothing is absolutely certain. And so it's hard to even speak about it because everyone I love wants to believe it's not true, and I'd give anything to be wrong about this, but I know deep in my heart that it's true, it's true, it's true. He killed her. My brother killed a little girl and dumped her body and now he's lying about it and I'm terrified my daughter will find out. And worse, he might even get away with it.

I sit there gulping wine as these words swirl around in my head, words I cannot possibly say, not even to someone as kind and good-hearted as Dominique, because such things are unspeakable. And next thing I know I'm once again sobbing and my face is all screwed up and tears are dropping into my lap and Dominique is sitting opposite me at the table, wide-eyed and saying softly, *Oh my God, I had no idea.*

And that's when I realise I have spewed up this torrent of words in a volcanic eruption of anger, shame, grief, fear, anxiety and confusion. Somehow, I have spoken all the unspeakable things. Because no matter how hard I try, I cannot hold them in anymore.

Oh my God, she says again. How awful. That poor girl ... and her parents. Have you told anyone else?

Celia, I say, wiping my nose on my sleeve.

You haven't told Paul yet?

No.

Should I call him? I'm sure he'll come over straight away.

Should she call Paul? Do I want Paul to know? He's my closest friend but he has a daughter more or less the same age as my own. Do I want his family to know that their dad's friend Alix has a brother who abducted and murdered his 15-year-old niece? Do I really want anyone to know?

Because right now, it feels that I will always be tarnished by association, that Stuart's crimes will forever warp my relationships, sowing doubt wherever I go.

Paul arrives and listens as I vomit it up once again.

He and Dominique ask questions and I fill in the blanks: our bleak family history, my father's drunken violence, Stuart's repeated incarceration and criminal record, the way he'd misled us all, why my mother feels he is innocent, how his wife Debbie was so quick to defend him, how I went down to Tilbury to speak with Stuart and looked him in the eye. Which is how I can be so certain, sitting here now, that he is guilty.

Except that I'm not, not 100 per cent.

How can I be?

*   *   *

The following Friday I'm packing to spend the weekend in London, as I'd told DS Keith Davies I would. But I haven't called him to arrange our meeting. I'm halfway out the door when my home phone rings, an English mobile number flashing up on the digital display. I let it ring and delete his message without listening to it. I have decided I can't keep doing this. I don't want to discuss this horrible business all over again. I don't want to hear what Keith Davies has to say about Stuart or Debbie or Danielle's parents. I don't want his sympathy, don't want him patting my arm like I'm a decent bloke but not that bright, bit of a soft touch. On the train ride he leaves three more messages on my mobile, which I delete unplayed. I get off the train and go straight to my London dentist to get a new crown fitted.

Then I go to Celia's. I don't tell her that I'm avoiding DS Davies, that I'm running away from the truth.

*　　*　　*

On Sunday I meet my Buddhist teacher and another student called Maya, and we go for dinner at Wagamama in Soho. As we're waiting for our food I tell Rinpoche – that's the honorific his students use to address him – there's something on my mind that I have to share with him.

Go on, he says.

My brother Stuart is in prison, charged with murdering his 15-year old niece Danielle, and various paedophile acts involving young girls. I believe he is guilty.

His brow creases as if he's suddenly struck by an intense headache. He looks down and says nothing for what seems like forever. I'm beginning to wonder whether he even heard me when he finally speaks.

That's very sad, he says. Especially for him.

That's all he says, but it resonates profoundly and the noisy room around us seems to fall away as my heart opens. Until this moment nobody except my mother has expressed compassion for Stuart. For the first time, I get a glimpse of the intense psychological pain my brother must be in right now.

Of course, he has brought this pain on himself through his own actions, and worse, those actions and his lies are causing others even greater pain. But his lies won't protect him from his own mind. He must confront the horror of his own making, or spend the rest of his life in denial. Either way, having extinguished an innocent life, he has destroyed his own.

Very sad, indeed.

Rinpoche, I say. There's one other thing.

Yes?

The young girl, Danielle? She disappeared on 18 June. Your birthday.

Oh, he says. That's a coincidence, isn't it.

Yes, I'd say that's quite an odd coincidence.

Of course, that's all it is. There's no bigger pattern at play, no deeper meaning to this awful fluke of fate, and therefore nothing much to be said about it.

But from now on my guru's birthday – an otherwise joyful anniversary, one I'd sometimes celebrated with other students – will forever be shadowed by my brother's awful crime, the murder of his niece.

Over dinner Rinpoche says he still expects me to stay with him early next year in the Himalayas. He had first proposed the trip months earlier – long before Danielle's disappearance – but it seems like perfect timing. Right now nothing would suit me better than to be far away from here, and for a long time. Three months, in fact.

As the cab pulls up, we say our goodbyes.

Thank you, Rinpoche.

See you in Bhutan, he says.

And then he is gone.

*　　*　　*

Back in Paris I call Stuart's solicitor to try and get some clarity on his situation. She explains that because bail has been refused, Stuart is still in Chelmsford Prison on remand. He'll be back in court on 5 November to enter his plea, she says, and a trial date should be set at that point, probably for late next year.

Although you never know, she adds. Something could still happen by the end of this year.

Okay, I say. But I've received a lot of conflicting information lately and I wondered if you would help me clear up some facts?

If I can, she says.

What exactly are the offences that Stuart has been charged with?

Ah, she says. That's confidential. I'll have to speak with Stuart and ask him if I can relate all the charges he faces. If so, I'll call you.

Confidential? He's all over the national press. This is a murder investigation, not a divorce settlement with a Non-Disclosure Agreement.

But, she continues, they're nothing like the police have said. No rapes or anything like that whatsoever.

Rapes? I hadn't heard about that before. The police are saying that he *raped* these girls?

Yes, she says. They seem to have been telling different people different things. And some of these charges are 20 years old.

Okay, I say. I'm just trying to clear up one thing. Has he been charged with Danielle's murder?

No, she says.

Really? Because the police are telling me that he has.

That's news to me, she replies. But I should be getting some papers soon from the Crown Prosecution Service, so I can see what statements have been made against him, and I'll be arranging to see him shortly after that. I'll ask him then if I can divulge to you the charges against him. But again, I can tell you the only charges so far involving young girls are over 20 years old.

Molly Sharkey aged 20, shortly before she met my father.
As a baby, her curly black hair and olive complexion led my
grandfather to dub her *Wops*, a nickname adopted
by family and friends – and even my father.

In the front room of 10 Seymour Road, my mother holds
baby Fraser. Despite the smiles, our clenched fingers betray
our deeply ingrained anxiety.

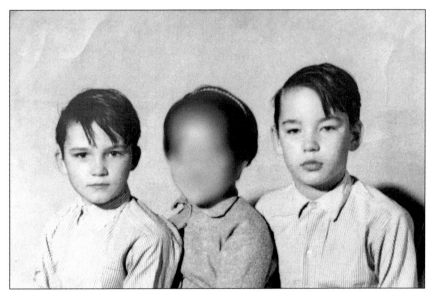

A family shot taken circa 1966 at St Mary's Roman Catholic
Primary School. It is already clear which of us has inherited our
mother's photogenic looks.

Palmer's Boys Grammar School, aged 13, sporting a brittle copper thatch with a jagged homestyle fringe. In the street, kids gawp at my terrible, half-abandoned hairstyle.

Alix (left) and Stuart (right), aged 18 and 17, outside 66 Darwin Road in August 1975, the last photo of us together, smiling and relaxed. Just over a year later Stuart would be in prison.

Tilbury's legendary pub The Ship, opposite the railway station on Dock Road. Beneath the Charrington's signage is the saloon bar, where in 1955 our mother and father first met.

Stuart in 1979, freshly paroled from prison, expert in numerous disco dances, but now estranged from his wife and baby daughter.

Stuart with our grandfather Jack Sharkey and Mum,
in the flat above the pub she ran, circa 1985.

Stuart's wedding, August 1996. Left to right: Debbie,
Stuart, Mum, Alix and 10-year-old Danielle Jones.

My interview with Stuart in the September 1985 issue of *i-D* magazine. The piece ran shortly after I'd secured a flat for him and Debbie in the housing co-operative where I lived.

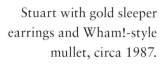

Stuart with gold sleeper earrings and Wham!-style mullet, circa 1987.

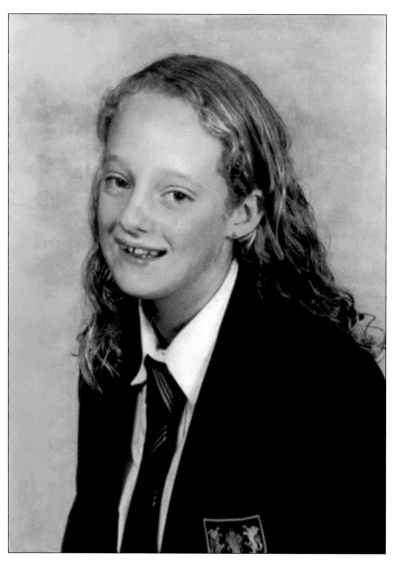

Danielle in her school uniform. This photo was
circulated by Essex Police in an effort to elicit the
public's help, and featured on the poster Stuart
pretended not to see at Lakeside.

An officer tapes a reward poster to the side of an Essex Police mobile incident room van. The *Sun* newspaper offered £25,000 for information leading to an arrest.

Over 400 volunteers, mostly locals, joined 60 police officers in a fingertip search of fields and marshlands around East Tilbury. No trace of Danielle's body has ever been found.

We agree to talk again in the coming days and hang up.

I just want this to stop.

This has been going on for months and I still don't understand exactly what's happening. All I know for sure is that Stuart is in prison again after all these years. But it's not like before. He doesn't write me those glib little letters, with a VO included, asking me to get him a radio. And I don't have any inclination to try and visit him.

Somebody, please, just prove to me that he's guilty or innocent. This weird limbo where he's both and neither at the same time, it's doing my head in.

And then I'm on my way back from the supermarket with my non-*haram* six-pack when I get a call on my mobile from DS Keith Davies.

Hi, he says, I just wanted to let you know that I checked and yes, the murder charges against Stuart definitely haven't been dropped.

Why are you telling me this?

Because you specifically asked me to check. Don't you remember?

Oh yeah, I lie. Of course.

Anyway, I checked, as you asked me to, and the charges are still on file.

Thank you, I say.

So, I was wondering if you were still up for writing that letter?

Letter?

Yes, we spoke about you writing a letter to Stuart and then going to see him, see if you can get him to talk, maybe get a lead on what he did with Danielle's body. Remember?

Right, yeah.

In a cracked whiny voice, I tell him I'm kind of losing track of all this and stop just short of saying I'm losing patience with the whole bag of tricks, and I'm sick of him calling me and assuming I'll drop everything and talk about this rotten business. Instead, I tell him I'll call him back some time in the next couple of days.

But we both know I won't.

At home, I open a beer and write in my journal:

I need to stop brooding on this, it's making me feel ill.

* * *

The following week I cover the Galliano and Westwood shows, where I smile and wave at all my fashion friends and pretend everything is just hunky-dory. And then my daughter arrives to spend half-term with me. Fiona still doesn't know about her grisly family connection to the Danielle Jones case and it feels increasingly weird to keep her in the dark. Not least because this whole business started with a dirty little secret, with people hiding the truth to avoid embarrassment.

On the first Saturday in November I call my mother, and as usual we spend the first 10 minutes talking about Spurs and her club West Ham and their respective fortunes, because after all these years, our sole common passion is football. She tells me she doesn't really understand people who don't like football. Best game in the world.

By the way, she says, I've changed my mind.

About football?

No, silly. About Stuart.

What do you mean?

I don't think he did kill that girl.

What? You told me just last week you thought he was guilty.

Well, I've changed my mind. I think the police have got it in for him. They've made up their minds and that's what they're going to do, pin it on him.

Fuck, here we go again.

Mum, I tell her, just give me his prisoner number and the address, so I can write to him.

Well, she says, I haven't got it to hand. Call me on Monday and I'll have it ready.

I call her on Monday and she gives me the address of HMP Chelmsford and Stuart's prisoner number. I sit down to write, trying to strike a non-judgemental tone in the hope of getting a response. My rage, my fantasies of beating the truth out of him, all that has been swept away by weeks of confusion, fuelled by conflicting narratives. My ambition at this point is simply to open a dialogue, which might then be leveraged into a prison visit. As DS Keith Davies has suggested, if I can get into a room and talk to him for an hour or two, perhaps I can get him to open up.

Tuesday 6 November 2001

Dear Stuart,

Congratulations to you on becoming a father. Despite your current sad circumstances, I'm sure you must be happy and proud of Debbie and little Simon. Apparently, you haven't even seen him yet, because the authorities are threatening to take the baby away from Debbie if she brings him to visit you. All very strange and frustrating, I'm sure you'll agree.

I wonder what life is like for you at the moment. I've never spent any time in prison, apart from visiting, so it's hard to imagine how cold and hostile it must be. Of course, being on remand is slightly less arduous, so I'm told, but even so it must be difficult for you. Do you get books and papers? What about exercise, can you use the gym? Are you locked up on the landing, or do you get time outside in the recreation area? If you want me to send you something, let me know.

If I was in prison I would certainly use the time to meditate. I have found that meditation is the only way to understand and control one's mind, which of course is a great skill when you are confronted with circumstances that are meant to intimidate and crush you. If you want, I can send you a book, but it would be best to get personal instruction from a qualified and practising meditation instructor. It's like lifting weights: if you try to learn from a book rather than someone who already knows, you're likely to strain yourself and end up weaker. Also, you could apply to Angulimala, a Buddhist group that sends trained meditation instructors into prisons. If you ask, they will send someone to see you (angulimala.org.uk). Or let me know, and I'll write to them, if you want.

As for these charges you're facing, Mum tells me most of them are really dated and that they've just been left on file, that there's not much in them. Personally, I don't know what's going on here. When I came to see you, I was hoping that you would be frank with me and tell me what had happened. I think we both know that you were evasive. That experience left me wondering how much you had to hide. And it's difficult to help someone when you don't know the whole truth.

I hope you won't take this as an accusation. It's not that at all. I just wish we were closer and you could have told me about this stuff. One thing is certain: whatever happens, you will always be my brother. I want you to understand this and to know that I will never desert you, no matter what happens. I will always be there to help you if you want me to.

Please write if you get a chance.

Alix Sharkey
45 rue Marx Dormoy
75018 Paris
France

Paris, Wednesday 14 November 2001
149 days since Danielle's disappearance

Nearly eight weeks after sending the letter I'm still going downstairs every morning to check the mailbox, but there is no word from Stuart. This morning I come back up and do some yoga, make coffee and log onto BBC News to find a headline that finally answers at least one of my questions:

DANIELLE'S UNCLE CHARGED WITH MURDER

And so, five months after Danielle Jones was last seen alive, Stuart James Campbell, 43, of Grays, Essex, is formally charged with her murder and remanded in prison to await trial.

His wife Debbie leaves the family home with their newborn son and, according to local rumour, moves in with her parents somewhere on the coast. Of course, I hear nothing from her about this, perhaps because she still believes I want to write a newspaper article.

She probably doesn't realise that even if I wanted to, I cannot write about the case. With the formal initiation of criminal proceedings the matter is now *sub judice*, meaning legal restrictions apply. Under penalty of contempt of court, there can be no further reporting on the particulars of the case, or about Stuart or his alleged victim, until the trial begins.

Having made national headlines almost every day for the last 21 weeks, the Danielle Jones story disappears from sight.

18

Bhutan, Sunday 10 February 2002
7 months and 23 days since Danielle's disappearance

I fly via Nepal to Bhutan, where I will spend the next three months in retreat, living in my guru's mountain house. Yet even 7,000 feet above sea level, I get online every few days. Although any discussion of the case against Stuart Campbell is forbidden, the search for Danielle's body continues, and reporting on that is fair game.

On the morning of 15 March I learn that workmen have discovered the decomposed remains of a young woman wrapped in a blue tarpaulin, at a disused cement works site in Northfleet, Kent – on the other side of the Thames, but less than five miles from where Danielle was last seen. Initial examination shows the deceased was between 14 and 20, with long fair hair.

In other words, a possible match for Danielle.

Five thousand miles away in the foothills of the Himalayas, I brace myself for a positive identification. It's a macabre situation, realising the best possible outcome might be the saddest possible news. I think about Tony and Linda Jones and how painful this must be for them, months after their daughter's disappearance, and how the best anyone can realistically hope for is the recovery of her body and to lay her to rest.

Over the weekend, DNA testing shows the remains are not Danielle's, but those of another young woman.

In a TV appeal to try and identify her, Kent Police describe the girl's distinctive clothing – a black sleeveless top with a gold leaf pattern under a denim jacket, with burgundy trousers and leather boots. Watching at home in Deptford, 46-year-old Bernadette Williams knows immediately that the police have found her 14-year-old daughter Hannah Williams, who had gone missing in April 2001, just two months before Danielle Jones disappeared.

Mrs Williams will later describe her horror at learning from a TV report that her daughter had been abducted and murdered and dumped like trash.

To find out that way was unforgivable, she will tell the *Guardian*. I screamed and then I cried and cried.

Within days, police arrest a 57-year-old serial paedophile and sex attacker. The following year he will be sentenced to life imprisonment for Hannah's abduction, rape and murder, and ultimately die in prison at the age of 71.

But for the Jones family, there will be no closure: their agony continues.

*   *   *

After three months in Bhutan I return to Paris. I collect a huge stack of mail from the concierge.

Still no letter from my brother.

Along with everyone else related to this case, I settle into a strange limbo, awaiting Stuart's trial.

19

Bermondsey, Thursday 26 July 1979

He turns his knee out and does that Michael Jackson hip-thrust finger snap. He skips and struts, then swivels forward and back, defying gravity. He spins on the spot and stops dead, then grinds his hips before exploding in a super-campy star jump. We laugh as he duck-walks backwards, his finger stabs punctuating the horns. He freezes in that iconic Travolta gesture, and ... pop! A hip bounce, head back, his face flashing in and out of profile. His moves are slick, his limbs slice the air, his torso oscillates with poise and grace, always in sync with the beat. He's an expert disco dancer, easily the best of the 40 or so in this room.

And that's strange, because I fully expected to fill that role.

I'm the dancer in this family. *I'm* the one with the moves. Or at least that's what I thought until now.

Until Stuart started dancing.

It's a Thursday night in the Dun Cow, a historic pub on the Old Kent Road that recently started pimping out its function room as a disco. The DJ spins dancefloor monsters like *Let's All Chant* and Top 40 hits like *We Are Family* and *Ring My Bell* and *Bad Girls*, and of course this summer's smash, the gay anthem *Born To Be Alive*. Dancing with us on this crowded tiny dancefloor – a dark sweaty room with red flock wallpaper and faux Victorian brass lamps – are two of my best friends. Justin I met a couple of years ago in art school, where we bonded immediately over our love of music. Andy I've known since he was 11 and I was 13 – the morning our paths crossed on our way to very different schools.

Tonight is a celebration of sorts, the first time I've gone out on the town with Stuart since he was paroled a couple of months ago. He'd called me from Tilbury a couple of days earlier, saying he wanted to come up and see me, and Justin had already told me about this pukka DJ working out of a South London boozer. It was a dodgy area but we could invite a couple of mates for safety in numbers – and Stuart was happy enough at the suggestion.

Having assembled at my Whitechapel squat earlier – quick toke on a joint and a cheeky line to set us all up – the journey south takes barely 10 minutes, roaring through empty City streets on two motorcycles, flying across Tower Bridge and howling with excitement at the glittering water.

I ride on the back of Justin's Yamaha XT 500, a stripped-down trials bike with insane torque, but we're barely keeping up with Stuart, whose Kawasaki Z1000 explodes out of each corner while Andy, the only rider with no helmet, clings to Stuart's waist for dear life. Stuart's hulking black beast is said to be the fastest production motorcycle available, top speed around 130 mph. Where he found the money for such an expensive machine – even this two-year-old model – is never firmly established. When I ask he shrugs off the question, muttering something about how easy it is these days to buy anything on tick, or hire purchase. I wonder vaguely about the down payment, normally 40 per cent, but push the idea from my mind. It's party time and his finances are not my business.

As we dance I can't stop looking at Stuart: how does he do this, how does he inhabit this space? He's filtering moves from *Soul Train* through some artful Essex self-mockery, all high camp, arch and impish. His kinetic energy seems effortless, like we could leave him here tonight and return weeks later to find him rocking and strutting in place, fingertips flashing and hips popping to the bass.

But perhaps the most amazing thing is that he learned these fancy little disco steps in prison, from a book purchased on mail order. He must have practised for hours in his cell.

Did he even have music in there? Did he finally get the radio he kept asking for?

Did I take it to the prison for him?

Not only are his movements graceful and powerful, his body has changed out of all recognition. Whereas he was once a smaller and slighter version of me, now he's the same height – but far more powerfully built. His chest is swollen, his shoulders are fleshy cannonballs, his forearms bulge like Popeye's.

This muscular body shape will one day become acceptable, but right now it's considered abnormal and deeply unfashionable. In the late seventies most guys want to look as long and lean as possible. Herculean brawn is for meatheads, wrestlers and fairground strongmen, or uncool athletes like shot putters. Cool kids want to look as if they breakfast on a line of coke, or its cheaper cousin, bathtub speed.

Watching him dance, seeing how graceful and powerfully he moves, realising he's no longer *my little brother*, I feel a surge of pride. The physical transformation, I realise, means he will surely transform his life, too. His powerful new bike and matching body symbolise his new future. He's only 21, still plenty of time to get back on track, and tonight this self-belief shines out of his pores.

This is the start of a new relationship between us. Instead of a recidivist criminal, he's going to become a success, an asset, a source of pride and support.

We're both going to succeed. In fact, everything seems to be going terrifically well for my whole family. My brother is back on the straight and narrow, my sister is training as a veterinarian, my mother is getting remarried – her boyfriend Gerry is a hardworking, easygoing man who treats her well, and they're all living happily together under the same roof, down in Tilbury.

Of course, I'm also aware that Stuart's marriage has irretrievably broken down: his wife Jennifer won't speak to him and he no longer sees their infant daughter, Jennie-Lee. But what I don't know is that, footloose and free to roam again, he has returned to his favourite stalking ground, the same place he'd found Jennifer just a few years earlier: the local school gate. He has bought himself a camera and started a sexual relationship with a 14-year-old girl called Cathy, even taking her back to our mother's home and posing her for a series of indecent pictures.

But all this will only come out years later. For now, everything seems golden.

When we take a break and head to the bar, I ask Stuart what he's drinking.

Mmm, I'll have a shandy.

You sure? One beer won't hurt, will it?

Yeah, rather not. Gotta ride home afterwards. And Andy's not exactly featherweight, eh?

Yeah, you're right. Shandy then.

He rarely drinks, and then only modestly. A half-pint here or there, a lager top that he'll nurse for an hour. I know it's not just because he's riding the bike. My guess is that he will always associate heavy drinking with his abiding hatred for the Old Man.

Lately he's been paying more attention to calories, too. He talks about his intake of carbs and protein and fats. A regulated diet must have played a significant part in his physical transformation and if there's one quality he has in buckets, it's self-discipline.

Again, I feel proud of him.

Another hour or so of strutting our stuff and we all agree to bail before closing time, always the diciest moment of any night out, when half-cut young geezers throng the pavement, eyeing each other up, eager for one last chance to make a mark. And so we mount up and roar back the way we came, over Tower Bridge and along Commercial Road until we reach Jubilee Street, where we pull over and bid farewell. Justin and I will head north, while Stuart and Andy will continue east along the A13 towards Tilbury.

A couple of days later I call Andy and ask him about the ride home.

Oh mate, fucking hell, that was scary.

Yeah, I bet he was going too fast, right?

Not just fast. We're coming up to Canning Town and there's this weird glow in the sky. As we get closer, we can see this huge fire, flames shooting up 30, 40 feet in the air. Hundreds of people, middle of the night, all lined up on the other side of the road, watching this factory burn down. There's sirens and alarms going off, and flashing lights everywhere. Fire engines and police cars everywhere and this copper standing in the road, turning all the cars around because the A13's closed, except for emergency vehicles. And there's this shiny grease or oil all over the floor, and the firemen are slipping and sliding and falling arse over tit as they try and get it all under the control. Stuart slows down and I'm thinking he's gonna turn back when this police car comes flying up behind us, siren blaring. As soon as it passes us, Stuart guns the throttle and fuck me, we're only following it, doing 50 right behind him. All lit up by the fire, hundreds of people watching us take the piss out of the law, right through the fire engines and out the other side.

Jesus.

Yeah, he doesn't give a fuck, does he.

Tilbury, June 1981

It never occurred to me that Stuart might have some perverse sexual attraction for underage girls. Back then, that thought rarely occurred to anybody. Take what was happening in the culture as a case in point.

In June 1981 the entire country seems on the verge of mass hysteria over the global media event of the year, the imminent royal wedding of Prince Charles and Lady Diana Spencer. In an interview just after their engagement, Charles recalls their first encounter, four years earlier. At that point the heir to the throne was still dating Diana's elder sister, Sarah Spencer.

Charles was 29, Diana was 16.

I remember thinking, says Charles, what a very jolly and amusing and attractive 16-year-old she was. I mean, great fun and bouncy and full of life and everything.

Asked her first impression of the future King of England, Diana replies with her trademark Bashful Schoolgirl gimmick: head down, doe-eyed, batting her lashes.

Pretty amazing, she coos.

This encounter is deemed wonderfully romantic by the respective families, the national media and the general public.

And so, as the nation hangs up its Union Jack bunting and gets ready to celebrate the Royal Wedding, Stuart cruises the streets of Tilbury on his powerful Kawasaki motorcycle. Ever more muscular, his shoulders burst from a sleeveless denim jacket or leather vest, his forearms covered with tattoos, his hands clad in fingerless black leather gloves. By now, as well as weightlifting, he has taken up Shotokan karate, an explosive full-contact martial art.

Astride his motorcycle Stuart wears aviator shades, his mullet tied back with a strip of black cloth, and a 7-inch hunting knife strapped to his thigh in a leather sheath. Cruising the town in this proto-Rambo outfit – *First Blood*, the first Rambo movie, won't be released for another 18 months – he recognises a girl walking along the road.

It's Cathy, the girl he had seduced and photographed at the age of 14 – before her parents threatened to report him to the police, ending their involvement. He pulls up in front of her. Now 17, she's on her way to college.

Stuart turns on the charm and offers her a ride.

She climbs onto his pillion seat.

But once again he takes her to our mother's home, where he tells her to undress so he can take some photos. When she refuses, he becomes abusive and slaps her. She tries to push past him, but he grabs her and holds his knife to her throat. Her screams of terror alert the next-door neighbour, who calls the police to report a woman being attacked. Within minutes a squad car arrives, and after questioning a sobbing and trauma-tised Cathy the police arrest Stuart for unlawful imprisonment and threatening behaviour. Given the terms of his parole, he seems certain to be returned to prison within weeks.

But Cathy, realising that Stuart knows her home address, tells police she is too scared to testify. Her parents reluctantly agree and the charges against Stuart are quietly dropped.

Yet again, he gets off scot-free.

20

Paris, Wednesday 14 August 2002
Almost 14 months since Danielle's disappearance

From my diary:

A few days ago the BBC website announced that the trial was expected to begin in October. This must be why DS Keith Davies left a couple of messages on my answer machine while I was in San Francisco earlier this month.

This afternoon my sister Sinéad called to say she'd been told by the police that she will be called as a witness at Stuart's trial. I had to give her something of a pep talk, explaining to her that no matter what Stuart might be guilty of, she is still innocent. In short, his actions were not her fault.

I told her, Whenever you start to feel sorry for yourself, or pissed off, or miserable about this whole affair, remember Tony and Linda. Remember how they feel, try to put yourself in their place. That's why you've got to do this, because until there's some resolution to this story, those people will never be at peace, they'll never sleep properly in their beds. Someone has killed their daughter, their little girl, and they can't even bury her because her body still hasn't shown up. Remember that, and you'll remember why you have to do this.

230

*I also ran through why I believe he is guilty as charged,
though I reminded her that all this was just circumstantial
evidence and not proof – and that I could be wrong, in
which case my brother would never speak to me again.*

*Then again, if he's guilty, the same is likely to be true. I've
written him a letter but had no reply, and a few months ago
I sent him a snide postcard with a photo of Samuel Beckett
above the slogan:*

When you're up to your neck in shit, there's nothing left
to do but to sing.

I don't suppose he appreciated the humour.

Paris, Wednesday 25 September 2002
15 months and seven days since Danielle's disappearance

From my diary:

*Spoke to my mum last week. She sounded quite bright and
reasonably happy. That made me feel better. But after
spending nearly 40 minutes talking about her life, matters
turned to Stuart. Or more specifically, to Debbie and Simon.
Such a lovely little baby, she says. So happy, always smiling.
Have you sent him a birthday card?*

I haven't, no.

Well, why not?

*Because I don't feel as if Debbie wants any contact with
me.*

*My mother tries to tell me this is ridiculous and a heated
exchange follows as I explain that, were it left to Debbie, I
wouldn't even know the baby had been born, let alone his
name and sex. When I called her, I say, she gave the distinct*

impression of not wanting to talk to me. She has never called me, not even once. And though I've written twice to Stuart, he hasn't even bothered to reply.

My mother starts making excuses on their behalf, citing reasons why they might not want to talk to me. She misses the obvious one, though: they both know that I suspect he is guilty.

Eventually we agree to disagree on whether my behaviour or theirs was at fault.

She says she has no idea when the trial might start and hasn't been in touch with Stuart's solicitor. This surprises me, since I'd imagined she would have been keeping tabs on the whole process – especially since she believes Stuart to be innocent and will therefore presumably attend the trial.

Paris, Thursday 26 September 2002
15 months and 8 days since Danielle's disappearance:

I'm scrolling the *Telegraph* online when I notice the following item. It seems like a grotesque joke. But no, it turns out to be genuine.

Danielle Detective Held Over Child Porn

A police officer who worked on the investigation into the murder of teenager Danielle Jones has been arrested in connection with allegations of child pornography.

The officer, who has not been named, was one of six men arrested at various locations across Essex as part of a continuing investigation into images of child abuse. It is understood the officer is a constable and not uniformed.

The arrests were made following information passed on by the American authorities following an investigation into child pornography websites.

Danielle Jones, 15, from Tilbury, Essex, was last seen near her home last June. Her body has never been found.

One of her uncles, Stuart Campbell, has been charged with her murder and is due to stand trial next week.

Paris, Friday 27 September 2002
15 months and 9 days since Danielle's disappearance

This morning I get an email from Jane, who is worried about our daughter Fiona. With Stuart's trial set to start in a couple of weeks, and a police officer on the Danielle Jones case recently arrested on unrelated child porn charges, the story is back in the headlines. Consequently, Stuart's photo and name have featured on TV news repeatedly over the last few days. Although Fiona has not yet recognised Stuart, it is only a matter of time. Jane's main concern is that Fiona could be at school or with classmates when the penny drops, and might be so shocked that she blurts out something like, *That's my uncle!*

Which, given the inevitable schoolgirl gossip, could easily lead the press to Jane's door, something none of us want.

I tell her that I'll be in London this weekend and will drop by to explain the situation to Fiona myself – that the man accused of Danielle Jones' murder is my brother, her Uncle Stuart. And that Danielle is the little girl Fiona met at his wedding. And how, months earlier, I had given Jane a sealed letter, to be given to Fiona in the event of her stumbling across these facts. In that letter I had tried to explain why her mother and I had held back, hoping to save her unnecessary distress and anxiety. The letter was far from ideal, but it would show at least that we'd put in place a plan to help Fiona make sense of the situation until I could speak with her in person.

But before I arrive, Jane decides she can't wait any longer, and explains to Fiona that Stuart Campbell, that surly-looking brute in all the papers, is her dad's brother. Jane tells me later that Fiona was shocked and broke down in tears. She started trembling uncontrollably when she realised that Danielle was *the other* little flower girl, and how the two of them had worn matching pink satin gowns and carried matching bouquets.

When Jane explains this, I wonder aloud whether Fiona had experienced the same horrified reaction that we'd had: the thought that, but for a matter of geography, it could have been either one of those two little girls.

What do *you* think, Alix?

God.

Yeah, she's a clever girl.

As insurance, I call the headmistress of Fiona's all-girls school to explain the situation, asking that she keep an eye on her – and watch out for reporters lurking at the school gates.

By now, I have become as paranoid as the rest of my family about the press.

21

Tilbury, 1980–81

Where is he? What is he up to? The last time I'd seen Stuart was the night we went disco dancing with Andy and Justin in South London, over a year ago. But now I have no idea. Maybe working as a labourer? Perhaps another factory job?

My trips to Tilbury are fewer and further between, but even when I come back for the weekend to see my mother there's rarely any sight of Stuart. All I know is that since his release on parole Stuart hasn't once seen his wife Jennifer or their daughter Jennie-Lee. When I ask my mother why not, she tells me it's because Jennifer has broken his heart. It seems that while Stuart was in prison, she grew tired of waiting for him and started dating a guy called Sid.

But my mother's version of events is incomplete. Whatever she may think, Stuart's wife Jennifer almost certainly knows the *real* reason for his incarceration – and it is not the handling of stolen goods, as we have been led to believe.

It is something much more serious.

Looking back, there was so much I didn't know and didn't think to question.

Ignorance, as they say, is bliss.

Grays, 1982

Blackshots pool is where Stuart and I first learned to swim on primary school trips. In our adolescence, we spent Saturdays there with dozens of other kids. The boys bombed and splashed and raced and wrestled each other. We loved everything about this pool, but most of all how it dissolved all tribal rivalries, reducing us all to wet-haired children, limbs pricked with goose-flesh, elbows clenched to sides, teeth chattering.

And it was at Blackshots that Stuart and I first encountered erotic desire, first became aware of female bodies. All the boys loved to tease the girls, to splash them or nudge them into the water. Sometimes we would swim up behind them, wrap our arms around their waists and pull them under. They would shriek and slap at us as we swam away laughing.

Overlooking one side of Blackshots is a public gallery that affords a panoramic viewpoint. After being released from prison in 1982, Stuart sits up here, watching the kids splashing around below, before going down to the locker rooms and getting changed into his swimsuit.

Is it really a surprise that he should return to this place, scene of our first erotic stirrings, our earliest physical interactions with the opposite sex? It certainly isn't difficult to imagine how events unfolded one particular Saturday afternoon as he emerges from the changing rooms.

Despite his time inside he still has his boyish looks, his long dark hair, narrow hips and powerful thighs. The prison weight-lifting regime has broadened his shoulders and thickened his biceps. As he paces the pool's perimeter in his Speedos, a teenage girl catches his eye. He smiles at her, beckons her, asks her name. He makes a joke, and she laughs.

The girl is barely 15 years old. Stuart is 24.

Her name is Debbie Jones.

Her girlfriends are used to Debbie getting attention – she's so beautiful, what with her blue eyes and lean frame and long slender legs. They all think Debbie should be a model and have told her so many times.

Trouble is, a lot of older men tell her the same thing. Just like Stuart, they stop her in the middle of the street and start laying on the sweet talk. Her friends have seen it many times. And so they mock Stuart, throwing their floats and armbands at him, calling him an old pervert.

He nods and smiles and ignores them, locking his gaze onto Debbie's.

And even though Debbie has heard it all before, this time it works. He persuades her to come to his house – yes, he's still living with his mum right now, but that's only while he's looking for a place of his own. What happens next? Does he enchant her with his trusty gimmick, offering to take some racy photos and send them to a fashion magazine – perhaps *i-D*, the hip publication where his brother Alix works? Whatever the con, it works like a charm.

Shortly after, Debbie introduces him to her family. And while they must be sceptical at first about Debbie dating someone almost a decade older, Stuart will soon put them at ease. Of course, he has those ugly tattoos on his forearms – especially that grinning skull in a top hat, cigar in his teeth, above a large red number 13. Why would he get such a creepy image tattooed on his arm? A bit weird.

Still, he gives the impression of being a decent bloke. Good-looking, nice manners, great sense of humour, always doing funny voices, doesn't take himself too seriously. And quick to lend a hand, always ready to help with a bit of DIY around the house or garden – trim the hedge, clean the gutters, that kind of thing. Nothing seems too much trouble.

And he treats her so well.

Calls her *Princess*.

*   *   *

In December 1982 the British film industry is galvanised by the UK release of *First Blood*, starring Sylvester Stallone as John Rambo. I can still recall my shock at seeing the poster for the first time:

Shit, that looks like Stuart.

Maybe he'd read the book in prison? Maybe it was just in the zeitgeist.

When I finally saw *First Blood* many years later, I was struck by certain themes. The violent loner, tormented by physical and mental abuse he suffered while imprisoned, refuses to conform and wreaks havoc on those who defy him. A tortured and orphaned son, he's unable to form stable relationships in a world devoid of any meaningful female character, much less romance or tenderness. Rambo's only moment of vulnerability and intimacy is in the final scene, when he breaks down and sobs in the arms of his long-lost father figure.

But then, maybe I'm simply projecting.

After all, what is my life at this point? Most days I get up late and go swimming at my local pool in Whitechapel. Then I sit around reading novels and writing lyrics and practising guitar. Later I'll ride the tube into the West End to rehearse with my bandmates Phil and Pete. Afterwards, we go to the pub with our manager, who buys all the drinks.

On weekend nights I go to nightclubs and dance until I'm drenched in sweat. I spend a lot of time thinking about clothes and like to imagine I'm leading some kind of avant-garde life, almost post-industrial. I figure if I just keep playing guitar and writing songs, everything else will come to me, just a matter of time. I periodically cheat on my long-suffering girlfriend. It's a pretty vacuous life with few responsibilities. And into this hedonistic existence comes the unexpected, a foreshadowing event.

It's gone midnight and I'm strumming my acoustic guitar when there's a knock at the door. A huge figure fills the doorway, one eyebrow cocked ironically.

Hello, stranger.

Wow, I say. Come in.

It's Stuart. And boy, does he look special. With his pretty boy features and puffed-up mullet and blouson leather jacket, he resembles those mumsy Wham! boys – but supplemented with an industrial quantity of steroids and carotene tablets. He removes the jacket and we sit at the table. He's wearing shell suit bottoms with a zigzag pattern, and a baggy yellow Golds Gym tank top ripped to reveal a bulging orange chest and grapefruit-sized biceps. He looks as if he's been inflated with a hydraulic pump.

Despite the breezy greeting, he's nervy and anxious, chewing his fingernails even more frantically than usual.

I open the fridge and hold up the last beer.

Just water, thanks.

Nice of you to drop by. Bit late for a social call.

Need a favour, he says.

No shit. What's going on?

Got into a bit of trouble with the law.

Fuck, again?

Nah, nothing too serious. Just need to get out of Tilbury for a while, keep a low profile.

How long's a while?

Couple of months, maybe a bit longer. Till it all calms down.
What's *it*?

Mmmm, he says. Better you don't know the whole story. That way, you won't be aiding and abetting.

I notice he's looking around my squat, maybe thinking about moving in. Which definitely is not happening.

So, I say, what's the plan?

Not sure, he says. Wondered if you had any ideas.

Maybe, I say. Let's talk tomorrow. You can have the sofa.

22

Paris, Tuesday 8 October 2002
1 year and 3 months and 20 days since Danielle's disappearance

After getting her mobile number from my mother, I phone Stuart's lawyer.

Hi, it's Alix Sharkey here. Stuart's brother.

Oh, hello. How can I help you?

I was wondering when the trial starts. Do you have a date?

A trial date has been set, yes.

When is it?

I'm afraid I can't discuss the case without Stuart's permission so I won't be able to give any information out.

He doesn't want you to talk to me?

I'm afraid I can't discuss the case without Stuart's permission.

*   *   *

Later that day I get online and learn that the trial had started that very morning.

That evening the *Yorkshire Post* leads with the headline: *Uncle's Sexual Obsession Led to Murder, Jury Told.*

The report describes a packed courtroom, with Stuart seated in the dock, impassive in his dark blue suit, dark tie and pale blue shirt. He has already entered a plea of Not Guilty to both charges, namely the abduction and murder of Danielle Sarah Jones. The case begins with Crown prosecutor Orlando Pownall

QC giving his opening argument: Stuart Campbell, a 44-year-old builder, had an 'irresistible sexual attraction' for his 15-year-old niece Danielle Jones, which led him to kidnap and murder the schoolgirl. Her body, he tells the court, has never been found.

Mr Pownall explains that Stuart Campbell had been fascinated with underage girls for decades and liked to photograph them in lingerie or school uniform. A forensic examination by police of his Packard Bell computer showed he frequented pornographic websites with names such as *Young Lolita Beauties*, with similar images. Stuart sits in the dock taking notes as the prosecution lists several women who have come forward – dating back 15 years – claiming he had approached them as teenage girls, successfully or otherwise, to pose for him.

It is the prosecution's case, says Pownall, that this defendant, Danielle's uncle Stuart Campbell, is responsible for abducting his niece and killing her.

He then outlines the relationship that developed between Stuart and Danielle, starting in the months leading up to her 15th birthday. How he became fixated by her, inserting himself into her life, driving her to and from school and her home, and sending her a constant stream of flirtatious text messages. How he kept a secret diary detailing the contact between them. How he ingratiated himself so thoroughly that Danielle's parents had loaned him a front door key to do some minor DIY work in the family home. How he had made a copy of that key, using it while the family was away on holiday to enter Danielle's bedroom, where he left handwritten notes for her.

And how, in the weeks immediately before her disappearance, Danielle had grown tired of, and started to reject, his advances.

Mr Pownall explains that a police search of Stuart's home led to the discovery of blood-stained white stockings that bore a mix of both the defendant's and Danielle's DNA.

Next, he points out the gaping holes in the defendant's alibi and how mobile phone signal triangulation proves Stuart could not have been, as he'd told police, in a DIY store several miles away when Danielle went missing.

On the morning she left for school, Pownall tells the jury, Danielle was seen talking to a man in a blue Transit van.

It is not coincidence, he says, that this defendant owned such a van and it is submitted that you can be sure that he abducted her that morning and took her to his home address, where he probably intended to take pictures of her. Although the manner in which she met her death is – by reason of the absence of her body – uncertain, it is submitted that you can be sure that he and he alone is responsible.

The presence of her blood on the white stockings, says Pownall, means she was either photographed wearing them or an attempt was made to make her wear them.

The trial adjourns, with the judge explaining to the jury that tomorrow the entire court will board two coaches and visit a number of locations – including the street where Danielle once lived, and was last seen alive.

Paris, Thursday 10 October 2002
1 year, 3 months and 22 days since Danielle's disappearance

From my diary:

Today's newspapers report on the two text messages Stuart supposedly received after Danielle's disappearance. The first:

Alix Sharkey

*HI-YA STU WOT YOU UP I'M IN SO MUCH TROUBLE
AT HOME AT MOMENT. EVONE HATES ME EVEN
YOU WOT THE HELL HAVE I DONE Y WON'T YOU
JUST TELL ME. TEXT BCK PLEASE. DAN XXX.*

The second, sent the following day:

*HI-YA STU. THANKS FOR BEING SO NICE, YOU ARE
THE BEST UNCLE EVER. TELL MUM I'M SO SORRY
LUVYA LOADZ DAN XXX.*

A professor of linguistics and English from the University of
Birmingham tells the jury the messages are not at all like
Danielle's normal text messages. There are several
discrepancies in style, he says, most obviously the fact that
Danielle always used lower case, while the messages are in
upper case. Crown prosecutor Mr Pownall points out that
mobile phone signals show the messages were both sent
from the vicinity of Stuart Campbell's home.

And why, he asks, would Danielle send text
messages only to the defendant, yet not to her family and
friends? Even if she were being held captive, who would
allow her to send two text messages, and why only to her
uncle?

Clearly, the text messages were meant to divert attention
from Stuart Campbell – yet they have only served to
underline his guilt.

I feel certain the police must have seen the embedded
statements in each of them, statements which leap out to me.
In the first, stripping away the jaunty greeting and fake
anxiety, my brother is literally sending himself a text
message which reads:

244

I'm in so much trouble at home at the moment. Everyone hates me. What the hell have I done?

The following day, in a fit of remorse, he sends himself another text which reads:

Tell Mum I'm so sorry.

And finally,

Why won't you just tell me?

Consumed by guilt, shame and horror, this question must have echoed through his mind. Why wouldn't he just tell someone – his wife, Danielle's parents, the police, anyone – the awful truth?

It's obvious.

These are not Danielle's words to Stuart.

They are Stuart's words to himself.

In his panic, dread and horror, he has betrayed the workings of his mind. This is what he wanted to tell Danielle's mother and perhaps his own: I'm so sorry. But he couldn't, because that would require admitting his guilt. Which in turn would have meant the loss of all that remained to him – his wife, and a son he will never know.

I call DS Keith Davies and tell him about the embedded messages in these fake texts. He says he hadn't noticed them, but thinks it might be worth pointing out to counsel. Also, he says he has checked the list of witnesses and our sister Sinéad isn't on it and so she is therefore unlikely to be called. He says he will call her this evening and let her know, to put her mind at ease.

Later that day, the members of the jury, along with prosecution and defence counsel and trial judge Mr Justice McKinnon, climb aboard two coaches outside Chelmsford Crown Court. They make the 45-mile drive south-west to East Tilbury, where they walk around the neighbourhood

surrounding the Jones family's home and retrace Danielle's
last steps on the morning of her disappearance.

Paris, Friday 11 October 2002
1 year, 3 months and 23 days since Danielle's disappearance

From my diary:

> *The trial has begun and it's getting me down, I feel very*
> *miserable and quite viscerally sick – much more than I*
> *imagined I would. In fact, I'm quite shocked at how sad I*
> *feel about the whole thing.*

The same day, *The Sun* reports:

> The mother of murdered teenager Danielle Jones wept in court
> yesterday as she recalled seeing her alive for the last time.
> Anguished Linda Jones broke down from the effort of describing
> watching her 15-year-old daughter set off for school on her final
> morning. Wiping tears from her eyes with her right forefinger, the
> 42-year-old mum told a jury: 'I saw her walk out the door.'

The following two lines land like a punch in the chest:

> As she spoke, the man accused of Danielle's murder, her uncle
> Stuart Campbell, 44, also burst into tears. He bowed his head
> and brought both hands up to his face as sister-in-law Linda
> sobbed loudly in the witness box less than 30ft away.

He burst into tears, bowed his head and buried his face in his hands?

Dear God, he knows what he has done.

Stuart still has a glimmer of shame. He knows how grotesquely he betrayed the love and trust of the Jones family, he understands the enormity of his crime.

And *still* he won't confess.

For the next 11 weeks, this is how I pass my days. Each morning, another heart-wrenching detail. Every afternoon, another gut-churning fact.

Every day I'm thinking, he must know that he can't possibly win. Even if he is now totally amoral, surely he's smart enough to see it's the only card he has left to play?

Surely he can't be stupid enough to think he'll be acquitted?

I hole up in my apartment trying to understand and then decide I don't want to understand and drown my confusion with wine until I stagger into the bedroom and pass out, fully clothed.

Then I get up and start again.

I wish I could talk about it. I don't want to talk about it.

I don't want to think about it, but I can't stop thinking about it.

I wonder if maybe I should write about it. Maybe that would help me process it.

Editors at the weekend supplements of national newspapers say they will pay me handsomely to write about it. One editor in particular, a man I respect who has shared with me his own story of fraternal loss, emails me to say he wants 5,000 words, a huge front cover story.

I tell him that while I want to write about it, I just can't. Maybe once Danielle's body is recovered and her parents have some closure.

But for now, I reply, *I can't see how it could be done without causing enormous suffering to people who have already endured a hellish ordeal.*

Back in Paris, I explain my reasoning to my friend Paul Rambali.

Okay, he says. But sooner or later you'll have to write about it anyway. Whether or not Stuart tells the truth.

No, I say. Not until my brother confesses.

Yes, you will.

No, Paul. I fucking *won't.*

He smiles in that superior, knowing way, a smile that never fails to piss me off.

One day, he says.

From my diary:

I have done nothing this week apart from go to parties and dinner. Most of the time I feel sick, literally quite sick in the stomach. It's a shock to me, this visceral reaction to my brother's trial. I'm not quite sure why I feel sick: it's something to do with understanding his state of mind, his panic, his dread and shame. And also knowing that I might still be dragged into this.

23

Whitechapel, 1982

Stuart comes looking for somewhere to stay and a job, so he can avoid the police while earning a few quid. I tell him he can count on me, no questions asked. I'm not sure how I justify it to myself, but I probably assume he has broken some minor law, like possession or intent to supply. After all, most people around me live on the edge of criminality – we all take drugs, and drugs are sold and taken everywhere we go.

Of course, I don't have a spare room or a job for him. But I know who to ask.

My band's manager has often told me tales about his time on the run. When I explain the situation, he tells me to bring Stuart to his office for a meeting. They speak briefly and my manager makes a few calls. Within 10 minutes Stuart has a place to stay for the next few months. He will hide out in Manchester, working for an old-school clothing manufacturer who'd made velvet jackets for my manager's boutique back in the seventies, back when he was spending a lot of time on the dancefloor of the Blackpool Mecca and velvet jackets were still a thing.

And so my brother buys a one-way ticket to Manchester, where he'll work as some kind of driver and assistant. It's unlikely that Essex Police will put out a national alert, but Stuart says he will get some new documents in a false name. In this paper era, before photo ID and computerised databases, it is still relatively easy to drum up some paperwork and create a new identity in a new city.

What name you gonna use?

He stops chewing his thumbnail and says, Scott.

Scott Campbell?

No, he says. Stuart Scott.

Why Scott?

Dunno, he says, I just like it. Sounds like a film star, doesn't it?

Oh, yeah.

But I'm thinking how weird it is to drop Campbell – a distinctly Scottish name, inherited from a father he detested, a name I have long since discarded – and opt instead for Scott. Almost like he can't let go of the past. I want to suggest the obvious alternative, his mother's maiden name, Sharkey. But I reconsider. Adopting the same surname as me?

Wouldn't that be even weirder?

We walk to Whitechapel tube station, where we hug and shake hands.

Stay in touch, I say. Let me know how you're getting on.

Yeah, he says. I'll send you a postcard. Don't worry, I won't sign it. But you'll know it's me from the message, *Wish you were here.*

I watch Stuart Scott as he disappears into the station, en route to his new life in Manchester.

The postcard never arrives.

After a couple of weeks, I forget all about it. I've done my bit and anyway, he's probably fine.

Looking back, I wonder what reason Stuart gave Debbie for his sudden departure, since at this point they had been dating for several months. I suppose he fobbed her off with some half-truth, just as he had with me. Of course, with hindsight it's obvious that I enabled his behaviour – as much as anyone, if not more – by helping him evade justice. Never once did I demand to know why he'd been arrested yet again, nor if he felt any shame or remorse.

Perhaps I avoided tough questions because I didn't want the truth. To this day I still don't know what he was running from – his criminal record is shielded by the Data Protection Act – but I suspect it involved the sexual assault of another minor. Whatever the charges, they were serious enough that he jumped bail and became a fugitive. Serious enough, too, that he would leave his pretty teenage girlfriend and uproot his life in Essex to travel 230 miles north-west to a city he had never seen, to work for a man he'd never met.

Maybe 10 months later, I get a call from my mother, one that I've been expecting for some time.

It's Stuart, she says.

What now?

He's been arrested in Birmingham and is back in prison, awaiting trial.

24

Paris, Thursday 31 October 2002
1 year, 4 months and 13 days since Danielle's disappearance

I'm looming over him and snarling, fists raised. He's on the floor, propped on one elbow and gazing up at me, stunned. A semi-circle has opened around us, wide-eyed, looking down at him and back to me, trying to understand what just happened.

Earlier that afternoon I'd taken the metro to Avenue George V and strolled through a cobbled courtyard into the palatial red-carpeted and gilded headquarters of Yves Saint Laurent. I told the security guard to call an assistant, and told the assistant I knew M. Saint Laurent personally, and since he was shuttering his couture business that very day, I wished to pay my respects. A blatant lie, but as expected, the assistant apologised profusely, saying Monsieur was very emotional and not up to seeing anybody right now, as I would surely understand.

But please, he said, have some champagne – he pointed across the foyer to a waiter with a silver tray – and take a seat in the *salon d'attente*, just in case.

Glass in hand, I wandered through empty offices towards the back of the building and climbed a series of tight staircases up to the workshops where *les petites mains* – the seamstresses, embroiderers and pattern cutters who had worked here for decades, bringing the master's creations to life – were gathered around cutting tables in rooms packed with gemstone-coloured bolts of silk. They sat drinking and reminiscing, laughing and weeping on this, their final day of employment at one of fashion's greatest houses.

I asked questions, took notes, drank more champagne.

Later, we all made our way down to the basement car park and lined up in a swaying guard of honour at the elevator door, applauding as a teary-eyed M. Saint Laurent, trembling and leaning heavily on his cane, hobbled out to his black limousine, exquisitely elegant as ever. We waved him off as he bade farewell to his staff and a lifetime's work – the *maison de couture* he'd founded in 1961.

I went home and wrote an 800-word fly-on-the-wall piece for an English newspaper about this historic moment, earning myself half my monthly mortgage.

That afternoon, just as I finish filing the piece, I'm scrolling the *Telegraph* website when I see Stuart's face under the headline

First Picture of Danielle Murder Charge Uncle.

He's smiling, tanned, healthy:

> Justice Stuart McKinnon ruled that only one picture of Stuart Campbell, Danielle's uncle, could be used. The photograph was taken while Campbell was on a family holiday.

I'm still processing this when I get a call from my friend Paul Rambali. He tells me about the embossed and gilt-edged invitation in his hand, one of dozens he receives every week as a producer for a TV company. He reads aloud in French:

Enter Larry Flynt's Hustler Club Paris and descend into an atmosphere of sensual hospitality.

But the most important words, he says, are in English: *Open Bar.*

And so just before midnight, in a glitzy neighbourhood just off the Champs-Élysées, we join American pornographer and free speech advocate Larry Flynt in celebrating his 60th birthday with the grand opening of his latest strip joint, a few minutes' walk from the flagship stores of luxury brands like Louis Vuitton, Chanel, Hermès, Dior – and yes, Yves Saint Laurent.

We are slumming it, of course, because strip clubs and lap-dancing joints – even the supposedly upmarket type – are not really our speed. But we tell ourselves that it's a free drink among the ageing Lotharios of the Parisian nightlife scene, an ironic gag.

After all, for almost a year now, high street fashion stores have been selling T-shirts for young women emblazoned with slogans like *Porn Star in Training* or *Porn Queen* or *Barbie Is a Crack Whore.* Within a couple of months, Hollywood director Sofia Coppola will direct a White Stripes video featuring Kate Moss as a pole-dancer. And given her enormous influence, it's no surprise that even teenage schoolgirls are getting hip to the hoochie mama hype. Rap and R&B videos invariably feature nubile women in so-called stripper heels and thongs, as sexual objectification becomes ever more blatant and normalised. This 'porn chic' has made the public's once-censorious attitude to strip clubs and the sex market far more ambivalent. Stripping and pole-dancing and porn and sex work might as well exist in plain view, it seems – not simply tolerated but celebrated. The days of hiding those smutty magazines in a cupboard are long gone. Having spent decades crusading for our right to drunkenly ogle barely clad young women, Larry Flynt has long since won this stage of the culture war and his attitude now prevails: what could be more wholesome than good old red-blooded lust, served up with a smear of irony?

The Hustler Club is reliably, cynically blatant. Red and white neon signage leads to a satin-quilted kiosk selling 'Beaver Bucks' – fake money for tipping servers, bartenders and hosts, 'although the most common use is for entertainer performances'. Upstairs, the cashier tells us, are the private rooms for one-on-one lap dances. Next to the kiosk is a souvenir store, like those airport gift shops, but with T-shirts, baseball caps, lubricant gel and flavoured condoms bearing the Hustler Club logo.

The main floor is your archetypal strip club: Big Hair stadium rock blares out across a cavernous uterine space, all raking pink spotlights and red velvet banquettes centred around two podiums, each with a lithe platinum blonde in a G-string swinging from a silver pole. Meanwhile, other girls in skimpy one-piece outfits strut back and forth with trays of drinks. We notice the clientele is somewhat younger and hipper than we'd imagined. Clearly, we're not the only media people to attend as a camp joke.

The bar menu offers whisky, vodka or tequila at €190 a bottle, around £120. Nothing by the glass. Fortunately, tonight's party is sponsored by Johnnie Walker Red Label, so we order whiskies on the house and down them rapidly. I order a couple more. Paul tells the barman that we're members of the press and we don't want to get drunk too quickly, so he obliges with two flutes of champagne.

The sexually charged atmosphere has a whiff of mercantile sleaze, that familiar aura of privilege and entitlement, as 20-something women in various states of undress smile at boozy middle-aged men and indulge their foolish chat-up lines, while other young women ply them with alcohol.

They're very professional, says Paul, still taking notes even off-duty. Nice midwestern girls. Wholesome, pleasant, chatty. Good teeth.

I'm already showing my empty glass to the barman.

Today was Day 19 of the trial.

For almost three weeks, the prosecution has been painting a picture of a strange, devious individual that I no longer recognise, even though I've known him all my life. A sullen and brutal man, apparently, with a long history of sexual violence towards underage girls. A man who for years has led a double life, his twisted criminal nature hidden behind an upbeat facade. For almost three weeks, this trial has dominated my waking hours and my dreams.

So even though this ridiculous environment – this cokehead rock music, these chatty girls in trashy outfits, this industrial-grade whisky – is starting to make me feel tense and uncomfortable, I'm glad to be here with Paul. Lately, I have been spending too much time at home. At least tonight I'm getting drunk in company, breaking up a routine which has become morbid and depressing.

But instead of having a laugh, I swiftly drink myself to near-oblivion. Like Paul's, my mind won't stop analysing, but along a much darker path. Here I am, surrounded by servile young women trying to please me, while I drink whisky and regard them as objects. I sink into a familiar pit of shame – the creeping sense that I'm not so different from my father after all.

Later on I'm leaning my stool back against the bar so I can watch the dancers, sipping my sixth or seventh free drink of the night. Axl Rose is screeching tuneless drivel about the Paradise City while the dancers swing their legs and whip their frosty hair, their gyroscopic motions defying gravity as they coil and uncoil, slithering up and down their poles. Little diamonds of light skitter off the mirrorball to wash over the blank faces around the base of the podiums.

On my left, his back to me, Paul is oozing charm all over an American girl in a scarlet satin one-piece and matching nails, with fishnet tights and strappy platform shoes.

Two stools to my right sits a dark-haired woman in her mid-twenties, bored lithic by her companion, a young guy who keeps shouting in her ear so loud I can discern his posh Parisian accent. He is leaner and taller than me, early thirties, artful stubble and long hair worn with a striped shirt and suit by agnès b. Very similar to mine, in fact. Maybe that's what throws him off, the assumption that similar taste indicates similar temperament.

Rookie error.

She sees me watching. I roll my eyes. She smiles and I smile back. He follows her gaze and glares at me. Since he is clearly a rich brat from the 16th arrondissement, I wink and pout at him. She laughs. He shouts in her ear, still glaring at me. I sneer.

Now enraged, he walks over and stands in front of me, blocking my view. I slide off my stool so we're eye to eye. He leans in until his nose is an inch from mine, teeth bared and index finger held up to my cheek, and shouts in my face that if I don't mind my own business, he will fuck me up.

It's all over in a blur, one-two-three.

Which is where we came in, with me looming over him, fists raised, snarling at him to get up again.

Suddenly, two arms enclose mine and I'm being swung around and steered towards the exit on the other side of the room. Paul is growling into my ear.

That's it, we're leaving now, let's go!

He steers me quick-march through a crowd too busy getting drunk for free and ogling female flesh to notice the fracas.

Seconds later we're in the cool night air on the rue de Berri, walking away briskly, having christened Larry Flynt's opening night with a brawl. As we cross the street towards his car, Paul turns to me.

Why are you smiling? he says.

What?

You're really pleased with yourself, aren't you?

He started it, I ended it.

You silly fucker. You could have just ignored him.

We climb into his bronze Mercedes 190E and Paul turns the key. Instantly the cabin explodes with the loping hypnotic bounce of *Let Me Ride* by Dr. Dre, from his debut album *The Chronic*, which Paul calls *a rap opera about revenge* and which he plays nonstop these days.

Seriously, what the fuck was all that about?

I lost control.

No, you knew what you were doing. You saw that guy and decided to fuck him up.

I look down at my bruised and swollen knuckles. Sheepish, I glance sideways, but Paul doesn't seem to notice.

We are not gangsters. We don't have tattoos or gold chains or bandanas or low-slung baggy jeans. We don't walk the walk or talk the talk. We're soft-bellied, middle-aged writers who live modest but easy lives in Paris, who share a love of Indian food, funky music and pop culture. We're grammar school boys who leveraged our literacy skills and streetwise nous to forge careers in London's early-eighties style press. We pride ourselves on *not* fighting, because words are our weapons. We can talk our way into any party, out of any trouble. And yet here we are in the Merc, with the rap blaring and laughing about the strip club fight we just left in our drunken wake, as if we're tough guys. Because irony, obviously.

I mumble something about the atmosphere of the club affecting me.

What do you mean, atmosphere? says Paul.

You know, the hustle. The sexual aspect, that whole cattle market thing, women for sale.

Alix, it's a strip club. You knew that, you weren't ambushed.

Yeah, but it was the taste and the smell of the whisky. It fucked me up. Whenever I smelled that as a kid, it meant my father would beat my mother. And that guy just made me angry, shouting at that girl, you know?

Don't sweat it, he says. He was only stunned, no real damage.

And so we smile our dumb stoner smiles and rock our heads to Dre's mesmeric beat, bathed in golden street light as we glide up the Champs-Élysées.

The strange thing is that ever since Stuart was last released from prison in the 1980s, he has never been involved in any kind of public brawl. Even though he was the one so quick to rage when we were kids, he must have learned another way to work with his anger, at least in public. Perhaps prison teaches you to keep your mouth shut and your head down, to pick your battles, rather than waste energy. Then again, maybe he was only violent in private, with defenceless young women.

Meanwhile, having never experienced prison life, I've been able to kid myself that I'm a civilised, intelligent rational human being with good manners and graces and the gift of the gab. And yet I'm the one sitting here drunk and ashamed, nursing bruised knuckles again after all these years.

Gazing out at dark empty boulevards I realise I'm lucky to have a friend like Paul, who has literally pulled me out of the fire tonight. More than that, his wit has helped keep me sane of late. We find grim humour in the fact that he and Stuart share a birthday, 21 February. A few days from now, I will write in my journal:

This was the year where I got in touch with my inner hooligan, as Paul so neatly put it. But having got in touch, I pulled back sharply and refused to answer his calls.

As we pass the Gare du Nord and approach my street, Paul turns off the music. He nods and strokes his chin.

I've figured out what happened, he says.

Oh yeah?

Yeah, he says. You want to hit your brother, but you can't, so you lashed out at someone giving you a dirty look.

No, no, I say. I told you, he was jealous, he got up in my face and …

But I can't finish, because we both know he's right: that's exactly what I wanted to do. In my darkest moments, consumed with rage, I have seen myself being let into his cell and attacking him, beating the truth out of him. He's bigger and stronger than me, but in my imagination, righteous fury makes me invincible.

You will confess. You will tell me what you did with her. I will beat you until you tell me, even if I have to beat you to death.

And then I catch myself in this sick fantasy, more lost and pitiful than ever.

We ride in silence for a moment and I ask Paul to keep going, past my apartment and around the corner, so we can stop at L'Olympique, my local bar.

You know, for a nightcap.

He looks at me and sighs.

Really?

Really, I say.

It's gross, I know, but I don't care. I'm going to need more alcohol before I can face the darkness tonight.

Paris, Tuesday 5 November 2002
1 year, 4 months and 18 days since Danielle's disappearance

Each day brings another revelation, another repulsive headline about my brother:

Danielle's Lipgloss Found in Uncle's Loft.

Danielle Uncle's Glamour Agency Claims.

Danielle Uncle's Topless Girl Photos.

This week Crown prosecutor Orlando Pownall is building a picture of Stuart's modus operandi, calling a series of female witnesses who provide devastating evidence about Stuart's decades-long predatory behavior. Yesterday the court heard that Stuart had taken topless pictures of two 16-year-old schoolgirls at his house after telling them he was a professional photographer.

Today a young woman weeps in the witness box as she tells the jury how Stuart had persuaded her as a 15-year-old to go to his home and be photographed. Caroline Thompson, now 22, explains that the defendant had approached her in August 1995 in Grays, Essex. After explaining that he was a professional photographer for a glamour agency, he persuaded her to come to his home, where he asked her to take her skirt off.

I said I didn't want to, she explains.

The next thing she recalls is being photographed topless, although she cannot recall how she got undressed.

A young woman called Neeley Bundock, now 20, tells jurors an almost identical story about Stuart approaching her as a

15-year-old on her way home from school. Again, he said he worked for a glamour agency and gave her his business card, offering to produce a free portfolio of photographs. Miss Bundock had agreed to be photographed, but the session was cancelled when she asked that her elder sister be present for the shoot.

Her mother, Susan Bundock, tells the court that despite her initial anger about this adult man approaching her daughter on the street, she had been convinced by his professional manner when he called at the family's house.

I'm intrigued by this phrase in the BBC report: *Her mother ... had been convinced by his professional manner.*

Of course, by this point I know that Stuart had often used my name in his con, telling his victims he could get them work with *i-D* magazine if they posed for him. The illusory connection between his *modelling agency* and his brother, a fashion magazine editor, added a patina of professionalism to his racket.

And the name of his bogus modelling agency?

Cinderella's.

The childhood fantasy of every little girl who dreams of escaping drudgery to become a princess – thanks to a change of clothes and the patronage of Prince Charming.

What was it Keith Davies had said?

He's a good-looking bloke, isn't he? And full of charm. Everyone says how charming he is, what a character.

Paris, Wednesday 20 November 2002
1 year, 5 months and 2 days since Danielle's disappearance

Today's revelations are in the *Thurrock Gazette*, the local news-paper for Tilbury and Grays, with the headline *Uncle Tried to Dump Porn Pics*. Apparently, Stuart had tried to wipe more than 2,000 pornographic images of teenage girls from his computer, just hours before Danielle vanished. Computer expert Russell May tells the court that my brother spent long hours surfing the web for images of underage girls. But the day before Danielle disappeared, he'd bought and installed Norton Cleansweep soft-ware. Still, police were able to piece together a detailed history of his online activity.

As always, the reporting ends with the phrase, *The case continues.*

*　　*　　*

Why do I follow the trial? I certainly don't want to. Reading about my brother and his grotesque secret life leaves me nause-ated, weary and miserable.

Still, I remain fixated.

Not because I expect any exculpatory evidence to surface at this point. Perhaps because I know how difficult winning this case may prove for the Crown Prosecution Service. After all, in 99 per cent of murder trials, the primary evidence is the victim's corpse: its location, condition and forensic status, the bruises, scratches, wounds, the body fluids, the skin under the victim's fingernails.

In this case, that evidence is non-existent.

Nearly 18 months since she disappeared, Danielle's body is still missing.

Everything feels sharp and jagged, rusty and tangled. I know my brother is guilty, yet in the darkest chamber of my heart, there's still a flicker of hope for some unexpected twist, hope that I'll wake up and log on to learn that Danielle's remains have been found in a remote part of the Scottish Highlands, hundreds of miles from Essex, proving beyond question that someone else must have abducted and killed her. At the same time, I want the prosecution to convince the jury beyond a reasonable doubt that my brother is Danielle's killer, so that justice is served and he is punished for his crime.

When I allow myself to feel anything for Stuart at all, I feel pity, knowing how lost and lonely he must be right now, and that deep inside his fearsome exterior there is still a frightened little boy unable to confess his crime. Yet I also feel a burning anger, a rage that wants vengeance, demands blood. Somehow I hold these incompatible thoughts and emotions simultaneously. I don't dare mention them, because people might think I'm losing my mind. More than that, they might be right.

Conflicting emotions literally stop me in my tracks. I find myself in the middle of a busy street, unable to recall how I got there, where I'm going, what I was doing. I feel an overwhelming urge to weep and then I wonder who needs or deserves my tears.

Who would I weep for? Certainly not myself.

How can I cry for Danielle, when I never really knew her? Why would I cry for Stuart, when I know he's guilty? I want to cry because it might make life more tolerable, but that would surely be self-pity. This is why my tears will not fall, why I can't unblock my emotions, can't unburden myself of this bleak and unrelenting sadness.

And so, of course, I drink.

Every evening I buy a couple more bottles and sit at home drinking myself into gormless anaesthesia. Sometimes when the booze kicks in, I call friends in America or England, drunk-dialling at ridiculous hours to talk about the good old days, or fashion, or football or politics. Anything but what's really on my mind, what I'm trying so desperately to forget, if just for an hour or so.

Every weekday morning, still hungover, I log on to follow the trial like a voyeur. Hidden from the courtroom, yet intimately present. For a long time I have struggled with the question of whether to go sit in the public gallery. Even after six weeks of testimony and evidence, I'm still conflicted, unable to answer my own questions.

Am I avoiding the trial out of sheer cowardice? It's a long haul but I could still catch the Eurostar and a connecting train to Chelmsford, there's nothing stopping me. But logistics aside, other questions arise. Would my presence be disruptive, even harmful? Would it cause a media distraction? Could it be misinterpreted as tacit support for the defendant, when in fact I'm certain of his guilt? Do I have a moral duty to be there, if only to bear witness? Am I, to use the biblical taunt, my brother's keeper?

In the end I decide my attendance could be taken as a gesture of support for my brother. Would I lend moral support if he asked for it, swearing on his life that he was innocent? Maybe. Probably. But since he hasn't reached out, the question is moot.

If I'm honest, I'm also worried about being roped into this vile story. On a slow news day, I'd be an easy target for the tabloids. I can imagine them raking through articles I'd written years ago for the *Independent* and the *Guardian* and then squeezing out a few sensational inches: *Murder Uncle's Brother Says Ecstasy Should Be Legal.*

Worse, they might use me as a conduit to pester my mother, or my sister – who may be called as a witness to one of his previous attempts at illegally detaining an underage girl.

But my greatest fear is that the press will hone in on Fiona. Although her mother has now explained the situation, Fiona is terrified that her classmates will learn that the man accused of murdering Danielle Jones is her uncle, and that she and her parents will become the object of school gossip.

Fiona's anxiety spiked recently when she found several copies of *Metro* scattered around the cloakrooms, discarded by girls who had picked up the free tabloid on their tube journey to school. That day's front page was dominated by a photo from Stuart and Debbie's wedding, featuring the couple standing with Danielle. Standing alongside the three of them was the Best Man, her own father. Her hands trembled as she wondered if any of her classmates had recognised me, perhaps from a school recital or theatrical production. Then she realised that in the original photo, she had been standing on the other side of me. By some fluke – or uncommon act of editorial probity – she had been cropped out of the picture.

Either way, it left her badly shaken.

For these reasons and many others, I follow the trial from my home, 200 miles from Chelmsford, in the heart of a city where nobody has ever heard of Stuart Campbell or Danielle Jones, in a country where nobody reads the *Sun* or *Daily Mail* or *Metro*.

25

London, March 1983

It's a sunny day in early spring and I'm talking with my mother at the Hertfordshire pub she now runs with Gerry, her second husband. While he is out at the cash and carry buying vodka, the two of us are catching up. I'm sipping a beer at one end of the bar while behind it she stocks the cold shelf with bottled lager, her back turned.

Without looking around at me, she speaks.

Did I tell you the Other Thing died?

Her casual tone throws me off guard for a moment and then I realise she's talking about my father.

Oh. Okay. No.

Yeah, I was down Tilbury last weekend and I bumped into this bloke from the Toot and he said to me, I heard Alec Campbell died a couple of months back.

How?

God knows. Finally drank himself to death, I imagine. Apparently he went back to his mother's in Gateshead to die.

Wow. That's kind of miserable.

I'm glad it's over, she says. I don't feel sorry for him, I don't feel anything. I stopped hating him years ago. Couldn't be bothered.

This news relieves some low-fi static which has been buzzing around me for years. Finally knowing my father is dead, I realise, answers a question I'd never really formulated, about where and how he was. And now I know. Despite this sense of a weight being lifted, I'm also silently appalled by my mother's delivery. Not that my father deserves anything like respect, but I feel cheated. Her icy dismissal leaves no room for dissent, annihilates any possibility of sadness, any sense of loss. Yet the thought of him dying in such pitiful conditions – limping back to his elderly mother, half-blind, terrified of dying alone – strikes me as unbearably tragic.

No wife, no children, no friend to hold his hand or soothe his brow. Unloved and uncared for, save by the woman who bore him, now approaching death herself.

He must have known he had squandered his life, leaving nothing but pain and bitterness and destruction in his wake, only to come full circle, crawling back to his mother. In that moment his life strikes me as unspeakably pathetic, deserving of pity. Still, having witnessed the horrors he inflicted on my mother, the years of misery and humiliation she suffered at his hands, I can understand why she would dismiss any thought of solemn words or noble emotions.

One thing she's not, my mother, that's a hypocrite.

So I nod and say nothing, and within seconds she is talking about football and I'm happy to join in. Tottenham this, West Ham that, and don't get me started on that bloody boring Arsenal.

My father is dead and we will never speak of it again.

Just one more unmourned death.

London, April 1983

I'm reluctant to make yet another prison visit, until my mother calls me saying she's worried about Stuart's safety. In his latest letter he says he fell and broke his hand. The prison doctor set it badly and now, weeks after it should have healed, the hand is still painful and his grip feeble.

You mean he broke his wrist?

No, it's the back of his hand.

How do you break the back of your hand in a fall?

He said he fell down some stairs, but I'm worried someone attacked him.

Mum, he punched a wall or something.

I think someone hurt him, he might tell you who it was.

And then? What am I gonna do about it?

Alexander, please.

*   *   *

A few days later we meet at Embankment station and take the tube to Tooting Bec, where we catch a cab to the nick. By now we're both familiar with the sordid standards of UK prisons. And we know HMP Wandsworth is Britain's biggest and most overcrowded – 1,500 prisoners stuffed into a Victorian building built for 950 – and dominated by violent gangs. Still, I'm shocked when we enter. The place seems to be rotting down to its stumps, a stinking warren of stained concrete, ancient brickwork, peeling paint, broken windows and rusted barbed wire. As we cross an inner courtyard I have the overwhelming sense that we're rattling the cage of some enormous wild beast. I can smell its foul breath, feel its seething anger.

For some time we sit waiting at a table in the middle of the visiting room, surrounded by a babble of prisoners and families. And then a haggard stranger flops down in front of us. I do a cartoon double-take:

Wait, this is my brother?

This bloke with ashen temples and a jutting grey jaw? This middle-aged con with a faint bouquet of piss and sweat?

What happened to my beautiful little brother?

Stuart is only 25, but this bloke looks 20 years older.

He nods at us, eyes half-closed, cold and reptilian.

Hey, I say, How you doing?

He grunts, shrugs.

Alright, he sniffs.

My mother smiles and makes cooing noises, trying to coax him into conversation.

How are you keeping? What's the food like, are you eating properly? Did you get enough time to exercise? Are you still doing your what's it called, weight-training?

He grunts and shrugs again. Before this, he'd always seemed glad to have a visitor. Now he seems to believe he's granting us an audience. Or worse still, he doesn't give a shit either way.

I'm shocked. Prison has finally made him its bitch, robbed him of whatever personality he once had, ground him down and made a bog-standard convict out of him, an old lag. Fighting down the urge to provoke him, I try another tack.

So Mum didn't really explain it, what happened to your hand.

He glances down at his hand as if to check it's still there.

He shrugs again.

Mum says you broke it in an accident.

Yeah.

What kind of accident?

Fell.

You broke your hand falling over?

Yeah.

How'd you manage that?

He sniffs and says, Metal stairs.

Right. Metal stairs.

I turn to our mother, expecting her to mirror my contempt. But she won't meet my gaze, focusing instead on Stuart, beaming love and concern at him in a misguided attempt to open his heart, or at least his mouth.

After another 20-odd minutes of monosyllabic grunting, I begin to look around the room and stare at the ceiling, unable to fake interest. He seems bored, yet he's insufferably boring. I feel outraged, cheated in some way. Having seen so little of my brother over the years, I don't have memories of growing older with him, of getting used to his face ageing, his hair greying. In my mind, Stuart is always that cute and cocky bright-eyed kid, with shiny black hair and sparkling dark eyes, forever 19. I can't accept what's in front of me. *This* is not my brother. *This* is some old zombie, a walking lobotomy with lousy hygiene and even worse manners.

I want to ask him who he thinks he is, this dead-eyed, charmless, pasty-faced con, sitting there and giving me attitude. Then I ask myself why I even give a shit and suddenly I feel angry but resolute. My mind is made up. We exhaust some thin gossip about old school friends and shift down the gears from parole to public transport to the weather, into an awkward silence as we acknowledge there's nothing left to say except the obvious.

Well, good to see you again, eh.

I can't get out fast enough. I want to get far away and never return. Of course, I won't say this to my mother. No need to upset her. But then, as we're walking down an echoing corridor with the other families, she makes some casual remark about our next visit, and I lose it.

You know what, I snap. I am fucking sick of prisons. I'm never coming back.

Alexander, you can't say that. He's your brother.

Mum, I growl, I don't even know that person back there.

He's just upset, she pleads.

Brother or not, I'm not coming back.

She says nothing, but pulls a wad of tissues from her bag, stopping every few steps to dab at her eyes, the way she has always wept.

Silently. Like a saint.

Now I'm furious. Now it's my fault.

Next time he gets out, I scowl, he better stay out. Otherwise I don't know him.

London, June 1983

At this point Stuart is in prison for a crime that he has never explained to me, and which I have no real urge to learn about. I'm tired of hearing every couple of years that Stuart is out of prison – and then shortly after, back in prison. Besides, my band is making progress, having negotiated a small deal with an independent label. And our manager's cutting-edge fashion store, which still underwrites our expenses and keeps us dressed like bohemian princes, has just got a mention on the fashion page of *The New York Times*.

When I visit my mother a few days later Stuart's recidivism is still a sore point. After his arrogance towards us a couple of weeks earlier I had sworn never to visit him in prison again, reducing her to tears. So my lip curls when she hands me a piece of ruled notepaper that I recognise instantly as a prison letter from HMP Wandsworth.

Why are you giving this to me?

Just read it, she says.

The letter is dated Wednesday 8 June, and addressed to *Dear Mum and Dad*. The opening line declares, *It was nice seeing you and Alix on Wednesday, Mum,* and then goes straight into asking whether I can remember to bring him a radio on my next visit.

Along with the letter is a Visiting Order.

He also attaches an addendum, addressed *To Whom It May Concern*, authorising me to collect his clothes and other belongings from the Birmingham police station where he was taken after his most recent arrest, presumably while making a delivery for his boss in Manchester, the job that my manager had fixed up for him after Stuart arrived at my squat a couple of years earlier, on the run from some undefined legal trouble in Tilbury.

But his main concern, it seems, is to convince my mother and Gerry not to go through with their plans to leave the area. During the working week the two of them stay in the small one-bedroom flat above the pub they run in Hertfordshire, but they still spend weekends at their three-bedroom house in Tilbury, purchased from the local council with their joint savings, and our last true family home. Recently, however, they have been thinking of selling up and buying a house in North London, closer to the pub.

Alarmed at this prospect, Stuart spends most of the letter trying to convince my mother not to move. *After all*, he says, *all of your friends and family still live in the Tilbury area*. Then, slipping effortlessly into first person plural, he asserts, *if we did move, we'd only end up with something nowhere near as nice as our house and in a rough area away from friends and the people we all know.*

The pleading becomes increasingly desperate, with dire warnings about how *you'd be left with nowhere to stay when you both went back home to visit friends, etc.*, and how it would mean *breaking away from everything and everyone you knew!*

Of course, he's not thinking about himself: *After living and working in Manchester, I know I can live anywhere, but ... come to think of it, my lady, Debbie, lives in Tilbury too.*

Two things strike me as odd. First, the way Stuart now refers to Gerry as *Dad.* Until this point, neither of us had ever regarded Gerry as a father figure. Indeed, we'd always shared the same attitude towards him: seems a nice enough bloke, but I don't need another father, thanks. One was more than enough.

And now Stuart is calling him *Dad*?

It's pretty obvious why. Stuart will need somewhere to live when he leaves prison, preferably somewhere in the Tilbury area, somewhere not too far from *his lady, Debbie.*

Who, despite the cheesy epithet, is still only 16 years of age.

I tell my mother I've got no intention of picking up Stuart's clothes and property from a Birmingham police station.

Well, she says, maybe Gerry can run that errand for him.

I can already picture Gerry tooling up the M6 in his gray Vauxhall Viva, anxious to keep his newfound son onside.

Otherwise, I say, maybe Stuart can work something out with his lawyer.

Oh come on, she says. His lawyer's not going to do it, is he.

Either way, I say, don't look at me. Same thing with the radio. I'm not interested in making his prison time more comfortable. I'll help him when he gets out. Provided he goes straight.

That's what I tell her, and it's what I tell myself.

But in a couple of weeks, I'll start writing to him again.

Next thing, I'm standing outside the prison gates again, clutching a VO.

City of London, October 1983

On weekdays the streets of Bishopsgate are thick with office workers, but on this cool Saturday morning the pavements are empty save for maybe a dozen women, some with small children, gathered loosely at a bus stop. Nobody speaks, except when a newcomer arrives and asks softly if this is the pickup point. Occasionally one of the women will glance warily at the solitary male figure, who stands in the shuttered tobacconist's doorway.

And I will pretend I don't notice her, fixing my gaze on the Marlboro between my fingers and thumb, hissing my disdain in a plume of blue smoke.

There's a little shudder of excitement as the coach pulls up, the air brakes exhaling a long weary sigh, and we shuffle onboard. Now it's official: we're all off to see our criminal kin. As the vehicle fills up, defences are lowered, judgements put aside and conversation breaks out. In the back row I slide into a corner seat, away from the chatty mums with their blunt and artless questions, the bored and sticky kids clambering over seats and laps, the snooty younger wives and girlfriends who snap their heads to avoid eye contact, as if anyone would try to chat them up on this trip. Most of them look as if they're off to a nightclub, dolled up with eyeliner and lipstick, reeking of hairspray and Charlie, wearing tight skirts or jeans, doubtless at the request of partners who need a reminder of what's waiting for them at home.

I hate being part of this ritual. I tell myself I'm not like these women – I have a choice, I have options. I'm not marking time until some two-bob drug dealer returns to rescue me from yearning boredom and gossipy neighbours. I have a life away from all this, I'm better than this.

That's what I tell myself.

But the truth is, I'm not.

I'm just like them. Clinging to hope. Telling myself he shouldn't be locked up, that it's not fair. That this will be the last time I'll make one of these trips. He'll go straight when he gets out this time, he said so.

Of course, we should know better, all of us.

As I sit there staring out the window, waiting for the stragglers to finish boarding so the driver can start the engine and set off, I find myself idly recalling previous visits. How many times have I sworn never to enter a prison again? And yet here I am, sitting on yet another coach headed to yet another clink.

By now Stuart is an inmate at HMP Highpoint, a Category C prison roughly 60 miles north-east of London. Category C prisons are relatively low-key as nicks go, designated for inmates who cannot be trusted in open conditions but are otherwise unlikely to attempt escape. Prisoners, in other words, who will do their bird in dutiful submission, heads down and noses clean, seeking time off for good behaviour. And of course, this time will be the last time.

No more bird for Stuart. *He promised.*

A support group for prisoners' families has laid on this free monthly coach from Liverpool Street station, so I have joined the otherwise all-female roster to make the 100-minute drive up the A11 to Stradishall. Slumped in my seat, head against the glass, staring out at empty office buildings, I'm wondering what version of Stuart I'll find sat across the table from me this time.

Excuse me, but is your name Alix?

A blonde girl has turned to peer at me from the seat in front. She's smiling like she's won some kind of prize. Before I can respond, she continues:

You're Stuart's brother, aintcha. I knew it was you. You look just like him. Well, kind of similar anyway. Definitely a family resemblance.

I want to tell this silly teenager she needs her eyes examined, that we don't look remotely alike. I want to tell her to keep her chirpy voice down, especially since a couple of the girlfriends and wives have now half-turned to see what all the excitement is about. But most of all I want to know how she knows my name and my brother's.

I'm sorry, but …?

Oh, she says, he said you'd be on the coach today, told me to look out for you. He's told me lots about you, he's always talking about you. Only good things though, hahaha.

Really.

I'm *Debbie*. Stuart's girlfriend.

I realise I should shut my mouth, which is hanging open.

Yeah, she says. I don't suppose he's had a chance to tell you himself. We've only been together a couple of months.

She's so gauche that I don't know how to respond to this girl, who seems to be a gushing mass of lanky limbs and freckles and Lady Di highlights and pale blue eyeshadow and bubbly charm.

Stuart told me you're a writer, she says, with that fashion magazine in London, *i-D*. It's really good, innit? Bit weird, some of the fashions, but I do like it. Some of the model girls are really pretty. I bet you must love your job.

Yeah, I say. Beats working for a living.

Haha, Stuart said you were funny. Is it alright if I sit beside you? I promise I won't be too annoying. If I talk too much, you can just tell me to shut up.

No, yeah, that's okay.

So, she says, flopping onto the seat next to mine, do you choose all the models, you know, in the magazine?

Er, no. That's not me, I'm a writer. I do interviews and stuff.

Yeah, but you must look at the photographs, you know, the portfolios the girls send in. Stuart said you look at some of the photographs, when they pick the girls.

He said that?

Stuart says I could be a model. Do you think I could be a model? You can tell me the truth, say shut up you silly cow, I won't mind.

Looking her over, I don't know where to start. This poor child.

How old are you, Debbie?

Fifteen, she says, sixteen in a couple of months.

My mind is reeling. Where did he meet this girl? Does she even know that he has a wife? That he married a girl not much older than her only seven years ago? That despite being separated, they have never divorced? That he has a seven-year-old daughter he never sees?

Before I can shape one of these questions into words, she's talking again.

So how did you become a journalist, anyway? Stuart said you went to art school.

The coach shudders as the engine roars, and we pull away.

This is going to be a long trip.

Whitechapel, November 1983

A few weeks later I get a letter from Stuart, thanking me *for coming up with Deb and making it such a pleasant visit*. Of course, I'd had no intention of *coming up with Deb*, and had been blindsided thanks to his manipulations. The letter slips instantly into his now-familiar default voice, a curious blend of vapid banter and casual duplicity.

I felt like an eighteen-year-old again (but I couldn't find one anywhere!), he tells me, before suggesting I join him in deceiving his new girlfriend: *I might be able to get another VO to send just to you, but don't let Deb know because she'd just get herself upset at missing a chance of seeing me, mad fool that she is to love me so much.*

This is followed by a request to bring him some cigarettes on my next visit, although once again he'd prefer it if I kept this information from Debbie, who has been led to believe he has quit smoking. A couple more feeble and tasteless jokes, including one about *the poofs in here*, and he switches as usual to his real concern, his latest parole hearing. *Somehow*, he tells me, *Mum has managed to get herself involved in the reports my probation officer is supposed to be writing about my home circumstances.*

Although his *home circumstances* are in fact one and the same as my mother's home circumstances, she apparently lacks his far greater understanding *of how the judicial system works*, and should not voice an opinion without consulting him first, especially *not to a man who I have been cultivating a friendship with for the past four or five months*. In other words, our mother should not meddle in his meticulous grooming of this probation officer. Stuart knows precisely how to play this. He doesn't need her cocking it up for him by blurting out the facts.

Finally, he signs off:
Lots of love,
(your good-looking brother)
Stuart

I remember being shocked by this letter. Not so much by the dishonesty, casual bigotry or his focus on parole rather than remorse or reform. No, what disturbs me most is Stuart's total lack of self-awareness or personal development. The person who sent this, I realise, is no different from the one who wrote me an almost identical letter five years ago.

Fuck, he just will not grow up.

And yet by early 1984, Stuart secures yet another early release on parole. Flat broke and without a place of his own, for the first few months he crashes on the sofa in my mother's one-bedroom flat above the pub in Hertfordshire, where she lives with Gerry.

Having spent much of his time in prison developing his physique, Stuart emerges bigger than ever, walking with an exaggerated gait, an invisible suitcase under each arm. His body mass and knowledge of gym equipment doubtless helps him quickly secure a job as a personal fitness instructor at a Mill Hill gym. Fortunately for him, criminal record vetting won't become routine for at least another decade.

Encouraged by his apparent attempt to go straight, I decide to help him. Even when he boasts about all the young women he's meeting at the gym, and how keen they are to have sex with him, I rationalise it by telling myself he's making up for lost time. After all, Debbie lives with her parents 35 miles away in Tilbury. Between her full-time job in the City, and his weekends and evenings spent on private training sessions, they barely see each other.

So he's cheating on his girlfriend? Who am I to judge? Anyway, logistics and morals aside, she's too young and naive to be with him. Their relationship is destined to fail.

Yet within a few months he and Debbie save enough money to get a place in Tilbury and move in together. She has just turned 17.

* * *

And then a door opens, one I'd never even considered. By November 1984, *i-D* magazine is so hip that New York's coolest nightclub, Danceteria, wants to throw a party in the magazine's honour, and offers return flights and hotel for four contributors. Along with Dylan, Caryn and Nick, I fly out on this fabulous freebie. But while the others dutifully return four days later as scheduled, I strike up a friendship with Haoui Montaug, the club's doorman and promoter, and move into another friend's apartment in Park Slope, Brooklyn. When I return to London six weeks later, I'm offered the role of a lowlife party promoter in a satirical BBC drama about a rake's progress from London night-life to a stellar media career.

It feels like irony turned inside out.

By year's end, playing in the band feels like a chore. Even if we resolve our musical differences, we'll need to borrow more money from our manager. And while he is offering to under-write a further £10,000 in recording costs, I can no longer go on spending money I haven't earned, money made by the people who work in the shop above us, while we play guitars in a basement rehearsal room. Besides, I want to try my hand at journalism without feeling I'm letting the side down.

So I quit the band to focus on writing.

London E1, July 1985

By now *i-D* is paying me £250 a month to write and edit and publicise the magazine, and already I see myself as a fashion and pop culture writer. As style magazines like *The Face*, *Blitz* and *i-D* start to carry real clout, fashion journalism is becoming a dream job. Working for *i-D* means free admission to nightclubs and private members' clubs, invitations to catwalk shows and gallery openings and book launches, *entrée* to exclusive parties thrown by publishers and record companies and fashion brands.

Meanwhile I'm wondering where I'll live next, because pretty soon I'll have to move out. Back in 1977 our ragtag band of squatters had become semi-organised and approached the Greater London Council, owners of our long-condemned Victorian tenement buildings, with a proposed amnesty. In exchange for a nominal rent we were allowed to form a housing co-operative, which meant we could secure a GLC grant to fully renovate the premises. Seven years later, we have started to vacate our flats, which will now be gutted and refurbished. Work is scheduled to start on my block in a few months.

Unexpectedly, my friend Rob Brown says he's moving to America, to take his chances in Hollywood. This means his one-bedroom flat will be vacant for several months even before it is due to be renovated. Spying an opportunity, I contact Stuart, urging him to attend our next monthly co-op meeting, and to bring Debbie with him. They should dress in smart casual but nothing flash, and let me do the talking.

I canvas my friends in the co-op, asking them to support Stuart's temporary membership, so he and Debbie can move into Rob's flat until it comes up for renovation. I explain that my brother has recently got out of prison and is trying to put his life back together, so I'm trying to help him out, get him on the straight and narrow. This way, I'll be able to keep an eye on him. And it would be perfect for Debbie, since she works just up the road at a City insurance firm. This would mean some stability for them, I say, the start of a proper life together.

Even though my friends laugh at this blatant nepotism, they agree to back me when I put Stuart's membership to a vote, and on Wednesday 3 July 1985 Stuart is granted temporary tenancy of Rob's old flat – the same premises Rob and I had broken into and squatted when we were still art school students. My friend Justin, who had joined us on the dancefloor at the Dun Cow a few years earlier, invites us all to celebrate with dinner at his place.

With Stuart and Debbie installed in a flat directly across the courtyard from my own, I realise there's more I can do to help him. A full-page feature in one of London's hippest magazines, I figure, will have clients lining up to hire him as their personal trainer. The following day I set to work on an interview-profile for *i-D*'s September 1985 issue. The feature runs with a small black and white photo taken by Debbie, showing a shirtless Stuart flexing his left bicep.

i-D Talks to Bodybuilding Instructor STUART CAMPBELL

Stuart Campbell is a bodybuilding and fitness instructor at The Body Factory, a gym and health centre in north-west London. He spoke to i-D about bodybuilding and fitness in general …

How long have you been bodybuilding?

Seriously, only since December last year. But I always used to read bodybuilding books and magazines and at one time I did power-lifting. That was with BAWLA – the British Amateur Weight-Lifting Association. I became Bucks County Champion and South Midlands Champion and Group 2 Champion for 1979. But that was really power/strength training rather than bodybuilding – although it was the basis for my later involvement in bodybuilding.

Why did you take it up? Did you just decide to change your shape?

There was a point where that came up, and I thought, 'Right, I'm gonna be something different.' Also, I had friends who were doing it and I'd noticed the changes in them: not only their size and shape, but also their personalities. That appealed to me.

How has bodybuilding changed you?

Well, I've got bigger and strong, and *I suppose I'm less aggressive than I was, although I've still got a lot of work to do in that direction.* [Italics added for emphasis] My personality *has* changed – I'm more aware, not only of health and fitness, but also my environment.

* * *

In the autumn of 1985, I feel certain that Stuart has turned over a new leaf. He seems happy and healthy, living with his young but sensible girlfriend in an inexpensive flat, a place where they can save some money and get ahead. And of course, I will be there for him, just 30 yards away, across the courtyard, ready to lend a hand if he needs it.

Still, he pretty much keeps to himself and we rarely see each other socially.

Many years from now, I will finally learn how he repaid me.

But for now, I have no idea that while I'm working the phone and typing up my notes at *i-D*'s Covent Garden office, and Debbie is at work in the City, Stuart is picking up teenage girls and taking them back to the flat I'd helped him secure, where he photographs and molests them.

26

Chelmsford Crown Court, Tuesday 3 December 2002
1 year, 5 months, 15 days since Danielle's disappearance

Yesterday, after almost two months of testimony and witness statements, the prosecution finally rested its case. Today, Michael Borrelli QC begins Stuart's defence. Forgoing an opening statement, Mr Borrelli calls a female witness who claims to have seen a schoolgirl resembling Danielle Jones several hours after her supposed abduction, weeping in Grays public library. However, under cross-examination by prosecutor Orlando Pownall, the witness concedes that the schoolgirl's clothing bore little resemblance to the clothes Danielle was wearing on the day she disappeared.

The defence continues in this vein for the next week, calling witnesses and introducing testimony that seeks to sow doubt in the jurors' minds as to whether Danielle has been abducted. Furthermore, Mr Borrelli argues, given the absence of a body, the jurors cannot even be certain that Danielle is, in fact, dead.

Chelmsford Crown Court, Monday 9 December 2002

1 year, 5 months, 21 days since Danielle's disappearance

Today is my 46th birthday. I wake up in Paris and get online to read that Michael Borrelli, Stuart's defence counsel, has already made his closing argument.

It is quite possible, he tells the jury, that this girl [Danielle] had simply decided not to go to school, simply decided not to go home and had not been kidnapped from Coronation Avenue [in East Tilbury]. The witness sighting of a girl who resembled Danielle raises a perfectly reasonable hypothesis that she may well not have been the victim of a crime when she set out at 8 a.m. that morning. The fact that Danielle's phone was no longer registering after 19 June proves maybe that her battery is dead but – we hope – it doesn't prove that she is.

Finally, Mr Borrelli tells the jurors, Unless you are sure that Mr Campbell was in East Tilbury on the morning in question, you cannot be sure he is guilty of these crimes. He did not do it and the prosecution cannot prove he was there to do it.

Reading this closing statement, I can't help but feel it's a desperately feeble defence. For a start, it implies that Danielle was not abducted, but chose to run away from the family she loved without telling even her closest friends. And, as the prosecution has established, without a change of clothes, her passport, or the £400 in savings she left untouched in her bank account.

And then, instead of phoning her parents or a girlfriend with a message of reassurance, the jury is invited to believe that she instead composed a pair of garbled text messages to her uncle, written in a completely different format with different spellings from her own, and sent from her mobile phone to Stuart's while they were within 50 feet of each other.

As a hypothesis, it's beyond absurd. It's an insult to the jury's intelligence. But it's all the argument that the defence can muster. Stuart cannot take the witness stand, since that would open him up to cross-examination, which would be a disaster.

So, Mr Campbell. When you were interviewed by Essex Police about your relationship with your 15-year-old niece Danielle and your whereabouts at the time of her disappearance, you refused to answer their questions. Indeed, you repeated the phrase 'No comment' at least 30 times, correct?

Like shooting fish in a barrel.

After reading Mr Borrelli's summation I don't much feel like celebrating my birthday, and decide to stay home. That evening I get a call from someone who identifies himself as Martin Wallace, Scottish crime reporter for *The Sun*. I don't ask who gave him my home number, although I suspect it is someone from Essex Police.

I wonder if you could give me a quote about your brother, he says, how you feel about him and *this difficult situation*.

I have no comment to make, I say, out of respect for the girl's parents. I don't want to get involved.

Jesus, did I just say No comment?

Oh, I can understand, says Wallace. I daresay you're upset about the shame he's brought upon you and your family ...

The oldest trick in the book.

I have to go now, I reply.

Well, if you change your mind, I'm ...

Goodnight.

Chelmsford Crown Court,
Wednesday 18 December 2002
1 year, 5 months, 30 days since Danielle's disappearance

Both sides have finished their closing arguments, and the trial judge has almost completed his summing up, explaining the applicable points of law to the jury in layman's terms. Finally, Mr Justice McKinnon tells the jurors what he expects from them when they return tomorrow to start their deliberations.

You must reach, if you can, unanimous verdicts, says the judge. Please put out of your minds any ideas of majority verdicts.

The following morning the seven women and five men of the jury file into a locked room deep inside the courthouse. Seven and a half hours later the foreman sends word: they have reached unanimous verdicts on both counts.

The court is quickly reconvened.

In the dock stands Stuart Campbell, grim-faced, wearing his sombre blue suit. Given that his defence had relied on sowing doubt and confusion, he knows that his only chance of an acquittal rests with a deadlocked jury, split between rival camps, with one or two holdouts arguing for days that there is still a reasonable doubt. Therefore, he and his legal team must know that the jury's remarkably swift and unanimous decision is an ominous sign.

The foreman stands to read out the jury's verdicts.

Stuart Campbell is guilty on both counts, namely the abduction and the murder of his 15-year-old niece, Danielle Jones.

As the judge confirms the verdicts, Tony Jones grimaces with relief and turns to comfort his wife Linda, who is sobbing.

Stuart displays no emotion.

For the first time since the trial began 11 weeks ago, Mr Justice McKinnon turns to address my brother directly.

You are no stranger to violence, he says, and merit the description *dangerous* ... You have been a blatantly deceitful and thoroughly dishonest smooth operator over many years.

He then sentences Stuart to a life term for Danielle's murder, with the tariff to be set at a later date. He also hands down a concurrent 10-year sentence for the kidnapping conviction.

Mr Justice McKinnon then takes the unusual step of telling Stuart that had the jury returned a verdict of manslaughter – as he feared they might – he would have asked for psychiatric reports with a view to imposing a life sentence.

Stuart calmly picks up his file and notepad before being led out of the dock to begin his sentence.

Outside the court, DCS Steve Reynolds of Essex Police talks to reporters.

Danielle's family, he says, have been left with a tremendous void in their lives, thanks to the cold, callous predator in their midst.

Undoubtedly, he says, Campbell did not want the relationship [with Danielle] to end. Worse for him, though, was the prospect of what might happen to him if she told his family and Debbie what her 'favorite uncle' had been doing to her. He was being rejected and he felt threatened. For an evil and inadequate pervert like Campbell, he says, it was a dual threat. He reacted as perhaps all the signs showed he would: he killed Danielle.

Next, Tony Jones speaks to the press.

He should have been a trusted family member, he says. It's terrible for someone to be murdered, but for someone in your family to do it, that is just unbelievable.

Finally, Linda Jones steps forward. Fighting back tears, she tells the press that while she's content with the sentence, she remains heartbroken, unable to move on.

We still don't have her back, she says. We need to find her so that we can lay her to rest and grieve properly.

* * *

Reading the news reports in Paris, I'm thankful it's over, but there's no sense of relief.

And even though the ghostly presence no longer seems to lurk in the dark corners of my apartment, my mood remains shadowy, my thinking dislocated.

Was it just my imagination, after all?

Does Stuart now wake up at night with that feeling of being watched?

Who cares.

I am numb. A throbbing mass of dull misery, a stump that has been cut off with a jagged blade and thrown into a landfill.

* * *

With the trial over and Stuart Campbell a convicted murderer, reporting restrictions are lifted, to reveal what was crawling under the rock. In the *Guardian* I learn of yet another betrayal.

Stuart Campbell had begun notching up convictions from the age of 12. A robber, burglar and car thief … for almost two decades he picked up girls on the street, claiming to be a photographer, and coaxed them into posing in lingerie … He was a practised liar. When he first met Debbie he was calling himself Stuart Sharkey …

The irony is not lost on me. When I'd helped him to evade justice in 1982 and he'd started calling himself Stuart Scott, I'd thought about urging him to adopt our mother's maiden name instead. And now, 20 years later, I find he had indeed become Stuart Sharkey. But only to sell himself as the brother of *i-D* style journalist Alix Sharkey, the better to dupe underage girls into posing for him.

Along with the story of his double life, splashed all over the press are details of his cold evasiveness under questioning about Danielle's disappearance, his callous indifference to her parents' agony. With his true nature exposed and any last shred of doubt obliterated, only one question remains.

Where is Danielle's body?

Tuesday 24 December 2002, *Evening Standard*

Danielle's Killer Stays Silent

The parents of murdered schoolgirl Danielle Jones suffered more heartbreak today when her uncle refused to tell police what he did with her body. Stuart Campbell has refused to speak to officers about the whereabouts of her remains.

Police family liaison officers have told them Campbell, from Grays, who is being held in prison in Chelmsford, refused to speak to them in his prison cell.

A police spokesman said: 'Mr Campbell didn't want to speak to us. There are ways we can make him sit down and have a conversation with us. But we are going to wait until the New Year and pursue him then.'

A police source said detectives were confident they would eventually persuade Campbell to speak to them. They said: 'Perhaps he will have a change of heart at Christmas. We will go back in the New Year, and if he won't speak to us we will go back and go back and go back until he does.'

He is under no legal obligation to speak to police, and even if he does he can simply answer 'No comment' as he did during all his previous police interviews. Detectives suspect his attitude may indicate that he plans to appeal against his conviction.

Police also reveal that since the trial began 11 weeks ago, six more women have come forward claiming to have been victims of Stuart Campbell. And even more sickening is another report in that same day's *Evening Standard*. Apparently, some time around 1990, my brother had gone looking for his young daughter Jennie-Lee. Not because he wanted to make amends for his dereliction of parental duty, nor to rekindle some kind of familial bond. Not even to simply check if she were still alive.

Campbell Photographed Own Daughter

Stuart Campbell was so obsessed with schoolgirls he even persuaded his own teenage daughter to dress up in lingerie for photographs ... Years after splitting up with [first wife] Jennifer, he re-established contact with their daughter Jenny [Jennie-Lee], whom he had not seen since she was a toddler.

Aged 14, she was persuaded to pose for indecent photographs on Campbell's promise of a future career in modelling – just as he did with other girls he picked up in the street and outside schools.

Jenny [sic], now 26 and a single mother of three, hates her father and refuses to have anything to do with him. When he was arrested, police found hundreds of similar photographs of girls, many of whom have not been traced.

Debbie – then pregnant with Simon, now 16 months – gave him an alibi for Danielle's murder, although she later retracted it.

She is still refusing to help police, who describe her as another of Campbell's long list of victims.

27

Blackshots Leisure Complex, Grays, February 1993

I was living alone in a one-bedroom flat in Bloomsbury, working full-time as a news editor at MTVEurope in Camden Town while writing a weekly column for the *Independent*. An insider take on nightlife, *Saturday Night* often profiled some DJ or illegal party host. My editors gave me plenty of rope, and I took more. We soon noticed the strongest reader reactions – positive or otherwise – were always in response to elements of my personal life. Looking back, it was a prototype of social media: a running list of likes and dislikes, snapshots of underground places and vivid nocturnal characters. Sometimes sly and knowing, sometimes confused and full of doubt. Either way, it struck a chord.

So when I was invited to join the family in celebrating my maternal grandmother's 80th birthday at a Saturday night gathering, that week's column began to write itself. My siblings and cousins, aunts and uncles – I would mention them all by name and sketch them in a few lines, in a good-natured preview. And then I'd turn up and hand out copies of the paper, revealing they'd made the national press. Sure, it was a bit cheeky, but I knew they'd see the fun in it.

My diary, though, records my doubts: this would be the most personal column yet and maybe a little too honest. After filing the story, I noted:

Wrote about Nan's 80th birthday for the Independent *column – previewed it, in fact. Very worried that it might be rejected, given its very personal nature. Simon Cunliffe says he likes it very much, but he'll 'show it to Anne and see what she thinks'. At home there's a message on the machine: Jane Taylor at the* Indy *says, 'I need to talk to you about this piece.' Oh shit, I think I've blown it.*

The following day, I was much happier:

'This is great … great copy and I love the ending,' says Anne Spackman, editor of the Weekend Independent.

The venue was a community hall in the Blackshots leisure complex in Grays, a place with familial ties. After his retirement our grandfather Jack Sharkey found himself a Saturday job here, renting out golf equipment. As kids, Stuart and I had learned to swim in Blackshots pool and spent long summer afternoons splashing around or clowning on the springboard. And it was at this pool ten years previously that Stuart – then 25 and still married to estranged first wife Jennifer – first met 15-year-old schoolgirl Debbie Jones. They now lived a 15-minute walk away.

The party was under way, pop music booming and kids running around squealing, when I showed up with two dozen copies of the paper under my arm. As I handed them out, my aunts and uncles peered at the column in disbelief. Most were a little shocked, but amused. *Typical Alexander* was the general reaction, along with, *Well, at least you spelled our bloody names right.* Uncle Chris chuckled and said, *You actually get paid for pulling a stunt like this?* My cousins seemed to like the cheeky tone. Everyone was pretty gracious about what was really an invasive and reductive piece of work. Everyone, that is, except those seated in one corner: Stuart and Debbie and her family – parents Jan and Phil, brother Tony and his wife Linda.

Watching his face from across the hall I could see immediately that my brother was not happy. He got up and exchanged some words with Debbie and then leaned over the table to talk briefly to her parents, who seemed to be asking serious questions. But before I could go over and talk to him, he and Debbie had crossed the dancefloor, heading towards the exit. They were intercepted by my mother who, sensing a problem, had moved rapidly to intervene. She spoke to them briefly before they left, said something to her husband Gerry, then followed them into the hallway. Leaning to one side, I could see the three of them engaged in serious discussion.

There had to be a problem with something I'd written. But what? I'd known that it was near the knuckle, and was already braced for some kind of irritation, but I certainly hadn't expected this reaction from Stuart. I'd been deliberately vague about his youthful indiscretions – as I naively understood them at that point – and had gone out of my way to emphasise his rehabilitation. For the record, the entire mention of Stuart amounted to four lines:

> Stuart got into trouble as a kid. 'Went away' for a while. He quit drinking years ago, and has since made good as a builder and decorator. Stuart pumps iron and dwarfs me, and is the only one of us still using my father's name.

Why would he be embarrassed? Wasn't it common knowledge by now? Having visited him in prison a dozen times, it would have been ridiculous of me to airbrush history. Anyway, I was proud of him. That T-shirt he'd given me, with his company name and phone number, and a cartoon of him with a power drill in hand? I wore it often.

I was on his side.

I saw him turn and exit the premises, Debbie in his wake. Then I saw my mother approaching, her face like thunder.

Why did you write that terrible stuff about him?

What terrible stuff?

About him going away to prison.

I didn't mention *prison*.

Well, they assumed it meant prison and now they're all upset.

But he did go to prison, Mum. Several times. Anyway, I said it was years ago.

But they were shocked – they had no idea.

Well, they should know the truth, don't you think?

It's not *your* bloody job to tell them.

Oh, you mean he would have got around to it, eventually?

That's not the bloody point! It's not your business to tell people about his past.

I shook my head and turned away. It wasn't worth arguing over. Either way, I couldn't undo it.

She was right. It wasn't my business. It was *his* business. But as we would all learn much later, first he lied by omission, and when challenged, he lied again.

But having read that Stuart *had gone away for a while*, Debbie's parents were immediately suspicious. When the party was over, they caught up with Stuart and demanded answers. This was why he'd been so incensed about the newspaper article. The last thing he wanted was people asking questions, or demanding explanations.

Yes, he admitted, he had been arrested and imprisoned. And yes, it had been for the alleged abduction of a minor. But he had been acquitted. The 14-year-old girl was a fantasist who'd completely misread the situation and overreacted. She'd invented the charges to save face. She had been lying all along, Stuart said.

In short, Stuart lied to Debbie and her family, and she had backed up his version of events. Worse, after slipping through the net, he realised he could get away with lying again, because Debbie would believe his lies.

Meanwhile Stuart was still stalking young girls and – impersonating a professional photographer – persuading them to pose for photographs, in lingerie that he provided, on the promise of a modelling career. Maybe he could even get them into trendy fashion magazine *i-D*, where his brother worked as an editor.

The same con he'd been using for over a decade.

28

Monday 20 January 2003
1 year, 7 months, 2 days since Danielle's disappearance

By now it looks likely that my brother intends to appeal and therefore has no intention of revealing what he did with Danielle's body, at least not until the appeal process is exhausted or – God forbid – successful. Meanwhile, in the BBC TV documentary *Missing Danielle*, Linda Jones can barely contain her rage. Her video diary, recorded during the trial, is scathing about Stuart and the trial process, which had required her to sit through hours of testimony, much of it speculative, about Danielle's relationship with the man who murdered her.

Watching, I try to understand how Linda must feel, but it's beyond me. I cannot imagine losing a child and not even having a grave to visit, a place where the body is laid to rest. Towards the end of the documentary Linda talks again about how Stuart had managed to hide his criminal history from herself and Tony. She urges viewers not to ignore warning signs in their own families.

For God's sake, she says, addressing the viewers, *don't let yourself be sitting where I am.*

Paris, Saturday 1 March 2003

*1 year, 8 months, 11 days since Danielle's
disappearance*

Ten weeks after the trial ends with Stuart's conviction, DS Keith
Davies calls, asking if I'd be willing to write to my brother again.
Having been sentenced to life imprisonment, Stuart is still awaiting his tariff, the minimum number of years he must serve before
he can be considered for parole. DS Davies suggests a friendly
tone would be best.

If you can get him to open up a bit, he says, maybe get a visit,
get him talking, maybe he'll tell you what he did with Danielle's
body. You know, if you still feel you want to help.

Of course, I say. But I don't hold out much hope. You really
think he'll speak to me?

Who knows, he says. But to be honest, right now we don't
have many options. He's refusing to speak to the police. I think
he's probably planning to appeal. But maybe he'll confide in you.
Worth a try, don't you think?

So I write the following letter:

Monday 3 March 2003
   Dear Stuart,
   I hope you are as well as can be expected, given your
circumstances. Now that the trial and media attention are
over, I hoped you might also be willing to write, or even to
see me in person.
   As I'm sure you can appreciate, the whole case has been
very difficult for everyone connected to you and Danielle.
Earlier this year, I was back in London on a job when the
documentary 'Missing Danielle' was screened. I don't know if

you saw it, but as you can imagine, it made for harrowing viewing.

Linda, in particular, was distraught.

I daresay you must be pretty miserable yourself. What are you doing to keep your spirits up? How are you feeling? Have the authorities set your tariff yet?

Well, it's been so long since we saw each other that this letter feels quite stilted and awkward. But basically, I'm trying to say that, as I told you before, I'm still your brother and you are still mine. And despite everything that has been said or done, I still care about your welfare and state of mind. The papers might call you a monster but we both know you're a human being, and on top of that you are my family. Nothing changes that.

So, I don't know what you think or feel about me, but if you want to write then I'll be happy to hear from you. If you want to arrange a date and send a VO then I'll come and visit you. Otherwise, I hope you will at least try to use your time wisely, and direct your mind to useful, constructive ends.

The worst thing you could do is to vegetate, or wallow in self-pity and anger at some perceived injustice.

Anyway, please let me know what you're doing, how you're doing, how you feel. And try to keep your chin up and look after yourself.

Alix Sharkey
45 rue Marx Dormoy
75018 Paris

As expected, he does not reply.

*　　*　　*

Almost a year later DS Keith Davies calls once more, asking if I will write to Stuart yet again. By this point my brother has been informed of his tariff: a minimum 20 years before he'll be eligible for parole. He has also been moved to HMP Wakefield, aka *Monster Mansion*, one of Britain's most notorious high-security prisons.

Perhaps, says DS Davies, now he's had a chance to reflect on the long sentence ahead of him, he'll be a little more willing to speak.

I agree, and write another letter.

No. FM7992
Stuart Campbell
HM Prison Wakefield
5 Love Lane
WAKEFIELD WFZ 9AG
15 January 2004

Dear Stuart,

I trust you are as well – or at least, as well as possible, given your circumstances. It's been over two years since we saw each other or communicated and naturally, I have been concerned about your health and your state of mind. I don't really have any experience of prison life, but I'm sure it can be quite depressing. Are you allowed to study anything in there? At least that would keep your mind active and sharp.

Mum told me that she received a card from you recently, which I took as a sign that you're starting to open up a bit. Who knows, maybe some day you'll actually let us come and visit! It's very strange, not being able to make contact with your brother. I imagine it's even more difficult as a mother not to be able to see your son.

Anyway, I just wanted to remind you, in case you've forgotten, that I'm still here and always ready to come and see you, if you want. Maybe I'm wrong, but it seems to me that if I were in your place, I'd like to see my family and have some kind of contact with the outside world. So if you'd like a visit sometime, you only have to say so and I'll come over on the Eurostar and take the train up to Yorkshire, bah gum.

Try to stay positive and look after yourself ...

Alix Sharkey
45 rue Marx Dormoy
75018 Paris

PS. Sorry about the typewritten letter but I can barely write longhand these days – because of my job I type everything.

As with my previous letters, I receive no reply.

Miami Beach, Sunday 12 December 2004
3 years, 5 months, 24 days since Danielle's disappearance

By now I have left Paris and relocated to Miami Beach, in an attempt to reset and restart my life. From there, I contact the editor of the *Observer Magazine* to pitch a story on the rumour of a new movie by cult director Alejandro Jodorowsky, starring goth rocker Marilyn Manson. The editor asks instead about a piece on Stuart.

Dec 13, 2004 at 9:26 AM

Subject: Re: Sons of El Topo

will try to warm to it, just seems too odd, does this mean you have given up on paris?

no chance of writing about your brother?

aj

Editor

Observer Magazine

3–7 Herbal Hill ECIR 5EJ

I reply, dismissing the idea:

Dec 13, 2004 at 10:17 AM

Subject: Re: Sons of El Topo

it is odd, but surely that is its strength?

and yes, no chance of writing about my brother yet. wrong time.

a x

29

Paris, April 1996

I first met Agnès in London when she was dating a friend of a friend. An aspiring film producer from Brittany, she told me she was planning on moving to Paris soon. I said I was thinking about moving there myself and we jokingly agreed to become flatmates. I thought no more of it. But a few months later, she contacted me to say she'd found an inexpensive two-bedroom near the Bastille. Did I want to split the rent?

Within weeks I was working as a Paris stringer for various English publications and covering the fashion shows. In those days, before airbnb and the internet news boom, this was still a viable lifestyle.

One morning in April, Stuart called me. I was surprised that he even had my number in Paris and wondered if he was about to break some bad news, but he sounded upbeat – and with good reason. After living together for 13 years, he and Debbie were getting married at the end of August.

Wow. Congratulations.

Yeah, finally making an honest woman of her.

Ho ho.

So, would you like to be my Best Man?

Of course. Yeah, it would be an honour. Brothers, after all.

Although I didn't say so, I knew he'd only asked because he had no real option. The previous year, Gerry had abandoned my mother, running off with a 40-something barmaid who'd worked for them briefly at the pub they managed.

So much for the guy that Stuart had once called *Dad*.

Which left Stuart with precisely one close male relative.

My brother had always been a loner. Never had any close friends, male or female. Not even a loose bunch of mates or colleagues from work. Like me, he was self-employed as a sole trader, a one-man operation. But unlike me, he rarely drank, and never went to pubs, cocktail bars or nightclubs. He had no interest in football or other team sports, so he'd never befriended other fans. I never once heard him talk about bands or concerts, artists or galleries, architecture or historical monuments. He seemed to take an interest in food – or at least in vitamins, supplements and nutritional values – but not to the extent that anyone could call it a passion.

As far as I knew, he did all his socialising with Debbie and her family. In many ways he seemed closer to the Jones family than his own. And why not? From my fleeting contact with Debbie over the years and what I'd heard from my mother and sister, I knew the Joneses were good people, decent and kind-hearted. Like many husbands, Stuart seemed to live a rich and rewarding life as part of the extended family unit he was marrying into.

Even though I felt vaguely fraudulent – wasn't the Best Man supposed to be the groom's closest friend? – I jumped at the chance to play the loyal and dependable older brother. At the very least it would get me out of Paris during the city's August doldrums, onto a train and back to England.

Oh, he said, and there is one other thing I wanted to ask. Actually, Debbie came up with this idea.

Go on.

You know Deb's brother Tony? Well, his daughter Danielle is

10, so she's roughly the same age as your daughter, right? Fiona's what, nine now?

Fiona? She's eight. Nine in November, another seven months.

Right, he said. So roughly the same age. Anyway, Debbie thought it would be really nice to have the two nieces as bridesmaids, dressed in matching outfits. Two little girls together, they'd look lovely in matching pink gowns, wouldn't they.

Yeah, I'm sure.

So, you think Fiona would be up for being a bridesmaid?

Yeah, of course. I mean, I'll have to ask her, but I'm sure she'll say yes.

Yeah, little girls love all that stuff, don't they? Weddings, dresses, flowers.

I suppose so.

Alright, let us know.

To ensure complete visual harmony at the event, he also wanted the two of us to wear matching morning suits and so he asked if I could come to Essex for a fitting sometime over the next couple of months. Of course, he and Debbie would cover my train fare and pick me up at the station, no way they'd expect me to pay for the trip.

It didn't seem an unreasonable request and I said it should be fine. No need to pay my fare, I could do with a trip to London anyway.

And so I sent a congratulations card and set to work on writing a decent speech. It wouldn't be easy. There were precious few happy memories to share about the groom, no breezy tales of teenage mischief, no raffish blowouts from our university days. Even though I might twist it into a joke, I couldn't see his new relations laughing at how he'd stabbed me in the leg with a hunting knife, or how I'd once bumped into him armed with an axe, off to confront a local thug. Would they warm to the hilarious tale of the time I smuggled speed into prison for him?

Oh, you should have seen our faces when those pills fell on the floor!

Yeah, maybe not.

The speech would have to be far more pop cultural and post-modern, full of clever nods to music and fashion. I tried quoting various songs and movies, but it was all too smartypants and self-referential. The problem was my own insecurity. I wasn't confident enough to write a simple heartfelt speech and stand up and deliver it in an honest, humble way. The truth was Stuart and I had long since grown apart and I no longer knew him very well. Worse, what I knew best about him was largely unsuitable for a PG audience.

I'd made the mistake of being too frank once before – with the *Independent* article that had caused so much upset – so this felt like a second chance and I didn't want to let him down. But more than that, I wanted to strike the right tone and put everyone at ease. And so I bought a how-to speechwriting book from the English-language bookstore on rue de Rivoli, and cobbled together a string of one-size-fits-all pleasantries and generic newlywed jokes.

On 26 May, I wrote to Stuart and Debbie to tell them I hoped their wedding plans were proceeding as expected and to apologise for not getting over to England a few weeks earlier, when he'd invited me to bring Fiona for her dress fitting, along with Debbie and Danielle. Instead, her mother Jane had taken her to the fitting session.

But, I reassured them, Jane tells me you all had a pleasant day together.

She'd also said that Stuart had taken great interest in the fitting session, although nothing he said or did aroused suspicion.

Just his typically fussy behaviour – he'd always liked things to be *just so*, neat and tidy, everything in its place.

A few weeks later I took the Eurostar to London, then the train to Grays, where Stuart and Debbie met me at the station on a sunny June afternoon. The pair of them were tanned and fit, and smelled good. He was wearing his normal off-duty attire – a sweatshirt with the sleeves cut off to reveal his massive shoulders and biceps, teamed with black track pants and clean white hi-tops. Debbie was slim and pretty, with a pair of acid washed jeans and a pastel crewneck sweater. She still wore her hair in that late-eighties Lady Di style, feathered with highlights.

We drove 30 minutes to the formalwear hire shop in Leigh-on-Sea and Stuart and I got fitted for our matching morning dress: tails, striped trousers and fancy waistcoats. I remember thinking it odd, his attempt to control every single aspect, right down to the cufflinks. He seemed determined to dress me like an accessory. I bit my lip while he told me what would look best on us, and why. But I drew the line at the wing collar and cravat, opting for a standard collar and tie.

Afterwards, on our way back to Grays, I asked them to drop me off in Corringham so I could see my old friend Andy. His elderly father Pete had recently won £3m on the lottery and the family had decided to open a boutique hotel and country club. Andy was overseeing the restaurant and wanted to show me around. Naturally, I invited Stuart and Debbie to come and take a look. It was just a couple of miles from their house, and if they wanted to make a reservation when it opened, it would be handy to know the manager.

Sounds like a good idea, said Stuart. I like a decent bit of grub.

After giving us a tour of the kitchen and showing off the stemware, flatware, linen, and tables and chairs he'd sourced from France, Andy insisted we raise a toast to congratulate Stuart and Debbie on their imminent wedding. We chugged Belgian beer while Stuart and Debbie sipped sparkling water. Stuart was driving, and Debbie only really drank if he did.

Which meant almost never.

After we'd waved them off Andy turned to me and nodded.

He seems to be doing really well, doesn't he. Got his business turning over nicely, finally settled down and she seems like a nice girl. Turned his life right round.

Yeah, he's done well for himself.

Yeah, said Andy. Got fucking big though, didn't he. Arms like lampposts. And his neck? Fucking hell.

That's his thing, bodybuilding.

Yeah, well. Looks much better for it. Really cleaned himself up.

What do you mean?

You know the way he used to look. That horrible rocker look, with the headbands and studded wristbands and all that shit.

Fuck, I'd forgotten about that. Yeah, that was some look.

And that big knife strapped to his leg. Did he copy Rambo or did Rambo copy him? Never could work it out. But he used to scare me, he looked so fucking weird.

He scared you?

Yeah. He looked like he might kick off at any second and slash your throat.

Grays Methodist Church,
Saturday 31 August 1996

As for the wedding? My sharpest memory is of stumbling through my speech with a dry mouth and trembling hands as I tried to convince everyone that I was normal and that my brother Stuart was normal, too. Just a pair of normal brothers, a couple of regular Joes. Which of course was not true.

Neither of us had ever been *normal*.

Debbie opted for a white ruched ballgown with leg of mutton sleeves, a mid-length white veil and tiara with matching choker. It seemed excessive, like a little girl's idea of a wedding gown, but who was I to critique a woman's bridal fantasy? Besides, my lasting emotional memory of that day is the warm glow of family life. Everyone seemed so happy, so keen to celebrate. And Stuart did his thing on the dancefloor, making us all laugh with his fussy little disco moves and camp gestures. He still had it, even after all these years.

But I guess I wasn't entirely convinced of the event's authenticity. Otherwise I would have brought along my digital camera and taken some photographs, or at least ordered copies from the official photographer. Maybe I'm just inherently selfish, but I returned to Paris and forgot about the entire event. It never occurred to me to ask for photos.

In fact, the first photograph I ever saw from that wedding was on the front page of the *Daily Mail*, published during his trial. And that photograph, I still have.

Five people are lined up on the lawn. From left to right: Debbie clutches a bouquet, looking pensive in her voluminous white gown. Stuart, hair swept back from his high forehead, wears a tight grin. My mother, in a scarlet bonnet and matching tunic, is still deciding how to compose her expression. Beside her, I look self-conscious and a little hungover.

Next to me, barely reaching my shoulder, a little girl in a pink satin gown clutches a bouquet. While everyone else faces right, she looks in the opposite direction. Peering out from under her fizzy blonde fringe, she seems to be scrutinising someone, or perhaps signalling impatience.

This is 10-year-old Danielle Jones.

My eight-year-old daughter Fiona, her fellow bridesmaid, had been standing on the other side, along with the Jones family. She has been cropped from the picture.

When I look at that picture now, knowing what Stuart was secretly doing in the weeks before and after it was taken, I think I understand why he asked me to be his Best Man. It wasn't that we were brothers, or that he didn't have any real friends. No, my presence was a ploy, a special kind of window dressing, a form of distraction.

By comparison, I made him look normal.

30

Royal Courts of Justice, London WC2, Thursday 20 January 2005

3 years, 7 months, 2 days since Danielle's disappearance

The tragically brief life of Danielle Jones and the story of her destruction by my brother, her seducer and killer, continued to reverberate for several years after his conviction. In 2004 Stuart was granted leave to appeal, allowing his barrister Michael Borrelli QC to argue that the trial verdict was unsound, since the judge should have dismissed one of the jurors and excluded potentially prejudicial evidence.

And so in early 2005, in *Regina v Campbell*, three Appeal Court judges heard argument from Mr Borrelli, and counterargument from original prosecution counsel Orlando Pownall QC. The first ground of appeal was that one of the jurors lived next door to one of the officers involved in the Danielle Jones investigation and therefore should have been dismissed, even though there was no evidence that they had discussed the case at any time.

The second ground of appeal concerned the admissibility of Stuart's history of deviant behaviour, including witness statements that indicated he was overheard pressuring Danielle to pose for photographs, as well as other evidence – including a trove of pornographic images discovered on his computer – that suggested he was obsessed by Danielle and had a perverted interest in young girls. At the outset of the trial, judge Mr Justice McKinnon had agreed with the prosecution that the prejudicial nature of this evidence was outweighed by its value as evidence.

Appeal judges Lord Justice Kennedy, Mr Justice Simon and Mr Justice Bean took just one day to hear and weigh the arguments, and delivered their verdict on the morning of Friday 21 January:

> In our judgment there is no substance whatsoever in the first ground of appeal [concerning the juror] ...
>
> In [the second ground of appeal] our judgment is the judge was right to rule as he did. The evidence which the appellant sought to exclude was relevant to establish a motive for the offences charged in the indictment, and evidence of motive is always admissible to show that it is more probable than not that the accused committed the offence charged (see *R v Ball* [1911] AC 47) ...
>
> So, neither of the grounds of appeal having been established, the appeal against conviction must fail and it is therefore dismissed.

After the hearing Linda and Tony Jones – who have travelled up to London to confront Stuart Campbell in court once again – tell the assembled media that they were confident the appeal judges would uphold his conviction and dismiss his appeal.

We now hope he does the decent thing, Linda tells reporters, and lets us have her back so we can put her in a place of rest, which she deserves.

But yet again Stuart retreats into silence, refusing to talk with detectives or say what he did with Danielle's body.

And so the Jones family must endure another painful step.

Normally under UK law, seven years must pass before a missing person can be declared *Presumed Dead*, even when there has been a conviction for that person's murder. But in an effort to spare Tony and Linda Jones further anguish, Essex Police secure an earlier hearing. On 28 July 2005, just over four years after Danielle's disappearance, coroner Caroline Beasley-Murray conducts an inquest. Having outlined Danielle's tragic story and Stuart's involvement, she records a verdict of unlawful killing.

As the year comes to a close Stuart Campbell's life sentence is subject to one final review, because of a change in UK law following his trial – namely the Criminal Justice Act 2003, Schedule 22. The new legislation means trial judge Mr Justice McKinnon is obliged to re-evaluate, explicate and, if necessary, modify his sentencing decision before the High Court of Justice at Birmingham Crown Court.

On my 49th birthday, Friday 9 December 2005, Mr Justice McKinnon writes that after deducting the 16 months the defendant spent in custody on remand, he had considered the accepted benchmark sentence for a 'normal' murder, then factored in both aggravating and mitigating factors.

Summing up, he states: The aggravating factors are that the victim was particularly vulnerable because of her age, the defendant abused his position of trust and concealed his victim's body. There are no mitigating factors.

He then concludes: I take as the first step the period actually to be served for the 'average', 'normal' or 'unexceptional' murder as 14 years. The next and final step is to look at the factors capable of mitigating the normal penalty and the factors likely to call for a sentence more severe than the norm. There are no mitigating factors. I would add at least six years for the aggravating factors to arrive at a minimum term of 20 years.

I do not have jurisdiction to increase the minimum term.

Accordingly, the minimum term the defendant must serve before the Parole Board can consider his release on licence is one of 20 years. That minimum term is the minimum amount of time the defendant will spend in prison, from the date of sentence, before the Parole Board can order early release. If it remains necessary for the protection of the public, the defendant will continue to be detained after that date. Where the defendant has served the minimum term and the Parole Board has decided to direct release, the defendant will remain on licence for the rest of his life and may be recalled to prison at any time.

Twice, the judge points out that *there are no mitigating factors*. But my eye is drawn to another phrase, one that indicates the judge's thinking:

I do not have jurisdiction to increase the minimum term.

The implication is clear: had he been empowered to do so, Mr Justice McKinnon would have added more time, perhaps many years, to my brother's sentence.

All the doors have finally closed on Stuart Campbell. Even given the best possible outcome, by the time he emerges from prison he will be 63 years old.

31

HMP Wakefield,
Saturday 3 December 2011
10 years, 5 months, 15 days since Danielle's disappearance

More than a decade has passed since he kidnapped and killed Danielle Jones, but as the Christmas season gets into swing Stuart Campbell is back in the national news. But not because he is finally ready to identify the location of his victim's remains. No, instead he complains from his prison cell about a 'disturbing' situation: his having to work in the prison kitchen over the festive period without receiving extra pay.

Having served almost half of his 20-year sentence for Danielle's abduction and murder, Stuart writes to *Inside Time*, the weekly national newspaper for UK prisoners and detainees. Now 52, and still refusing to reveal what he did with the body of his teenage niece, he whines about working 'unsocial hours' over the holidays, complaining that other prisoners with non-kitchen jobs get paid time off at Christmas.

Conversely, as a kitchen worker, he will receive neither paid time off, nor extra pay. He questions how HMP Wakefield administrators can expect him to work on public holidays without paying him a bonus.

Unsurprisingly, there is little public sympathy for Stuart's complaint, which is widely ridiculed in the tabloid press.

32

Los Angeles, Monday 13 April 2020
18 years, 9 months, 26 days since Danielle's disappearance

This morning I call my sister Sinéad to explain that I'm going to write a book about growing up with Stuart and how our relationship evolved and atrophied as we became adults. I tell her that she will be mentioned, if only in passing. She agrees to help me by sharing her memories and we find ourselves discussing an issue we had never directly confronted before: the point at which Stuart's personality first became darker and more dangerous.

I ask, When would you say Stuart started to change?

I never really understood it, she says, but everything seemed to change after he went off to that boarding school when he was 12 or 13.

Oh yeah, I say. That fancy school. We all drove up there with him.

Yeah, she says. I remember how sad it was when we left him there.

Right, I say. I remember he had that big blue trunk, to put all his stuff in?

That's right, she says. We were so jealous of that trunk. And he knew it, acting like he was all clever and special. We weren't allowed to even look inside it.

And until he went to that school, we were all pretty close, if I remember?

Oh yes, she says. When we were seven or eight, we all used to play together, even in the house. Don't you remember? We'd all get our dolls out and play together.

Dolls?

I had my Sindy dolls and you and Stuart both had those Action Man dolls, remember? Though of course you wouldn't call it a doll, not back then, because boys didn't have dolls. What did we call them instead?

Action figures?

That's it, action figures. Anyway, before he went away to that boarding school he was a nice little boy.

Our conversation almost over, I ask my final question:

You know, Sinéad, I've been trying to recall the name of that boarding school. Do you remember what it was called?

Yes, she says, it was called Eccles Hall.

And it was somewhere near Ipswich, right?

I think it was Norfolk.

We say goodbye and minutes later, I get online to find the New Eccles Hall School, described in a clunky ESL idiom on a dual-language website apparently aimed at Russian parents who want their children to get a solid education and a passable British accent:

The New Eccles Hall School was founded in 1945 and is located in Norfolk County (eastern part of England), occupying a picturesque territory of more than 30 acres. There are a few students studying here – about 200 people – which allows keeping a friendly, warm atmosphere at all educational levels (the school is open to students of 7–18 years old and offers a full British educational cycle).

Alix Sharkey

In fact, the school is now called Aurora Eccles Hall and provides specialist education for students aged seven to 16 *who experience difficulties learning in mainstream school environments.* This, I realise, was pretty much the definition of Stuart's condition back in the early seventies.

And then, just as I'm about to log off, I finally stumble across the fault line in this story, the yawning chasm of horror that I'd always felt lay just below the surface.

Beneath the Aurora Eccles Hall website, the next seven Google results are news items from late March 2015, reporting on the suicide of David Tuohy, an elderly former headmaster. Having been convicted a few weeks earlier of historic sex attacks on young boys – all of them pupils at his school during the 1970s – Tuohy had flung himself into the Thames to drown before he could be sentenced to prison.

Friday 28 March 2015, *Daily Mail*

Headmaster Who Molested Boys Found Floating in the Thames

- David Tuohy was due to be sentenced next week for historic sex abuse.
- 83-year-old has been found dead in River Thames near to his Oxford home.
- Headmaster convicted of 15 counts of indecent assault against young boys.
- He indecently assaulted five special needs pupils, under 13, at Eccles Hall.

A former headmaster who was found guilty of molesting boys as young as ten at a special needs school in the 1970s has been found dead just days before he was due to be sentenced.

The body of David Tuohy, 83, was found floating in the River Thames close to his home in Oxford earlier this week.

Norfolk police said his death was being treated as 'unexplained but not suspicious'.

Tuohy was due to be sentenced at Norfolk Crown Court on Monday after earlier being found guilty of 15 counts of sexual assault following a nine-day trial.

He was in charge of Eccles Hall School, in Quidenham, Norfolk, in the 1970s when he carried out the indecent and serious sexual assaults against five pupils, who all had special needs and were under 13.

Last month, Norfolk Crown Court heard how Tuohy liked to discipline boys who came to the school from different parts of the UK and found themselves alone, isolated and separated from their families.

He was also said to be 'obsessed with spanking' and the prosecution said he had a 'particular deviant sexual fascination with the bottoms of very young boys'.

I scroll through the various reports for key dates. Finally I find what I'm looking for, what I'm dreading.

David Tuohy had started at Eccles Hall School in 1970, becoming headmaster in 1974.

Precisely when Stuart was enrolled there as a boarder, 100 miles from home.

33

Houses of Parliament,
Wednesday 13 June 2018
16 years, 11 months, 26 days since Danielle's disappearance

Stephen Metcalfe, MP for South Basildon and East Thurrock, stands in the Commons and urges MPs from both sides of the House to expedite new legislation known as Helen's Law, also known as the 'No Body No Parole' law.

This legislation, he says, is very important to my constituent Linda Jones, as the location of her daughter Danielle's body has never been disclosed by her killer. This new law would close off any possibility of parole for convicted murderers who refuse to disclose the whereabouts of their victims' bodies.

As a grace note Metcalfe adds, There is something peculiarly disgusting about the sadism involved when an individual murders somebody and then refuses to reveal the location of the victim's body.

He doesn't mention his name, but everyone knows the disgusting and sadistic individual he has in mind: Stuart Campbell.

Helen's Law is the result of two decades of tireless campaigning by Marie McCourt, whose 22-year-old daughter Helen McCourt disappeared in February 1988 on her way home from work. The investigation soon focused on Ian Simms, who owned a pub close to Helen's Merseyside home. After police found Helen's blood and one of her earrings in his car, Simms was convicted of her abduction and murder, and jailed for life, with a minimum of 16 years before being eligible for parole. Despite this, he refused to reveal the location of Helen's remains.

Thanks to Marie McCourt's efforts, Helen's Law had seemed certain to reach the statute books in summer 2018, until being swept aside by Tory Party infighting over Brexit. A few months later, in the wake of Prime Minister Theresa May's resignation, the Parliamentary timetable is cleared once again for the December 2019 General Election. With that resolved, the law is due for another vote – until the Covid-19 pandemic leaves the country in lockdown and its government in quarantine.

With Helen's Law consigned to legislative limbo, Linda Jones does her best to maintain media pressure on Stuart Campbell to reveal his final secret.

On 1 April 2019, she tells *The Sun*:

> I wrote a letter to [Stuart] early on pleading with him to tell us, but he never responded. We haven't spoken to him, his wife [Debbie] or Tony's parents [Jan and Phil] since he was arrested. My sons have lost that whole side of their family too. It's been catastrophic.

On 8 April 2019, in *When Missing Turns to Murder*, a one-hour documentary about Danielle's murder on the Crime+ Investigation channel, Linda tells her interviewer:

> He's still alive and will come out with a life at the end of it, and [Danielle] never will. But to say where her body is, he's got to admit he's done it. And I don't know that he ever will. We still haven't got our daughter back and that is torture.

By November 2019, with Ian Simms having served almost 32 years, the Parole Board recommends that he be released. Outraged that her Helen's killer could walk free without disclosing the location of her body, Marie McCourt and her family launch an urgent legal challenge to the Parole Board's decision.

At the High Court, the family's lawyers argue that Simms should remain in jail until their legal challenge is concluded. Lawyers representing Simms reveal he has been in open prison conditions since 2016 and has already been released under supervision several times, arguing that he represents no further threat to the public.

On 4 February 2020, just short of the 32nd anniversary of Helen's murder, Lord Justice Dingemans and Mr Justice Fordham refuse to postpone Simms' release. Based on psychological reports, the Parole Board accepts that he will never disclose the location of Helen's remains, even if he must spend the rest of his life in prison. And as the law stands, there is no reason to deny his parole application any further. Two days later the McCourt family's worst fears are realised: Ian Simms is freed on parole.

A Ministry of Justice spokesman issues a press statement:

We completely understand the pain and anguish that the Parole Board's decision has caused Marie McCourt and her family. The High Court's ruling means we must now release Ian Simms from custody though he will be recalled if the Court later decides to quash the Parole Board's decision. He will be on licence for life, subject to strict conditions and probation supervision when released, and he faces a return to prison if he fails to comply.

This is the nightmare scenario for the Jones family and others like them, as Linda Jones explains to the *Daily Mirror*:

Helen's Law has to be pushed through now as a matter of urgency. We are all in this awful limbo but at least for now our loved ones' killers are still behind bars. Until the right decisions are being made, I just want time to stand still. It's not just the murder they need to take into account, but the refusal to give up the body and allow us a funeral. It's an ongoing torture.

And so Ian Simms walks free without giving up the location of his victim's remains. Although he will be supervised, he can resume some kind of normal life – while the family of the young woman he murdered will never know closure, comfort or solace.

Is this Stuart's strategy?

If so, will it succeed?

These are the questions that hang over me for several months as I write this book. And then, in a sudden rush of legislative action, the loophole is abruptly closed with the passage of three short clauses.

On 4 November 2020 the Prisoners (Disclosure of Information About Victims) Bill receives Royal Assent and becomes law. From now on Parole Boards will have a statutory obligation to take into account an offender's non-disclosure of certain information when making decisions about their release from prison. And the law may yet be further tightened in the near future, to ensure that victims' families are heard during Parole Board deliberations.

Unfortunately, the passage of Helen's Law comes too late for Marie McCourt and her family. But for Tony and Linda Jones there is a glimmer of hope. The new law comes into force just weeks before Stuart Campbell becomes eligible for parole. If he was gambling on emulating Ian Simms, he now faces a very different scenario. He can no longer serve out his minimum sentence and expect to walk free without revealing the location of Danielle's body.

A new question presents itself.

Will he finally see reason and do the right thing?

Epilogue:
My Last Prison Letter, Part Two

And so we come to the end of the book, Stuart, if not the end of the story. But before I sign off, I want to explain how it felt to write this book and why I did it.

This story took me more than a year to complete and writing it has been a kind of hell. Raking over our early lives, trawling through years of emotional trauma and then confronting your predatory nature – all this has frequently left me feeling drained and disgusted and profoundly miserable, nauseated by this story and my unwilling involvement in it. It has caused me long nights of self-loathing and self-hatred, as I was forced to examine in detail my own multiple failings, in an attempt to get closer to your mindset and try to understand how you could murder a young girl and then dump her body in some godforsaken void, thereby aggravating the agony of her parents, inflicting decades of pain and despair on top of your already monstrous act.

Is there no limit to your depravity? How could you be so heartless, so cruel?

Tony and Linda Jones trusted you. With their home, with their children.

And you killed their little girl because your sexual fixation with her went horribly wrong. How can you live with yourself without begging their forgiveness? How can you sit in that stinking cell, stewing in your phoney denial, having refused them for two decades the only thing they want?

All they want is their daughter's body. So they can lay her to rest, and place flowers on her grave.

How do you imagine your own grave, Stuart? Are there flowers? Do you see a headstone? What legend would you like engraved on that stone?

Is anyone standing there, weeping for you?

A brother, a sister?

A son, perhaps, that you've never met?

As much as I dared without hurting others, I have laid myself bare. You may call me cowardly or vain, or complain that I twisted certain facts or left out others. If you feel that's the case, I invite you to respond with your version of events.

But only if you tell the *whole* truth.

Meanwhile, there are four questions I tried to address across these pages, but which I'm not sure this book has answered.

First, how did you manage to conceal the predatory side of your nature for so long? I think one reason is our family's tendency to hide shameful secrets. You took advantage of our mother's attempts to protect you, her willingness to give you chance after chance. And in order to spare your feelings and save your reputation, she was less than forthright with the rest of us. She minimised your savagery and euphemised your crimes. Although I'm sure you manipulated and lied to her, too.

Another element of your double life was that you led us to believe prison had reformed you. After your transfer to HMP Grendon, a psychiatric prison, we believed your therapy had helped you, enabling you to address your issues and change your criminal ways. For reasons only you can know, it clearly didn't work.

Additionally, back in the late 1970s and 1980s, you benefited from cultural norms that were far more sexist and misogynistic, as well as various legal loopholes that allowed you to prey on young girls. Having met her when she was 15, you groomed a schoolgirl named Debbie Jones, gaslighting her into accepting your lies. Was it a coincidence that, after another 15 years, you finally married Debbie in 1996 – barely a year before the Sex Offenders Act 1997 was signed into law, creating a database of sexual offenders?

And then there's the simplest of reasons: we all wanted to believe the best of you rather than the worst, simply because you were such a beautiful young man. You once wrote me a letter signed *Your good-looking brother, Stuart*. It was a joke, of course, but that glib sign-off told me a lot about you. You've always known that our culture rewards good looks, that we almost all have that subconscious tendency to believe the best of people we find attractive, to assume they are honest and kind and intelligent – even when the evidence tells us otherwise. That's the lesson you learned early: because you were handsome and charming, because you could crack a joke, you would always get another chance.

And another, and so on.

The second question is more difficult to answer: what started you on this path?

I can never really know, but many child abusers have a history of being abused as children. You were certainly abused physically and psychologically by the Old Man. Still, there is no predestined path from a violent upbringing to the sexual grooming and murder of a minor. If there were, I'd be in prison with you. So was your obsession with underage girls some twisted attempt to recover lost innocence, to regain youthful promise and potential? Or were you acting out some far darker and deeper impulse? While writing this book, I discovered an ugly fact about the school you attended between the ages of 12 and 15. Your former headmaster David Tuohy was convicted in 2015 of molesting schoolboys at Eccles Hall during the early 1970s – when you were a boarder there. Did you see this news? Did you feel the shock of recognition? You must have known something was going on.

Kids talk, especially kids who live together in a boarding school.

Or perhaps there's more?

I can't help but wonder if something terrible happened to you at that school, something that deformed your personality and made you a far more secretive, manipulative and vindictive person. Was Eccles Hall where you first experienced the sexual dynamics of the older man and the adolescent object of desire, first learned that you had to take control and dominate? And if you suffered sexual abuse at the hands of David Tuohy, could that have set you on a path to the sexual domination of underage girls, and ultimately the abduction and murder of Danielle?

My third question concerns your state of mind: why have you chosen to maintain your obstinate silence, and to inflict such pain on the Jones family? You're not stupid and you're not insane. You know the difference between right and wrong. And no matter how deeply you may have buried the knowledge, no matter how powerful your sense of denial, we both know that you killed Danielle and disposed of her body.

The last time I saw you, in Grays, six weeks after Danielle disappeared?

I knew you were guilty. I knew you were lying.

At this point, *everybody* knows.

For what it's worth, I still can't believe you actually set out to kill Danielle. I still want to believe it was a confrontation that got out of hand, and that you panicked and tried to cover up your horrible crime. But you killed her, there's not a shadow of doubt.

My final question is the most important: will you do the right thing and reveal what you did with Danielle's body?

Our mother thinks not. You have caused her so much anguish and pain, but still she loves you. What else can she do?

I know you love her, too. I know you always send a card for her birthday, and for Christmas and Mother's Day. You even send her small amounts of money that you save from your wages, money you earn working in the kitchens at HMP Wakefield.

At this point, though, she has given up on the idea that you might one day confess.

She told me recently, Once Stuart decides on his story, he'll stick with it. He won't ever change his mind and admit he was wrong. I think he'd rather go on insisting he didn't do it.

I said, But surely he understands that means he'll die in prison? That he'll never walk through a park or sit on a beach or eat in a restaurant, never look up at a blue sky and ask himself what he'd like to do with the rest of his day, ever again.

I don't think he cares, she said. He's lost his wife and son, so there's nothing left for him.

For your sake, Stuart, I really hope she's wrong. I hope there's still something out here in the real world that you think is worth living for.

So my last question hangs in the air: will you do the right thing?

And only you know the answer to that, Stuart.

Only you have the power to bring this terrible story to an end.

Choose wisely.

Your brother always,

Alix Sharkey

Los Angeles

12 February 2021

Acknowledgements

Across three decades of journalism I have worked with many exceptional journalists and editors who helped me become a better writer. Though too many to name, they include Terry Jones, Claude Grunitzky, Don Atyeo, Steven Wood, David Jenkins, Anne Spackman, David Robson, Dylan Jones, Susannah Frankel, Allan Jenkins, Louise Chunn, Randall Koral and Allan Jenkins – as well as the late Peter Browne and the late Deborah Orr.

I am thankful to everyone at Elite of Los Angeles, where I taught English grammar and critical reading for seven years. Several individuals and families gave support at critical moments, including Lee Brian Schrager, François Guenet, Phil Ox and Mayerly Marquez, and Fiona Scott. I am indebted to Rex and Jeena Chung, and their children Maxwell, Alex and Isabella, and the Seret family of Sylvia and Ira, Isaiah and Jesse.

Mark Sarvas, my friend and tutor at UCLA Extension, got me to look deeper into the craft. Paul Rambali helped me envision this book with his invaluable feedback and encouragement, and also provided the title. Christian Kiki Nagy read early sections, offering both fiery enthusiasm and cool-headed advice.

I'm infinitely grateful for the vision and judgement of my incredible literary agent Cathryn Summerhayes at Curtis Brown, and her tireless assistant Jess Molloy. Thanks also to Luke Speed for extending this work into audiovisual media.

At HarperCollins, I'm indebted to my UK editor Joel Simons and my US editor Sara Nelson, both of whom helped me hone this book until we found its essence. I feel extraordinarily fortunate to work with such peerless professionals.

A hearty thanks to my vajra brothers and sisters, especially those in the Los Angeles sangha, with extra props to John Solomon, Julie Adler and Kathleen Pratt.

I could not have written this book without the love, kindness and endless indulgence of my wife Sarah Guenet Sharkey, who was with me on every step of this difficult journey.

Above all, I pay homage to my guiding light, HE Dzongsar Jamyang Khyentse Rinpoche, to whose outrageous elegance I will always aspire.

Credits

While every effort has been made to trace the owners of copyright material reproduced herein and secure permissions, the publishers would like to apologise for any omissions and will be pleased to incorporate missing acknowledgements in any future edition of this book.

Picture Credits
Page 6 bottom: PA Images/Alamy Stock Photo
Page 7: Shutterstock.com
Page 8 top and bottom: PA Images/Alamy Stock Photo

All other images courtesy of the author

Text credits
p.164 Extract from *Daily Telegraph*, 'Missing Danielle's Uncle Re-Arrested' by Stewart Payne (18 August 2001) © Telegraph Media Group Limited 2021

p.233 Extract from *Daily Telegraph*, 'Danielle Detective Held Over Child Porn' by Sean O'Neil (26 Sept 2002) © Telegraph Media Group Limited 2021

p.284 '*i-D* Talks to Bodybuilding Instructor Stuart Campbell' by Alix Sharkey (September 1985) © *i-D Magazine* 2021

p.292 Extract from *Evening Standard*, 'Danielle's Killer Stays Silent' by Harriet Arkell and Justin Davenport (24 December 2002) © *Evening Standard* 2021

About the Author

After grammar school and art school, ALIX SHARKEY began his writing career at *i-D* magazine, eventually becoming coeditor. Over more than three decades in journalism, he has filed hundreds of features on crime, popular culture, and fashion for the *Guardian*, the *Observer*, the *Sunday Times*, and the *Sunday Telegraph*, as well as various UK and international magazines. In 2004, he moved to Miami Beach to write about the contemporary art scene for *Ocean Drive* and fashion for *Harper's Bazaar*. After a brief stint as a magazine editor in New York, he relocated to Los Angeles in 2009. He has studied creative writing at UCLA.